ENGLISH ELECTRIC
CANBERRA

ENGLISH ELECTRIC
CANBERRA

THE HISTORY AND DEVELOPMENT
OF A CLASSIC JET

BRUCE BARRYMORE HALPENNY

Pen & Sword
AVIATION

First published in Great Britain by
PEN & SWORD AVIATION
an imprint of
Pen & Sword Books Limited
47 Church Street
Barnsley
S. Yorkshire
S70 2AS

ISBN 1 84415 242 1

A CIP catalogue record for this book
is available from the British Library.

Printed and bound in Great Britain by
CPI UK

Colour profiles created by Dave Windle

Pen & Sword Books Ltd incorporates the imprints of
Pen & Sword Aviation, Pen & Sword Maritime, Pen & Sword Military,
Wharncliffe Local History, Pen & Sword Select,
Pen & Sword Military Classics and Leo Cooper.

For a complete list of Pen & Sword titles please contact:
PEN & SWORD BOOKS LIMITED
47 Church Street, Barnsley, South Yorkshire, S70 2AS, England.
E-mail: enquiries@pen-and-sword.co.uk
Website: www.pen-and-sword.co.uk

Contents

INTRODUCTION

Since the 1950s the Canberra has played a major role in Britain's contribution to peace and security. In those early years these were broadly classified as colonial policing operations and action in support of bilateral treaty commitments entered into by Her Majesty's Government, with, for example, the sheikhdoms of the Persian Gulf and those under the Malayan Defence Agreement signed in October 1957, which brought the Canberras to war.

In the Middle East Great Britain had alliance commitments and treaty undertakings, and was also frequently involved in internal policing actions. To meet all these commitments the Royal Air Force needed a variety of aircraft. The Canberra's primary duty in the Middle East was to provide support for the Baghdad Pact, for which they were based in Cyprus. They also performed many other duties within the area, which included such places as Aden and Gan, in the Indian Ocean, which at that time was being developed for Royal Air Force use.

The United Kingdom deterrent strategy was based on the striking power of Bomber Command, and in the 1950s there was a continued need for high-performance long-range reconnaissance/strike aircraft of great versatility. These aircraft were tasked to provide Britain's atomic strike and reconnaissance contribution to the NATO shield forces and the Baghdad Pact, and were also available to the South-East Asia Treaty Organization.

The Canberra was an extremely good aircraft and had the capabilities necessary to carry out these duties. During the Canberra period it was the duty of the Royal Air Force to provide air forces in support of these alliances, and it served well as a front-line aircraft for many years and gave faithful service.

In the past, military aircraft, and engines developed for them, made valuable contributions to Britain's exports, and the Canberra was an outstanding example of this. In 1946, the United Kingdom exported aircraft, aero-engines and equipment valued at £14,704,686, and in 1957 it was £116,471,110. The Canberra was exported to fifteen countries, earning over £90 million.

From the following pages, you will see how the 'Day One' problems nearly put paid to the Canberra, but, once solved by Squadron Leader Ken Wallis, you will see how the mobility and flexibility of the Canberra has stood the test of time, just like the Rolls-Royce Avon engine, which has its own chapter. It was a matter of producing either a technical book on the Canberra or one that would appeal to a wider readership, just setting out the true Canberra story: marks, variants, overseas orders, Canberra squadrons, miscellaneous units, experimental Canberras, camouflage, markings and, told for the first time, the truth about bombing-up of Canberra aircraft; and the serious problems with which the Canberra was sent out to operational stations. I chose the latter, and trust that you will enjoy reading the book, as much as I did writing it.

During my research for the Canberra update (I started the book in 1987), I interviewed many people, one being my best friend, Wing Commander Ken Wallis, better known to millions around the world as the man who flew *Little Nellie* in the James Bond 007 film *You Only Live Twice*. On 12 January 2005, he had this to say:

Nice close-up picture, and the pilot in WT329 gives a contented glance for the camera.

As the armament officer on the first Canberra station, I certainly have strong memories of the aircraft. It was generally a good aircraft, but as you'll know, it had a deadly, possibly armament-related, feature that caused some early fatal crashes. Also, there were some short-comings in the armament design and to which there is quite a story. I have probably told you all about this before, ages ago. Anyway, I am glad to have been able to make some contributions to the efficiency of the Canberra as a bomber, and to have received some small credit for it. However, it was a long and uphill struggle; and for a while I was very unpopular with the Air Ministry and English Electric for raising so many comments. There was eventually a showdown.

Modestly put – by the man who saved the Canberra. Ken says '...as you'll know, it had a deadly...'. Yes, they thought at first that the Canberra crashes were sabotage. Well, that was not so; and, now you can read the 'Showdown: High Noon at RAF Binbrook' – the real truth about those with ideas on paper, and the Ken Wallis's of this world who make them work. Wing Commander Wallis never got the rightful recognition for saving the Canberra, and this book will set the record straight: the facts, told here for the first time.

Bruce Barrymore Halpenny
former Royal Air Force Police Provost
 (RAFPD) Special Security Duties
 (Atomic & Chemical Weapons) SS

Rome, 1983 to March 2005

Bruce Barrymore Halpenny

ACKNOWLEDGEMENTS

Once again, to all the many people who have given valuable assistance in the production of this book, I extend my gratitude for their readiness to help without question.

Argentine Air Force: Group Captain Daniel A. Paredi, Air Attaché, Argentine Embassy, London.

BAE Systems (formerly BAe): to all at BAE Systems 'Thank you', with special mention for Julie Cowell for getting my update request into the right hands, Alison Hawton, Head of Communications, and Jon Bonnick, Communications Manager, Military Air Solutions and Support, who found the answers to my questions and the photographs.

Group Captain Nigel B. Baldwin at RAF Wyton during the Canberra era.

My good friends, Edward Montegue Stephen Beaumont, and Roy Butler – Butler Engineering Heighington Garage – for putting their personal Mercedes at my disposal during research for the Canberra. Cheers Lads, a case of Italian vino rosso on its way with copy of Canberra.

Karlheinz Böckle, Leiter der Pressestelle, Auto & Technik Museum Sinsheim, Germany, for the photograph.

Terry Brown for his kind offer to help, for the photographs and for permission to quote from his Canberra articles.

Business Press International Ltd, for permission to quote from the article about the Rolls-Royce Avon in *The Aeroplane* magazine.

Flight Lieutenant M.A. Carter, RAF, for No.3 Squadron's history and photographs.

John Crampton DFC, AFC, MRAeS, RAF, Rtd, for much valued help with information and photographs.

Squadron Leader Brian Fern, for taking me to BAe at Warton many times.

Flight Refuelling Ltd: Tom Brook-Smith for photograph and material.

Brian Forway, for his help. Having worked on the Canberra at Handley Page and witnessed the crash of Canberra WJ622.

A. Foster & Son (Horncastle) Ltd: Matthew Ryder for his speedy, professional help.

Alan W. Hall, for permission to quote from Paul Jackson's Canberra article, 'Scale Aircraft Modelling', in *Aviation News* magazine.

German Air Attaché, London: Flight Sergeant Joerg (George) Noppens, who helped solve the 'village Kermis' mystery regarding Canberra WT335.

The High Commission of India: the officials and staff at India House in London, who were most helpful regarding information and photographs, and permission to publish same.

Indian Air Force (IAF) for its help with my request.

Paul A. Jackson, aviation historian and colleague, for permission to quote from his Canberra articles in *Scale Aircraft Modelling* and *Aviation News*.

Jane's Publishing Co. Ltd: the Canberra B(I)Mk 8 details reproduced from Jane's *All The World's Aircraft 1962 – 63*, by kind permission of Jane's Publishing Co. Ltd.

Fabian Jones, CPRO/PR2, Headquarters Strike Command, RAF High Wycombe, for clearance onto RAF Wyton during the Canberra era.

David Kirkpatrick, former RAF groundcrew for the photograph.

Kirkstall Productions Ltd: Chris Ellis for permission to quote from the Canberra article in *Airfix* magazine.

Hermann Laage, my German colleague, for his support and cigars.

Godfrey Mangion, Malta, for his fine selection of photographs and permission to publish as I wished.

The Author's son, Baron with Squadron Leader Sowells, pose in front of 100 Squadron Canberra at RAF Binbrook on 8 March 1983... The picture that started the Canberra book.

Royal Air Force Marham: Commanding Officer No.39 (1 PRU) Squadron, Flight Lieutenant Paul Morris, and Flight Lieutenant Jodie Gladki (CRO).

Marshall of Cambridge Ltd: Harold Fairbrother, Chief Electrical Designer, for his help in tracing some of the Canberras, and for material and photographs. Nothing was too much trouble. Much valued.

Alan Parkinson, Senior Project Engineer, British Aerospace, Warton, for his valued help in searching the records.

Air Commodore H.A. Probert MBE, MA, RAF, Rtd, at the Ministry of Defence AHB (RAF) London, and his staff at AHB, for their help with the squadron histories.

Tony Regan, for Canberra information from the side of the groundcrew and for the photographs of Tony at work on the Canberras.

Rolls-Royce Ltd, which was most helpful at all stages: with particular mention for Mr M.H. Evans at the Derby factory, and Robert (Bob) Gray, Service Engineer, Military and Commercial Avon Service, at the East Kilbride factory, for the Avon engine data and photographs, etc.

Royal Aircraft Establishment, Bedford: Mrs Enid Cawdron, for her help in dealing with my request for information and photographs.

Stewart Scott, for his offer to help with photographs.

Comodoro Jorge Julio Segat, Argentine Air Force (FAA), for his recollections of his part in the Falklands War, and for help with all FAA information and photographs regarding the FAA crews; with special mention for Captain Alberto Baigorri for his recollections of the war.

Short Brothers Ltd, Belfast, during my early research in 1987, 1988 and 1989: to all Shorts staff, with special mention for Mr Roberts, Marketing Director, Mr Richard Gordon, Marketing Manager, and Mr Tom Goyer, Assistant Publicity Manager. A special thank you for quick action with my request for Canberra information and photographs, and for permission to use them as I wished. Very much appreciated.

Shorts-Bombardier Aerospace, during the Canberra update in 2003 and 2004: Alan McKnight, Corporate Community Investment Manager, for expeditiously furnishing the answers to my questions, and for the photographs with permission to publish; and for the present of BOMBARDIER AEROSPACE-SHORTS Special Edition (1903-2003) Centennial of Flight Photographs and books.

Terry Senior, for helping with some of the photographs and for being ever ready with his camera.

Wing Commander K.H. Wallis MBE, DEng (hc) CEng FRAeS FSETP PhD (c) RAF, Rtd, my good friend, for his friendship and support over the years, Canberra armament information and photographs with permission to publish as I wished; for always a welcome cigar, drink and snack in his club when I am over in England from Italy. Always a stop to see Little Nellie and her sister with Ken.

Carmella for typing; and thanks to my son Baron for sorting out all the hundreds of photographs, putting onto CD (his world not mine) and his enthusiasm for creating the Canberra book.

GLOSSARY

A&AEE	Aeroplane and Armament Experimental Establishment
ACU	Acceleration Control Unit
AEW	Airborne Early Warning
AFC	Air Force Cross
AI	Airborne Interception
AMAC	Armament Monitoring and Control
ANG	Air National Guard
AOC	Air Officer Commanding
AOC-in-C	Air Officer Commander-in-Chief
AOP	Air Observation Post
AUW	All-up Weight
AVM	Air Vice-Marshal
BAC	British Aircraft Corporation
BAe	British Aerospace
BCDU	Bomber Command Development Unit
BOAC	British Overseas Airways Corporation
BPC	Barometric Pressure Control
CAACU	Civilian Anti-Aircraft Co-operation Unit
CENTO	Central Treaty Organization
CO	Commanding Officer
Daughter Firm	means built at either A.V. Roe, Boulton & Paul, Handley Page or Short Brothers.
DFC	Distinguished Flying Cross
DFM	Distinguished Flying Medal
DSO	Distinguished Service Order
ECM	Electronic Countermeasures
ESM	Electronic Support Measures
ETPS	Empire Test Pilot School
FAA	Fuerza Aerea Argentina
FAE	Fuerza Aerea Ecuatoriana
FAP	Fuerza Aerea Peru
FEAF	Far East Air Force
FF	First Flew
FRADU	Fleet Requirements and Air Direction Unit
GR	General Reconnaissance
HF	High Frequency
IAS	Indicated Air Speed
IR	Infra-red
JPT	Jet Pipe Temperature
KCB	Knight Commander of the Order of the Bath
kg	Kilogram
LABS	Low-Altitude Bombing System
lb	Pound
MAP	Military Assistance Programme

Met.	RAF slang, abbreviation of meteorological
Mk	Mark
MoD	Ministry of Defence
MoS	Ministry of Supply
MOSAP	Ministry of Supply and Production
MRAF	Marshal of the Royal Air Force
MU	Maintenance Unit
Musketeer	operation, the code name for the Suez War
NATO	North Atlantic Treaty Organization
NCO	Non-commissioned Officer
NZ	New Zealand
OCU	Operational Conversion Unit
OTU	Operational Training Unit
PDU	Photographic Development Unit
PR	Photographic Reconnaissance
PR Blue	Photographic Reconnaissance Blue, which was used during the Second World War as an underside colour on PR Spitfires in Germany and the Middle and Far East. PR Blue was the brainchild of Sidney Cotton, who invented PR
PRU	Photographic Reconnaissance Unit
QRA	Quick Reaction Alert
RAAF	Royal Australian Air Force
RAF	Royal Air Force
RCM	Radio Countermeasures
Recce	Reconnaissance
RNAS	Royal Navy Air Service
RNZAF	Royal New Zealand Air Force
RPM	Revolution per minute
RR	Rolls-Royce
RRE	Royal Radar Establishment
RSR	Relay Set Receiving
R/T	Radio-Telephone
RWR	Radar Warning Receiver
SBAC	Society of British Aircraft Constructors
SEATO	South-East Asia Treaty Organization
SAAF	South African Air Force
SFC	Specific Fuel Consumption
SOC	Struck-off charge
Sqn	Squadron
SS	Static Thrust
TOS	Tactical Operations Squadron
UHF	Ultra High Frequency
UK	United Kingdom
US (A)	United States (of America)
USAF	United States Air Force
USAAF	United States Army Air Force
VHF	Very High Frequency
W/T	Wireless Telegraphy

CHAPTER ONE

English Electric Canberra

The English Electric Canberra is one of the truly great aeroplanes of all time, and was the first jet bomber to enter RAF service (the world's first jet bomber was the Arado Blitz), the origin of its design going back as far as 1944. At that time the war was running in favour of the Allies, but was by no means over, and the Ministry of Aircraft Production was looking for a high-altitude jet bomber to replace the Hawker Typhoon in the fighter-bomber role.

The Air Ministry issued the specification, and W.E.W. Petter, then chief designer at English Electric, started to investigate proposals put to him by Sir Ralph Sorley, Controller of Research and Development at the Ministry of Aircraft Production. Neither English Electric nor Mr Petter was a newcomer to the business, for Petter's previous appointment had been with Westland Aircraft, and English Electric had vast experience in aircraft manufacture through substantial sub-contract work on the twin-engined Hampdens and the four-engined Halifaxes. Out of the 6,178 Halifaxes built, English Electric Co. Ltd built 2,145 – more than a third. And at that time English Electric was preparing to build its first jet aircraft – the Vampire fighter – under licence from de Havilland.

The initial proposals for the high-altitude jet bomber had been for an aircraft of about 40,000 lb (18,144 kg) AUW (all-up weight), powered by a single engine of 12,000 lb (5,443 kg) thrust mounted in the rear fuselage. However, by the autumn of 1945 the design had undergone a great many changes and was now put forward to meet the B3/45 specification for a high-speed two-crew bomber, and from the proposals received from the aircraft industry the most ambitious was that tendered by the English Electric Company.

By mid-January 1946, a contract had been placed for four prototypes of the English Electric A.1 as it was then known, and work soon began on a wooden mock-up. The beautiful clean lines of Britain's first jet bomber took shape in a converted commercial garage in Coronation Street, Preston, far away from Samlesbury, where Vampire production was well under way.

Radical though the aircraft undoubtedly was, Petter relied for the most part on skilful use of proven techniques to achieve the desired performance without incorporating untried aerodynamic or constructional features. Functional in appearance, with a cylindrical fuselage and conventional tail surfaces, the A.1 was provided with broad wings of low loading, which endowed it with a truly impressive performance more normally associated with fighter aircraft. Two of the new axial-flow Rolls-Royce engines, forerunner of the Avon, where chosen. These were mounted on the wing outboard of the undercarriage, which allowed a longer bomb bay and greater internal fuel tankage. The crew was to consist of pilot and navigator, with the blind-bombing radar mounted in the nose.

This low-speed wind tunnel in the English Electric Company's aircraft and development centre at Warton played a vital part in investigations for the Canberra.

Over the next three and a half years detailed design and building of the prototypes continued, and by May 1949 the first of the four prototypes had been constructed at the company's second airfield at Warton, a former USAAF aerodrome on the banks of the River Ribble.

After a series of taxiing tests and short hops down the runway, the first 400-yard (366 m) 'hop' being on 11 May, the great day came on Friday, 13 May. A Halifax B.111, LV907, christened *Friday the 13th* – so named because it was delivered to No. 158 Squadron at Lissett, Yorkshire, on that date – carried various unlucky omens on its nose and in the cockpit, but these seem to have worked in reverse, for far from bringing the crews who flew it ill fortune, *Friday the 13th* completed 128 sorties. For the superstitious, it was not the best day to begin test flying, but the all-blue A.1 Canberra prototype, VN799, took to the air with English Electric's chief test pilot, Roland Beamont, at the controls and made a successful first flight of twenty-seven minutes. As with 158 Squadron's Halifax, *Friday the 13th* proved lucky, and the only problem encountered during the test flight had been that of a slightly over-balanced rudder, this being remedied by removal of part of the horn balance, giving the aircraft its well-known square-cut fin and rudder. The other three prototypes were modified before their first flights.

Test flying of VN799 continued during the summer of 1949, and in September of that year it made its first public appearance at the Farnborough Air Display. Roland Beamont put the Canberra through its paces, and after a short take-off, near vertical climb and high-and low-speed passes, nobody was left in any doubt about its flying qualities and the soundness of its design. The Canberra was originally unarmed, the intention being to follow the Mosquito tradition, with the light bomber flying too fast and too high to be caught by contemporary fighters.

The Canberra had won the day, designed and built by a company that had not built an aircraft of its own design for more than twenty years. Time was to show that they were right, and numerous variants of Canberra appeared at Farnborough until well into the 1970s. So well was VN799's demonstration received – its performance was such that the then current fighters would not have been ashamed of it – that it was later demonstrated

Canberra B. Mk1 takes to the air and banks over the airfield.

at the USAF base at Burtonwood before a party of USAF officers and government officials. This was later to lead to an aircraft going to America to take part in trials against American aircraft types.

The remaining three aircraft of the initial batch made their first flights at Warton in the final two months of 1949, and to guard against failure of the new Avon engine, one of the prototypes had been fitted with two Rolls-Royce Nene engines.

The test programme progressed so well that it gave problems of another kind. The proposed radar bombing equipment was so far behind in its development that a revised version of the aircraft was called for, and a further four pre-production aircraft followed, with the first of these, VX165, emerging to B. Mk2 standard under specification B5/47. The stillborn B.1 had been intended to have a crew of two, seated side by side, but in the B. Mk2 version provision was made for a third crew member, a bomb-aimer, along with the installation of optical bomb-aiming equipment in a new glazed nose section, necessitated by the absence of the projected radar bombsight. The bomb-aimer reached the bombing position by crawling from his position behind the pilot. It was a step backwards in time to the duties of a Second World War bomb-aimer. However, substantial contracts had already been placed for the Canberras to replace the rapidly ageing Lincolns of Bomber Command even before the very first Canberra had flown. The first prototype B.2, VX165, made its first flight on 23 April 1950, less than a year after the original prototype, and was soon followed by VX 169, the second prototype B. Mk2. These aircraft were powered by Rolls-Royce Avon RA3s, as were the production B. Mk2s already on the production line.

WD929, the first of an initial production batch of seventy aircraft, made its first flight on 8 October 1950, and it was released to service on 5 April 1951. It was WD929 that was christened 'Canberra', after Australia's capital city, by the then Prime Minister of Australia, Robert (later Sir Robert) Gordon Menzies, at RAF Biggin Hill in January 1951, and after a long career as a trials aircraft, it appropriately ended its days on a scrap dump at Adelaide in 1967. The first seven aircraft were mainly used for tests and experimental purposes, and WD930 was taken on charge by the Handling Squadron at Manby on 8 March 1951, for preparation of Pilot's Notes. On 25 May, the first operational unit began conversion when Roland Beamont delivered WD936 to RAF Binbrook for No. 101 Squadron and by so doing became the first Royal Air Force Bomber Command squadron to be equipped with jet bombers, thus starting a new era in the history of the service. Many of the Canberra pilots were specially picked for the first jet bombers, and Binbrook, through the superb influence of Group Captain (later Air Commodore) Hetty Hyde and his wife, achieved something of a wartime spirit during those early Canberra days. There were lots of problems, but the place was lively and there were many very memorable parties to go with the first jet bombers. At this period Bomber Command still had only piston-engined aircraft, mainly Avro Lincolns and Boeing Washingtons, so jet conversion was undertaken by the Bomber Command Jet Conversion Unit. Later the Canberra Operational Conversion Unit was formed for this purpose.

Some of the early aircraft were used for development and trials work, including WD933 with Armstrong Siddeley Sapphire SSa6s in place of the B. Mk2s' Avons: WD929 at the Telecommunications Research Establishment at Defford; WD932 and WD940 as evaluation and pattern aircraft for US production as the Martin B-57; and WD935 and WD939 for similar roles in Australia, where forty-eight Canberras were built. A Canberra, WD952, fitted with two Bristol Siddeley Olympus engines, set a world height record of 63,668 ft (19,406 m) on 4 May 1953, while at the end of its officially sponsored work with English Electric. This record was raised to 65,890 ft (20,083 m) on 29 August 1955, and almost two years later, on 28 August 1957, another Canberra, powered by two Rolls-Royce Avon turbojets and a Napier Double Scorpion rocket motor, raised the world height record to 70,310 ft (21,430 m). The Canberra was a sensational aircraft from the start, and between 1951 and 1958 set twenty-two world records for speed, height and range, a record its designers and manufacturers can be justly proud of. Like the Mosquito, it was unarmed, relying on speed to evade fighters. WD937 appeared on the civil register as G-ATZW for a twelve-month period beginning in October 1966.

Bomber Command waited eagerly for the Canberras, for it was keen to trade in its ageing Avro Lincolns, but deliveries did not get fully under way until the latter part of 1951. The need now was for large-scale crew training, and this began in December, when the first two B. Mk2s arrived at No. 231 Operational Conversion Unit at Bassingbourn. By January 1952, the second Canberra Squadron, No. 617, the famous 'Dam Busters' – also at Binbrook – began to get its Canberras, with WD961 arriving on the 21st of the month. By March, WD980, WD982, WD984 and WD986 had arrived, these being the last Canberras to be delivered in the grey and black colour scheme. By May 1952, Nos 9 and 12 Squadrons, also based at Binbrook, were trading in their Lincolns for Canberras.

As the Canberras began to arrive at Binbrook, Squadron Leader Ken Wallis, the Senior Armament Officer, began to find many faults (see Chapter Eleven). A problem that they had, as armourers, in the early fatal Canberra crashes, was to find in the wreckage the pitch control rod severing charge. This was an explosive charge, in a Tufnol clamp, which was fitted around the pitch control tube. In the event that a bale-out was necessary, this charge would have to be blown before firing the ejection seat. If not, the pilot's knees would strike the spectacle roll control on the typical bomber-type control column.

Cutting the control rod enabled the control to go fully forward and clear of the pilot's knees. Inadvertent firing of this charge (it was electrically initiated) was often suspected as being the cause of the aircraft just flying into the ground. Ken Wallis spent many hours searching in wreckage in Lincolnshire before finding this charge unfired, even if somewhat broken up. Squadron Leader Wallis believed that runaway tailplanes would eventually be found to be the cause.

With the outbreak of the Korean War in 1950, orders for the Canberra were increased, and three sub-contractors were called upon to produce additional aircraft in order to hasten the build-up of the Canberra squadrons. Short Brothers and Harland built a total of sixty Canberra B. Mk2s, beginning with WH853, flown on 30 October 1952; A.V. Roe at Woodford built seventy-five B. Mk2s from serial WJ971, which first flew on 25 November 1952; and Handley Page at Radlett assembled sixty-six from serial WJ564, which flew on 5 January 1953. Contracts for a further 150 B. Mk2s divided equally between A.V. Roe and Handley Page were later to be cancelled.

Thus, as production built up, Bomber Command increased its Canberra strength as the Avro Lincolns and Boeing Washingtons were replaced. The Mosquito B35s of Nos 109 and 139 Squadrons at Hemswell in Lincolnshire were also replaced by Canberras. In addition six squadrons, Nos 10, 18, 21, 27, 40 and 59, were re-formed with Canberras, and by March 1955 twenty-five squadrons were flying Canberra B. Mk2s, including four units which made up No. 31 Wing at RAF Gutersloh in West Germany. The Canberras were part of the 2nd Tactical Air Force and consisted of No. 149 Squadron, which received its Canberras in the spring of 1953 and in August 1954 became the first Canberra squadron to be permanently based in Germany with the 2nd Tactical Air Force; No. 102 Squadron re-formed as a Canberra unit in October 1954, and No. 103 the following month. Both squadrons re-formed at Gutersloh. The final squadron of the Gutersloh Wing was No. 104, which re-formed in March 1955. But their stay was short-lived, for in August 1956 they all disbanded.

The Canberra was to make a number of tours and goodwill visits, and it was No. 12 Squadron which started the ball rolling when four aircraft, WD987, WD990, WD993 and WD996, left Binbrook on 20 October 1952 for 'Operation Round Trip', which lasted for over six weeks and involved flying more than 24,000 miles (38,600 km) to South America – the first South American visit by RAF jets. The tour included the first jet crossing of the South Atlantic in both directions. Countries visited were Brazil, Uruguay, Argentina, Chile, Peru, Colombia, Venezuela, British Honduras, Mexico, Cuba, Jamaica, Dominica and Trinidad.

On 22 September 1952, WD987 made a record-breaking flight to Nairobi, carrying the Bomber Command Commander-in-Chief, Sir Hugh-Pugh Lloyd. The Canberra was again in the news on 3 June 1953, when it rushed films of the Coronation to the USA. More tours followed in November 1953 – No. 57 Squadron at Cottesmore sent six Canberras on a tour of the Middle East, giving flying displays at Baghdad (Iraq), Amman (Jordan) and Idris (Libya).

In June 1954 it was the turn of No. 27 Squadron, which took six aircraft on 'Operation Med. Trip', a tour of Europe and the Mediterranean area that included visits and displays in France, Italy, Greece, Turkey, Yugoslavia and Portugal. The following year it was No. 139 (Jamaica) Squadron, which did a tour of Jamaica. During its tour the squadron was given the freedom of Kingston, the capital city. No. 9 Squadron flew the flag in 1956 with a tour of Nigeria, which also coincided with the tour by Her Majesty the Queen and the Duke of Edinburgh. During the tour the squadron made ceremonial fly-pasts over Lagos, the Nigerian capital. It also gave flying demonstrations and, after the Royal Tour, visited other territories in West Africa.

In the mid-1950s the Canberra went to war. It is one of the few RAF jet aircraft to have actually been in action. During February 1955, No. 101 Squadron became the first RAF jet bomber squadron to fly on war operations, when four of its Canberra B. Mk6s were deployed to Butterworth, Malaya, for anti-terrorist bombing missions in Operation Firedog. On 23 February, Canberra WH948, flown by Squadron Leader Robertson, became the first RAF jet bomber to drop bombs in anger. That same day the other aircraft also flew missions. An example of the Canberra at war is given in Chapter Six (No. 101 Squadron).

Other Bomber Command squadrons deployed to Malaya to take part in the air war against the terrorists included No. 9, detached to Butterworth from March to June 1956, and after its anti-bandit tour No. 5 Squadron Canberras paid a goodwill visit to the Philippines; No. 12 detached to Butterworth from October 1955 to March 1956, and during that period made twenty-four successful strikes; No. 617 was also detached to Butterworth, from July to November 1955, to operate against the Communist terrorists. In November 1957 No. 45 Squadron moved to Tengah to re-equip with Canberra B. Mk2s, and it used these on anti-terrorist operations in Malaya.

The Canberras also saw war operations in a different area – in the Middle East – and on a much larger scale when the Suez War occurred in 1956 and they went into action against military objectives in Egypt. In October and November 1956, Bomber Command squadrons were detached to Cyprus and Malta. The Canberras – mostly the longer-range B. Mk6s of Nos 9, 12, 101, 109 and 139 Squadrons – were based at the Maltese airfields of Hal Far and Luqa, while shorter-range B. Mk2s of Nos 10, 15, 18, 27, 35, 44, 61 and 115 Squadrons went to Nicosia, Cyprus.

Egypt refused to accept the terms of a ceasefire that Britain and France put forward, and so, on the evening of 31 October, Canberras of Nos 10 and 12 Squadrons and Valiants of No. 148 Squadron attacked airfields in the Canal Zone. The first bombs were dropped on Almaza airfield by Canberra B. Mk2 WH853 of No. 10 Squadron. Over the next two nights attacks were made on airfields, including four in the Nile Delta, by which time the Egyptian Air Force was largely destroyed. Attacks were then made on fuel and ammunition dumps. During the conflict some of the aircraft were hit by small-arms fire, and a Syrian MiG-17 claimed Canberra PR.7 WH799 of No. 13 Squadron on 6 November.

Although the bombers encountered little opposition from fighters or ground defences, the operations showed many weaknesses in equipment and techniques. The Canberras had not been designed for that kind of radar warfare, and because there were no ground beacons in the war zone for their main navigational aid, Gee-H, target marking was carried out in the same way as it had been done in the Second World War.

Canberras were also used in the reconnaissance role in the Gulf and the Aden Protectorate and during confrontation in the Far East, as well as other trouble spots, and in support of earthquake, hurricane and flood relief operations. Canberras of the Royal Australian Air Force and licence-built B57s of the USAF flew extensively during the Vietnam War. Canberras also saw action during the Indo-Pakistan War, and those of the former Rhodesian Air Force made long-range attack missions.

As increasing numbers of V-bombers, Valiants and Vulcans became available for

Bomber Command, they assumed the nuclear strike roles that had been allocated to the Canberra B. Mk6s, and a number of the Canberra units began to disband before becoming part of the V-Force.

During the latter half of the 1950s many B. Mk2s from disbanded units became available, and after being overhauled at MUs a number of B. Mk2s replaced the de Havilland Venoms of four squadrons, Nos 6, 32, 73 and 249, on Cyprus. They were the Akrotiri Strike Wing, and Canberras of various marks were to remain in service with the Cyprus strike wing for the next eleven years.

During this period No. 45 Squadron, stationed at Tengah, Singapore, traded in its Venoms for Canberra B. Mk2s and used these on the final anti-terrorist operations in Malaya.

As the B. Mk2s were traded in for other marks with the remaining Canberra squadrons, they became available for sale to overseas customers and for conversion to later marks in order to continue in service with the RAF. The final Canberra bomber squadron stationed in Britain was No. 35, equipped with B. Mk2s, and it remained with these until it disbanded at Upwood on 11 September 1961. By this time many of the B. Mk6s had changed role from strategic to strike. As more B. Mk2s became available they were relegated to second-line duties, some being for radar calibration, while more than twenty were converted to dual-control T. Mk4 trainer configuration to augment the production batch of this type. T. Mk4s were used by No. 231 OCU in large numbers, and most Canberra squadrons received a T. Mk4 for continuation training. No. 56 Squadron, equipped with supersonic Lightnings, obtained three Canberras to act as target facilities aircraft for its Lightnings while they were based in Cyprus during the late 1960s. In the mid-1950s the OCU formed an aerobatic team with their Canberra T. Mk4s and gave many displays throughout the country.

As the development of the B. Mk2 went ahead, a second line of Canberra variants was also planned, the first of these being the PR. Mk 3 a reconnaissance variant. This

The one and only B. Mk5, VX185, in a new coat of paint for the Farnborough display immediately after the double Atlantic flight.

Canberra WH793, PR. Mk7 was released to service on 20 April 1954 and became the prototype PR. Mk9. Shown here with Mk9 wings, which were needed because of the different engines and also to get better lift. Note the extended wing tip and extended leading edge to cater for the Avon R.A.24 engines.

was basically a B. Mk2 and was designed as a replacement for the final marks of high-flying reconnaissance Mosquitoes. The first production aircraft, WE135, first flew on 31 July 1952, and in December 1952, No. 540 Squadron at RAF Benson started to replace its Mosquito PR 34s with Canberra PR Mk3s. From 1953 to 1955 five more squadrons were equipped with PR Mk3s, together with a reconnaissance flight of No. 231 OCU. By the summer of 1958 four more squadrons were flying Canberra PR Mk3s, and they also served with No. 237 OCU, which was absorbed by 231 OCU.

Most notable of the PR Mk3s was WE139, flown by Flight Lieutenant R. L. E. Burton AFC, and Flight Lieutenant D. H. Gannon DFC, which won the speed section of the London to Christchurch (New Zealand) air race of October 1953 in 23 hours 51 minutes at an average speed of 494.5 mph (797.5 km/h). Retired from service, it was placed in storage on 24 April 1969, and is now preserved in the Royal Air Force Museum at Hendon. Several point-to-point records were set up during the race, and it is interesting to note that the five Canberras (two PR Mk3s RAF; one PR Mk7 RAF; and two B. Mk20s RAAF) that took part in the race were only separated by fifteen minutes in actual flying time.

Canberra B(I). Mk8 WT329 which was issued to service on 1 January 1956. Note standard wing profile for B(I). Mk8 and other marks with integral tank and Avon R.A.7 engines.

As the Canberra B. Mk2 was transformed into the B. Mk6, which entered service with No. 101 Squadron at RAF Binbrook in Lincolnshire and then with Nos 6, 9, 12, 21, 76, 109, 139, 249 and 617 Squadrons, so the PR Mk 3 gave way on the production line to the PR Mk7. Many went to earlier customers of the PR Mk3, and they served in all areas of operations where the Royal Air Force was engaged at the time.

Naturally, PR Mk7s undertook their fair share of long-distance flying, including WT528 Aries V of the RAF Flying College, Manby. This aircraft took over from Canberra WH669 (Aries IV) in 1956, and it was already a record breaker, having broken the London to New York and New York to London records on 23 August 1955 – 7 hours 29 minutes 56.7 seconds and 6 hours 16 minutes 59.5 seconds respectively – and it had also achieved the first two-way Atlantic crossing in a single day, covering 6,915 miles (11,128 km) in 14 hours 21 minutes 45 seconds (including a 35-minute refuelling turn-round at Floyd Bennett Field), an average of 481.52 mph (775 km/h).

Canberra WT528, Aries V, went on to break more records. With increased tankage to give a total fuel load of 4,065 gallons (18,479 litres), it flew over the North Pole from Haneda airport, Tokyo, to West Malling in Kent on 25 May 1957, as an experimental navigation exercise covering a total of 5,942 miles (9,562 km) in 17 hours 42 minutes 2.3 seconds (335.7 mph 540 km/h).

In the spring of 1958, WT528 made a round-the-world flight and then went on to visit Rhodesia, South Africa, Australia and New Zealand, developing navigational techniques and working out training methods with Commonwealth air forces. After its record-breaking run, WT528 was converted to PR.57 standard and sold to the Indian Air Force in the mid-1960s as BP746.

In the UK Nos 58 and 540 Squadrons at Wyton received a number of PR Mk7s, and No. 542 Squadron also served at Wyton for a short while with PR Mk7s.

Abroad, PR Mk7s replaced the Meteor PR.10s of No. 81 Squadron at Tengah, Singapore, the Far East's reconnaissance squadron. In January 1958 Canberras, along with some Meteors and Valiants, completed for the Colonial Office and Directorate of Military Survey, a photographic survey of Aden Colony and Protectorate (112,000 square miles/290,080 km²).

In the Mediterranean Nos 13 and 39 Squadrons received Canberra PR. Mk7 aircraft, and RAF Germany proved to be the largest user of the PR. Mk7, with three squadrons based there during 1956, 1957 and 1958. No. 31 Squadron re-formed at Laarbruch in March 1955, and was soon joined by 80 Squadron, which also re-formed at Laarbruch in June 1955. A third squadron, No. 17, re-formed at Wahne with PR. Mk7s in June 1956. Following on from the PR. Mk7 came the B(I). Mk8, the first Canberra with a fighter-style canopy. No. 88 Squadron received the first B (I) Mk8s at Wildenrath, Germany, in January 1956, and was redesignated No. 14 Squadron in December 1962. Similarly, No. 59 Squadron, which started to receive them in early 1957, became No. 3 Squadron in January 1961 at Geilenkirchen. The wing came up to full strength when No. 16 Squadron re-formed at Laarbruch in March 1958. This squadron was the final unit to use Canberras of any mark in the bombing role, and was disbanded in June 1972.

When a political whim forced the cancellation of the TSR2 – an aircraft decades

Canberra PR. Mk7 WT528 'Aries V', which was released to service on 21 September 1955.

In this unique picture we see the one and only TSR-2. Chase aircraft is the Lightning (which is left standing), and trying to catch it on film are the Canberras. One Canberra never saw it. It had gone.

The last production version of the Canberra was the PR. Mk9 seen here on the production line at Short Brothers, which produced twenty-three of them.

before its time and that left everything we had standing, as if they were powered by rubber bands; and that included the English Electric Lightning, as seen in my unique photograph, published here for the very first time – the Canberras were forced to soldier on as front-line aircraft until the early Seventies, when they were replaced by Hawker Siddeley Harriers, Phantoms and Buccaneers. Most Canberras came back to the UK, either for refurbishing and resale overseas or for scrapping.

Canberra 'new build' ended in 1964, with refurbishment work continuing into 1982. The last 'basic' version of the Canberra was the PR, Mk9, which was the ultimate high-level development of the reconnaissance Canberra theme, and these were engineered and built by Short Brothers in Belfast. The last 'basic' version built in England was the B(I). Mk8, but a mixture of these, T.4s, B.6s, PR.7 (or their export equivalents) B(I). 12s and T.13s were included in the later production orders. Other versions were created by modifying existing aircraft, for example TT.18 up to the Mk22.

The first Shorts-built Canberra, a B. Mk2, made its maiden flight on Thursday 30 October 1952. The last Shorts-built Canberra, a PR. Mk9, made its maiden flight in December 1960, when production of new Canberras ceased at Airport Road. In addition to manufacturing the Canberra, Short Brothers also made a very considerable design contribution to the Canberra programme, being responsible for the major modifications involved in transforming the standard bomber into the PR.9 high-altitude photographic reconnaissance aircraft, and later, for the entire design programme on the U. Mk10 high-speed target drone conversion.

In the case of the PR.9, Shorts did a lot of the design work, including structural modifications, layout of hydraulic and air systems and installation of electrical, photographic and radio equipment. One very important task was the provision of an automatic ejector seat for the navigator.

The first PR. Mk9 squadron was No. 58 Squadron at RAF Wyton. It re-equipped at Wyton in early 1960, while later Canberras augmented Nos 13 and 39 Squadrons in Malta. As attrition took its toll, No. 58 Squadron disbanded in September 1970, and No. 13 Squadron went back to using the PR. Mk7 Canberra.

When Britain reduced its commitments in the Mediterranean, Canberra XH136 of No. 39 Squadron became the last of the type to leave Malta, flying home on 21 October 1976; while Canberra XH174, of the same squadron, was the first to be noted with fin-mounted ECM pod in 1977.

In November 1983, Shorts at Airport Road, Belfast, started work on the first of five Canberras PR. Mk9s, destined to 'Only Live Twice' and to see out the Canberra era in RAF service. They are the magnificent five, and in the foreground (see pages 24 and 25) is XH131. Shorts refurbished them for the Royal Air Force under a Ministry of Defence contract. It included, in addition to major servicing, reconditioning and replacement of stock parts, the manufacture of components and embodiment of modifications involving design work by Shorts, and provided a valuable extension of the company's work on the Canberra aircraft. The contract was worth in excess of £3,500,000 and gave work for many years; the final PR.9 was handed over on 14 December 1989.

The Canberra, having flown into the twenty-first century, is proof that it is an ageless aircraft; and on 21 January 2004 the Command Secretariat, Headquarters Strike Command, at Royal Air Force High Wycombe, told me:

> Firstly, the out-of-service date for the Canberra is anticipated to be towards the end of the decade. Secondly, future provision of the capability provided by the Canberra has been under consideration for some time, and as yet, no conclusions have been finalised.

The last of the few. End of Canberra production at Shorts. A nice head-on view. Rare picture.

Canberra B. Mk6 WH952, released to service on 29 January 1955 and served at Farnborough. Photographed 28 November 1983 at RAE Bedford.

The call of the Mayfly – Lilian Bland in her 'flying machine'.

The beautiful Lilian Bland, the first lady in the world to fly.

Now I have known for some time that No. 39 (1 PRU) Squadron will disband on 31 March 2006, thus bringing to an end the Canberra era in the RAF. Not before time, for during the summer of 1975 the Canberra airframe had many Category 3 problems; and at RAF Cottesmore No. 71 MU had to call in a contractor's working party to help iron out the many problems. These were so difficult that many airframes were still being worked on in hangars, long after the station had been placed on care and maintenance.

Having said that, on the plus side, the Canberra in service, like the de Havilland Mosquito, became a 'Jack of all Trades', though not as the old adage goes, 'Master of None', for the Canberra took all these diverse roles with ease, which bears glowing testimony to the design team who produced this 'Jet Mosquito'. From flying as a medium conventional bomber, tactical nuclear bomber, night intruder, radar trainer, ground-attack aircraft and target tug; from photographic reconnaissance aircraft to countermeasures, the Canberra has proved itself a very worthy successor to the de Havilland's twin-engined, wartime all-rounder, which was one of the best aircraft ever produced by the British aircraft industry.

The year 2003 marked the Centennial of Flight; and the Canberra has been flying for over half that century of flight. Wing Commander K.H. Wallis, who was destined to fly and be involved with the Canberra aircraft, has been a pilot for well over two-thirds of that century of flight, the Wallis family being involved from the start. In the picture above we see his father, H.S. Wallis, holding an airscrew 'tractor' (not 'propeller') with his left hand and, with his right hand, a good cigar.

Lilian Bland, a native of Kent, England, designed, built and flew a 'flying machine' which she named the Mayfly, for she said at the time, '*It may fly or it may not*'. She lived with her relatives in Carnmoney, near Belfast, and later emigrated to Canada.

Like Lilian Bland, the first lady in the world to fly, the Canberra is another lady to have flown into the history books; and to that I will raise my glass:

To the Lilian Blands and Kenneth Wallises of the world'
and to that Grand Old Lady, the Canberra,
Cheers!

CHAPTER TWO

Rolls-Royce Avon
A History of its Development

The Avon, the name most frequently found among Britain's rivers, is, in effect, the modern Merlin, and like the Merlin, it had its early troubles, but it was soon to be established as one of the most reliable aero engines of all time.

Two things are of prime importance to an aircraft turbine engine – that it works and that it is available at a time when it is needed. Compared with these criteria, all other considerations are of lesser consequence. An outlook such as this towards business may be regarded as the theme behind the success of Rolls-Royce as an outstanding aero-engine manufacturing company in Britain, and it is undoubtedly the reason why the Avon turbojet became such a huge success.

Two factors may be said to have led to the initiation of the Avon as a project design: firstly, the opinion of Rolls-Royce engineers at the end of the war that the future for the turbojet engine lay in the use of an axial-flow compressor rather than a centrifugal unit; and secondly, the requirement for a suitable engine for the high-altitude light bomber set out in a Ministry of Supply specification of 1945.

Rolls-Royce was designing axial gas turbines as long ago as the Battle of Britain; for example, the CR.1, an engine of exceptional technical interest, was on the drawing board in September 1940, and an experimental prototype ran on the test bed in 1942. It was felt that by using an axial compressor based on the latest design concepts and applying it to an engine bearing all the developed and well-tried features of the company's centrifugal Derwent and Nene turbojets, an engine could be obtained of particularly low diameter and weight. The higher efficiency and pressure ratio of the axial compressor would also result in the attainment of an exceptionally low specific fuel consumption (SFC).

This basis for a new engine was set out in a company technical memorandum shortly after the end of the war by Dr A.A. Griffith, then Rolls-Royce's chief research engineer. Dr. Griffith, who is well known for his early work on compressor aerofoil theory at the Royal Aircraft Establishment, is also known as a protagonist of the small engine, and for the new engine he further suggested that its overall diameter could be made sufficiently small for it to be suitable for installation in the thin wings of the high-altitude jet bombers then being projected.

Such were the apparent advantages of this new engine that the 13,000 lb (5,896 kg) two-stage centrifugal engine already projected at Rolls-Royce was dropped and the design of the English Electric light bomber, which was ultimately to become the Canberra, was reconstituted to take two axial-flow engines in nacelles in the wing (just how they fit into the Canberra wings can be clearly seen in the photograph on page 37), and in this way the Avon was born. It was designed in Derby and was, in its original form, known as the AJ65, an abbreviation of Axial Jet, 6,500 lb (2,948 kg) thrust, this figure being approximately the highest output that was likely to be achieved eventually by a single-stage centrifugal engine. In configuration the Avon R.A.1, as it was designated in its first form, utilized a 12-stage compressor of constant mean diameter, i.e. blade tip and hub diameter reduced progressively towards the rear of the compressor. With a pipe chamber combustion system of similar design to the Nene, the total cross-sectional area required for combustion showed that eight chambers constituted the optimum number.

A single-stage turbine was used, it being possible to design this within the maximum engine diameter of $41\frac{1}{2}$ in. (105.5 cm), as dictated by the combustion system. Three main bearings supported the rotative assembly. The shape of the engine was such that the progressive reduction in compressor casing diameter provided adequate space to mount and drive the engine accessories on the compressor delivery casing, within the combustion system diameter. Following Dr Griffith's memo, many of the proven mechanical features of the Nene were also incorporated, such as the turbine shaft coupling and the main bearing oil seal systems, etc.

This R.A.1 engine, which weighed 2,400 lb (1,089 kg), first ran in March 1947. However, as Rolls-Royce's first axial design, certain running troubles were experienced, which meant that neither the brochure thrust nor the SFC of 0.89 lb/hr/lb was achieved. A further version of the engine was produced, having a reduced-capacity compressor. This Avon, the R.A.2, first ran in January 1948, and, in addition to air bleed valves, the compressor now also incorporated two-position inlet-guide vanes. The addition of these devices was to improve the running conditions of the compressor.

By August the same year, the R.A.2 became the first Avon to be flight tested, installed in the outboard nacelles of an Avro Lancastrian (VM732) in place of the normal Merlin power-plants. It was in this aircraft that the Avon made its public debut the next month at the 1948 SBAC Flying Display.

For the same weight and diameter as the first Avon, the R.A.2 eventually produced 6,000 lb (2,722 kg) for an SFC of 0.98 lb/hr/lb, it being at this rating that it was released,

Left-hand side of Mark 1 engine.

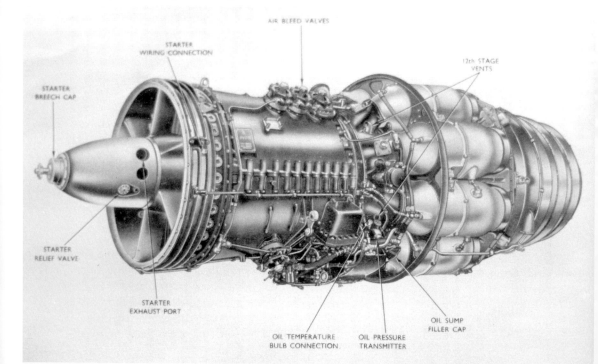

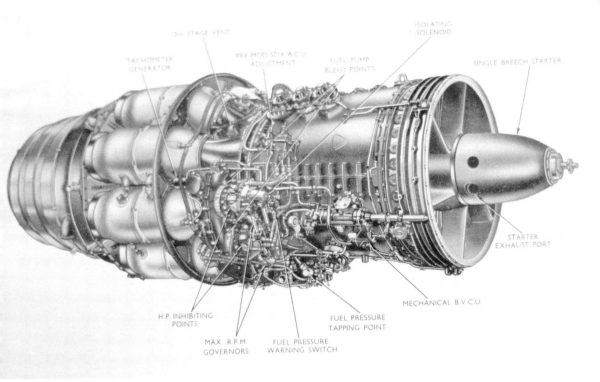

13th STAGE VENT

TACHOMETER GENERATOR

PRE-MOD 5014 A.C.U. ADJUSTMENT

FUEL PUMP BLEED POINTS

ISOLATING SOLENOID

SINGLE BREECH STARTER

STARTER EXHAUST PORT

MECHANICAL B.V.C.U.

H.P. INHIBITING POINTS

MAX. R.P.M GOVERNORS

FUEL PRESSURE WARNING SWITCH

FUEL PRESSURE TAPPING POINT

Right-hand side of Mark 2 engine.

in January 1949, for 100 hours' flying in the Canberra. It powered the prototype Canberra B.1 (VN799) on its first flight in May 1949, and it can be seen that Dr Griffith's contention that it should be possible to bury the Avon within the aircraft's wing had all but been achieved. This aircraft, together with an Avon-Meteor 4 flying test-bed (RA491), provided very impressive evidence of the Avon's power at the 1949 SBAC Flying Display.

Rolls-Royce, however, was still aiming at the Avon going into production at its originally specified thrust of 6,500 lb (2,948 kg). A new engine was produced, with the turbine redesigned as a two-stage unit of consequently smaller diameter. This was known as the R.A.3, and it first ran in April 1949. By October that year sufficient further development had been completed for the engine to take to the air in the Lancastrian flying test-bed.

Such was the progress of the R.A.3 that it entered production, as the Avon Mk1, in July 1950, the same month in which it flew in the Canberra B.2, both the aircraft and engine having been ordered in quantity for the Royal Air Force. This move was made on the evidence of engine test results, confirmation in this confidence placed in Rolls-Royce being provided in November that year, when the R.A.3 became the first Avon to pass a test successfully. At 6,500 lb (2,948 kg), it had an SFC of 0.88 lb/hr/lb; its weight was reduced to 2,240 lb (1,016 kg) and its diameter increased to 42.2 in. (107 cm).

By November 1950, with the onset of the Korean War and the initiation of Britain's rearmament programme, the orders for the Avon and the Canberra were greatly increased. To cope with this new production requirement, the Engine Division of the Bristol Aeroplane Co. and D. Napier and Son were given Ministry contracts to manufacture the Avon. Later, the Standard Motor Co, was included in the list as well. Rolls-Royce, in addition to Avon production at its Derby and Hillington (Glasgow) factories, increased its capacity by building a new factory at East Kilbride.

In January 1951, the Canberra entered squadron use with the Royal Air Force, the Avon thus becoming the first British axial turbojet to see service.

Returning to Avon development, the R.A.3 with its redesigned turbine was basically an underrated engine. In the course of structural development and other tests, R.A.3s had been run incorporating various modifications. These had enabled considerably higher thrusts than 6,500 lb (2,948 kg) to be achieved.

As a consequence of these, a 25-hour special-category test in August 1950 cleared the R.A.3 for 7,800 lb (3,538 kg), and two of these engines in the flying Meteor test-bed provided an outstanding performance for the SBAC Show of that year.

On the basis of a further type test of a modified R.A.3 at 7,950 lb (3,606 kg), and to provide a more powerful engine for the forthcoming Hawker Hunter and Supermarine Swift fighters, a new Avon, the R.A.7, was initiated. To fit the engine for this purpose, some fairly considerable redesigning of the R.A.3 had to be carried out. At the same time the R.A.7 was arranged to incorporate the modifications developed on the higher rated R.A.3s. The pressure balance piston behind the compressor was also eliminated.

An addition of major importance was the introduction of anti-icing equipment in the R.A.7. Typical of Rolls-Royce's methodical approach to engine development were the extensive compressor inlet icing tests that were performed. After initial investigation on the ground, in which ice cubes as large as 1½ in. (3.8 cm) were fed into the intake with no damage to the compressor, flight tests were performed in a second Lancastrian test-bed, fitted with a water-spray grid. These were to assess just how much ice the Avon could swallow.

After various anti-icing schemes had been investigated, a hot-air system was developed. This used hot compressor-delivery air for heating the starter fairing, intake struts and compressor inlet guide vanes. A separate bleed of compressor air was provided for anti-icing the aircraft air-intake lip.

By August 1952, the R.A.7 had been sufficiently developed for it to pass its 150-hour official type test. It entered production the same month, and the R.A.7 and its descendants became known as the 100-series Avons. Its rating was 7,500 lb (3,402 kg) thrust for an SFC of 0.92 lb/hr/lb. Weight had been necessarily increased to 2,460 lb (1,116 kg) because of the general all-round increase in engine operating stresses when used at transonic and supersonic aircraft speeds. The diameter of the R.A.7 was unchanged at 42.2 in. (107 cm).

Returning to 1951, during that year the Avon-powered Canberra P.R.3 and Canberra

Canberra B. Mk2 WD943 used as the Reheat Avon Canberra for trials of the Avon R.A.7R engine.

B.5, Short S.A.4 and Vickers Valiant B.1 medium bombers, Supermarine 508 naval fighter and Hawker P.1067 and Supermarine Type 541 (respectively the forerunners of the Hunter and Swift) all made their first flights. Also, in April that year development running started with an after-burner version of the Avon, the R.A.7R. This form of thrust boosting had been necessary to provide the forthcoming fighters in their interceptor role with a sufficiently high rate of climb and altitude performance. Reheat, or after-burning, provides a means of increasing thrust without increasing the engine's frontal area. Unlike a piston engine, the fuel in a jet engine is burned in an excess of air, so there is still a certain amount of oxygen present in the exhaust. These gases will therefore support combustion, and it is possible to burn additional fuel in the jet pipe to increase the exhaust velocity and consequently increase the thrust of the engine.

Development of this equipment, using Rolls-Royce's previous after-burner experience on such engines as the Derwent, had progressed sufficiently far by June the next year for the R.A.7R to be flown in the Canberra test-bed. Canberra WD943 was used for the Reheat Avon trials.

This forceful combination played a loud and persuasive part in the 1952 SBAC Flying Display, as also did the Avon-powered first prototype Avro Vulcan B.1 medium bomber, the de Havilland 110 naval fighter, the Canberra T.4, the Hunter F.1 and the Swift F.1.

By March 1953, further experience with the after-burner enabled the R.A.7R to pass its official 150-hour type test and enter production some while later, being the first British after-burner turbojet to do so on both counts.

The basically 7,500 lb (3,402 kg) R.A.7R was rated at 9,500 lb (4,309 kg), with after-burning in operation. The weight of the engine with the additional equipment rose by 500 lb (227 kg) to 2,960 lb (1,343 kg), and its length was 120 in. (305 cm), compared with 102.1 in. (260 cm) for the basic R.A.7.

Further development of the R.A.7

While an updated 7,150 lb (3,243 kg) version of the R.A.3, known as the R.A.22 Mk101, had not been proceeded with, development of the R.A.7 took two lines. The first of these was the R.A.9, a 6,500 lb (2,948 kg) civil engine for use in the de Havilland Comet 2X jet airliner, the pre-production aircraft for the Comet 2. Designated the Mk502, it flew in the Comet 2X on its first flight in February 1952. A later version of this engine, the R.A.25, was a 7,100 lb (3,175 kg) engine intended for production Comet 2s. With its original designation of Mk503, it flew in the Comet 2 in August 1953. Later R.A.25s for the Comet were the Mks 504 and 505.

Both the R.A.9 and 25 differ from the R.A.7 mainly in installational details and in the provision of a higher standard of anti-icing equipment for the flight let-down requirements of civil aircraft, where the engine would be operated at a lower rpm. Development of this and later anti-icing systems for civil Avons had been performed on Rolls-Royce's rotor icing test rig at Hucknall, the company's flight test establishment.

The second major line of development of the R.A.7 was the military R.A.21 of 8,000 lb (3,629 kg) thrust, introduced to compete with the higher ratings of the Armstrong Siddeley Sapphire turbojets. This engine entered production as the Avon Mks 113 and 115.

A new Avon

Although by 1950 the Avon had increased its thrust rating by 33.3 per cent from 6,000 lb (2,722 kg) to approximately 8,000 lb (3,629 kg), it was doubtless apparent that for the

Canberra B. Mk2 WH671, which was used by Rolls-Royce for development flying with R.A.24 and R.A.28 Avons.

engine to maintain its ascendant position insufficient thrust potential would be forthcoming. For this reason work was started on a redesign of the engine based on the use of a new and larger compressor and a cannular combustion system.

From an initial project for an 8,500 lb (3,856 kg) engine, the R.A.14 of 9,500 lb (4,309 kg) thrust was evolved.

Development running of this new and potent addition to the Avon family started in November 1951, and sixteen months of intensive and progressive testing enabled the R.A.14 to make its first flight in February 1953, in a second Canberra flying test-bed (WD930). The engine was shown at that year's SBAC Flying Display both on Rolls-Royce's stand and in the Canberra. Other Avon-powered newcomers were the Swift F.3 and F.4 and the Valiant B.2.

The last-mentioned aircraft had flown with R.A.14s in April 1953, the same month in which the engine successfully passed its type test. The R.A.14 had then the highest official rating of any British turbojet, giving 9,500 lb (4,309 kg) for an SFC of 0.84 lb/hr/lb. Its diameter was $41\frac{1}{2}$ in. (105.5 cm), the same as the early R.A.1, and its weight was 2,860 lb (1,297 kg). By July 1953, R.A.14s were in production as the first of the new 200-series engines. It was then the most powerful engine being manufactured in this country.

Two civil versions of the R.A.14 were projected, the de-rated 9,000 lb (4,082 kg) R.A.16, which flew in the Comet 3 prototype in July 1954, and the 9,500 lb (4,309 kg) R.A.17, which was never built. The Comet 2 and 3, together with the Canberra B.6, PR.7 and B.8, and the Hunter F.4 and Supermarine 525 naval fighter, were included among the Avon-powered aircraft that flew at the 1954 SBAC Show.

Further development of the R.A.14 via an intermediate engine led to the 10,000 lb (4,536 kg) R.A.28, having an SFC of 0.86 lb/hr/lb. This engine became the first British turbojet to pass a type test at a five-figure thrust rating. It had entered production by September 1954 as the Mk204. Its diameter was the same as that of the R.A.14, and its weight was increased by only 30 lb (13.6 kg) to 2,890 lb (1,310 kg).

A civil version of the R.A.28, designated R.A.26, was developed, also with a 10,000 lb (4,536 kg) thrust and an SFC of 0.86 lb/hr/lb. This engine was scheduled as the Mk521 for the production versions of the Comet 3; however, as this aircraft was to be superseded by the Comet 4, R.A.26s were flown in the prototype Comet 3 only, as the Mk524, it being these engines which were used for the Comet 3's record-breaking flight to Australia.

The R.A.29 was specifically developed by Rolls-Royce for use in Comet 4 production aircraft. Two other versions of the Avon family are the R.A.18 and 24, the latter being the Avon Mk206 and used in the Canberra P.R.9. The Avon Mk206 is a turbojet engine intended for use in fighter aircraft, the principal features of which include a 15-stage axial-flow compressor driven by a two-stage turbine, a turbo-annular combustion chamber containing eight straight-flow flame tubes and an exhaust unit. The principal features of the engine carcase consist of an air intake casing, compressor casing, combustion casing, nozzle box and exhaust unit. The axial compressor is carried on a two-piece shaft and the turbine shaft couples with the compressor shaft assembly by screwing into it.

The main features of the Avon fuel system consist of an inlet filter, a twin fuel pump, a fuel-cooled oil-cooler and a flow control unit. Other features of the fuel system include the acceleration control unit, which limits the over-fuelling of the engine during accelerations, a top temperature control, which maintains the jet pipe temperature within limitations, and a fuel drains connection.

The oil system is essentially an integral part of the engine, and includes a combined sump and tank, pressure and scavenge pumps, filters and a fuel-cooled oil-cooler, incorporating a bypass valve for low-temperature operation. To prevent ice formation in the engine air intake, hot air, tapped from the compressor outlet, is distributed to the critical surfaces by an engine anti-icing system. Hot air from the aircraft anti-icing and pressurizing system is also available from the engine compressor. The engine is started by an iso-propyl-nitrate starter in conjunction with a high-energy ignition system. The starting sequence is controlled automatically.

The Avon has now ceased production. The most popular Avon type built was the Mark 1.

Jet Propulsion

Fundamentally a jet propulsion engine propels an aircraft in the same way as a propeller does. In each case air is accelerated rearwards, and the forward thrust on the aircraft is due to reaction to this acceleration. The thrust obtained is proportional both to the amount of air and to the acceleration imparted to it.

A jet propulsion engine takes in air, compresses it and then mixes it with fuel to form a combustible mixture that is burnt continuously. The heated gas then expands and accelerates backwards, producing the reaction that, acting on the airframe structure, thrusts the aircraft forward.

Rolls-Royce Avon

The differences between the various marks are related mainly to the installation features of the aircraft and include such items as handling rollers, alternative accessory drives, turbo or electric starting, reheat equipment and top temperature control.

General description of the Avon

A cross-section through the engine shows it to be built around a central shaft carried by three large bearings. On the front part of this shaft is a multi-stage air compressor and on the rear end is a two-stage turbine. Forward of the compressor is the air intake – between compressor and turbine are the combustion chambers – aft of the turbine are the exhaust unit and jet pipe.

Clear view of the Rolls-Royce Avon Mk206 engine.
These engines were only used in the PR. Mk9.

How the engine works

The engine has three main components – a compressor, a combustion chamber and a turbine.

Compression

Air entering the compressor from the forward-facing intake first passes between the variable-angle swirl vanes, which ensure that it approaches the first rotor blades at a suitable angle.

Compression of the air takes place in twelve separate stages, each consisting of a ring of rotor blades that accelerate the air, followed by a ring of stator blades in which the air is slowed down again, caused to increase in pressure, and directed at the correct angle on to the next stage of rotor blades.

Some distance along the top compressor casing will be seen a number of bleed valves, which open to allow the escape of air from the middle stages of the compressor at low rpm, when the early stages of the compressor are required to pass more air than the remainder of the engine can accept.

The axial-flow compressor engine claims two important advantages over the centrifugal flow type: (a) Engine efficiency is higher, less power being needed to compress the air and the specific fuel consumption being reduced by perhaps as much as 20 per cent; and (b) Air consumption is about twice as much for the same frontal area, much smaller installations with lower drag being therefore possible.

Combustion

From the compressor the air is delivered to the eight combustion chambers, where it is heated by burning fuel. About one-quarter of it is burnt with the fuel and the remainder mixes with the hot combustion gas to reduce its temperature to a safe value for the turbine nozzles and blades.

In each chamber most of the air required to support combustion enters the centre of the flame tube and is thoroughly mixed with finely atomized fuel from the Duple burner to give a short, intense flame at a temperature of about 3,632 °F (2,000 °C).

The remainder of the air first flows between the air casing and the flame tube to form a heat insulation and is then admitted to the flame tube by a series of holes to dilute the primary combustion products. Some of this air also completes the combustion, helping to give correct flame shape and size and prevent hot streaks reaching the turbine. The temperature of the gas reaching the turbine is between 370 and 426 °F (700 and 800 °C), and the turbine nozzle guide vanes are normally at red heat.

Despite the extreme temperatures within the combustion chambers, their outer surfaces are relatively cool. For extra safety, however, a fireproof bulkhead, forward of the combustion chambers, separates the fuel system and electrical equipment from the hot section of the engine.

Expansion and exhaust

After leaving the combustion chambers the gas passes first through the nozzle passages formed by the first-stage ring of nozzle guide vanes, and is guided on to the first-stage turbine blades at a velocity of about 2,000 ft/sec (610 m/sec). The gas then passes similarly between the second-stage nozzle guide vanes and through the second-stage turbine. At take-off conditions the gas imparts over 17,500 shaft horsepower to the turbine for driving the compressor.

At exit from the turbine the gas has an axial velocity of about 900 ft/sec (275 m/sec), and this remains fairly constant throughout the length of the exhaust unit and jet pipe, but is increased to about 1,800 ft/sec (550 m/sec) by the jet pipe final nozzle, which converts the remaining pressure energy of the gas into velocity energy.

Gas temperature is measured in the jet pipe and is referred to as jet pipe temperature (jpt). It would be more useful to know the exact temperature at the turbine nozzles and blades, which are, of course, the critical points as regards temperature, but it is both safer and more convenient to place the thermocouples in the jet pipe.

A small quantity of air is piped direct to the turbine from various stages of the compressor and is used to cool the turbine discs and to prevent gas leakage.

Fuel flow

Before the fuel system is described, it will be helpful to consider the way in which fuel flow must vary over the working range of the engine. Fuel flow is required to bear a fairly steady relationship to the airflow, although the air-fuel ratio varies over a much wider range than in a piston engine.

Assuming for the moment that air density remains constant (that is at constant altitude and constant aircraft speed), more fuel admitted to the burners by opening the throttle results in more turbine power, rpm, airflow and thrust. The engine takes up an rpm at which air and fuel are correctly related and the correct gas temperature is obtained. The throttle valve of the jet engine is, of course, very different from the throttle of a piston engine, which controls the airflow directly by the throttling effect of a butterfly in the air intake. The throttle valve is merely a form of tap controlling the fuel flow.

Fuel flow, however, is only one of the two factors that determine engine rpm. The other factor is air density at the engine intake which depends on the altitude and on the intake ram due to aircraft speed. When a change in intake air density occurs, the airflow undergoes a similar change. For example, at maximum rpm and 600 mph the airflow changes from about 150 lb/sec (68 kg/sec) at sea level to about 25 lb/sec (11 kg/sec) at 50,000 ft (15,240 m). In this example the airflow at 50,000 feet is one-sixth of the sea-level value, and fuel flow must be reduced in about the same proportion. Variations of intake air density, and therefore of airflow, must all be accompanied automatically by proportionate changes in fuel flow, because if the fuel flow remained unchanged this would cause either a rise or a fall in the engine rpm originally selected by the throttle. This automatic variation of fuel flow is a most important function of the fuel system.

The fuel system

The only manual control over the fuel consumption is the throttle, which selects the required rpm. Automatic adjustment of fuel flow made necessary by variations of altitude and aircraft speed, as previously mentioned, is accomplished by changes in fuel pump delivery pressure, so that the rpm selected by the throttle will be maintained within relatively close limits.

Fuel is delivered to the engine pumps under pressure from tank pumps, and the main pumps discharge it at a much higher pressure to the throttle valve. From the throttle valve it passes via the high-pressure cock to the pressurizing valve, which apportions it between the two jets of the Duple burner.

The main fuel pumps

The two fuel pumps are engine driven, and have a variable stroke which is controlled through the medium of a servo system by three units – the barometric pressure control (BPC), the acceleration control unit (ACU) and the overspeed governors.

These units are each able to alter the pump stroke, and thus vary the fuel delivery pressure to the throttle and therefore the fuel flow to the burners.

The barometric pressure control

The BPC is the unit that automatically keeps the correct ratio between fuel consumption and airflow and thus ensures reasonably constant rpm and jet pipe temperature for a fixed setting of the throttle. The BPC, through the servo system, varies the stroke of the fuel pumps in such a way that the fuel delivery pressure is proportional to intake air pressure. If intake air pressure remains constant so does pump delivery pressure, regardless of throttle position. If intake pressure falls, as it does on a climb to altitude, pump delivery pressure is also made to fall, and less fuel gets past the throttle valve to the burners.

The acceleration control unit

The ACU prevents an excessive amount of fuel being admitted to the combustion chambers if the throttle is opened rapidly, at low altitude only (the ACU is only fully effective up to about 3,000 ft (915 m)).

When the throttle is opened the fuel flow increases immediately, but the airflow can only increase as the engine accelerates. During this brief period of acceleration the ACU limits the rate at which fuel flow can increase and thus prevents too much fuel being burnt in too little air. It allows the fastest possible acceleration but eliminates the risk of compressor surge and unduly high gas temperatures.

The ACU works in the same way as the BPC, by adjusting the fuel pump stroke.

The overspeed governors

Each of the two fuel pumps has a built-in governor, which prevents the engine from exceeding its maximum safe rpm. The governor of the bottom pump is set to a slightly lower rpm than that of the top in order to avoid instability, and when maximum rpm is reached the governor opens a servo system valve to limit the stroke of the pumps.

The isolating valve

The two fuel pumps normally work at the same stroke, since they use the same servo system and are jointly controlled by the BPC, ACU and the overspeed governors.

If a servo system fault were to develop in one of the pumps or in one of the controlling units, both pumps would move towards minimum stroke and fuel delivery might be lost. In such an event the isolating valve could be closed to isolate the top pump, which would then go to maximum stroke, thus ensuring that about 60 per cent of the maximum take-off fuel demand would be available at sea level.

The Duple burner

The Duple anti-carbon burner consists of two concentric jets surrounded by a shroud that causes air to blow across the jets and prevent fuel from burning on the burner surfaces. The Duple burner gives good fuel atomization, even at the very low flows required at high altitude, without requiring unduly high fuel pressure at the high fuel flows. Low flows are handled entirely by the small jet, and large flows by both together. The fuel is apportioned between the two jets by the pressurizing valve unit.

The oil system

The Avon has no heavily loaded bearings of the type met with in a piston engine, and is thus able to use a thin oil at low pressure to obtain the necessary lubrication and rate of flow. Consumption of oil is very moderate, the normal maximum being less than 1½ pints (1 litre) per hour.

The duty of the oil system is to flush, lubricate and cool the ball and roller bearings of the main shaft and to lubricate the various wheelcase gears and bearings. Oil is delivered by a pressure pump at about 30 lb/sq in. (2 kg/cm²) via the fuel-cooled oil cooler and pressure filter, and is returned to the sump by the two scavenge pumps and gravity drainage. The use of the main fuel flow as a means of cooling the oil avoids the need for an external oil radiator.

Suitable measures are taken to prevent oil loss from the main bearings, including pressurizing with air tapped from the compressor. Very effective de-aeration of the oil is accomplished in the centrifugal breather to prevent loss of oil.

The starter system

The engine is started by a small cartridge-driven turbine, and ignition of the main fuel sprays is accomplished by flames from two torch igniters. An automatic time switch controls the starting cycle upon pressing the starter button. The turbo-starter is housed inside the engine nose fairing, where it is readily accessible for reloading and also conveniently situated for driving the compressor shaft through its compound gear train and an engagement dog. About 200 horsepower is developed by the starter at a rotor speed of 45,000 rpm, and the engine is accelerated to about 1,700 rpm in two seconds. At this rpm the engine is self-sustaining and able to accelerate to idling under its own power.

Ignition takes place in combustion chambers 2 and 7, and flame spreads to the other chambers via interconnector tubes. The torch igniters consist of a small fuel atomizer and a sparking plug; they receive fuel from a separate feed pump and high-tension current from booster coils.

The automatic time switch runs for 30 seconds after momentary pressure of the starter button. It simultaneously fires the cartridge and switches on current to the torch igniter valves, torch igniter feed pump and booster coils.

For relighting in flight the ignition services only are required, as the engine will already be windmilling. These services are brought into operation by using the relight button.

Use of fuel pump isolation switch

If a sudden drop in engine rpm is experienced in flight, there may be a fault in the fuel system. Normally, the servo side of the fuel system controls both pumps, and if the servo pressure falls, the stroke of both pumps will be reduced and the engine rpm will fall. By switching to the ISOLATE position, one of the fuel pumps will operate at maximum stroke, making available at least 60 per cent of engine thrust at sea level, increasing with altitude to 100 per cent thrust at about 12,000 ft (3,658 m) and above.

When in isolate the BPC has no control over the top pump, and provided this pump is not faulty it will work at full stroke, regardless of the altitude. This means that engine rpm will rise as the aircraft is climbed at part throttle, and will necessitate throttling back if operating conditions are required to remain constant.

For this reason the engine has to be throttled back when isolating at altitude, and opened up again slowly, watching the JPT while setting up the required thrust. This will avoid a sudden increase in fuel delivery to the burner, which would cause a rapid rise of jet pipe temperature.

Engine performance

It should be remembered that fuel consumption when idling on the ground and taxiing is very high compared with that of piston engines. Each minute at ground idling uses enough fuel to travel about 4 miles (6.5 km) at 40,000 ft (12,192 m), and taxiing is even more extravagant.

Careful use of the throttle, particularly between idling and 6,000 rpm at altitude, is necessary. One of the reasons why mistakes resulting in overfuelling can easily be made is that the increase of thrust for a given rpm increase is much greater in the high rpm range. Thus, in the early stages of the acceleration there is a natural tendency to attempt to increase rpm too rapidly, owing to the disappointing initial thrust response.

Mk No.	Rating	Canberra Mks	Nom. Thrust (lb)	Significant Features
AVON ENGINES USED IN CANBERRA AIRCRAFT				
1	R.A.3	B.2, T.4	6,500	Basic R.A.3. Air bleed operated via a mechanical connection from IGV ram. 12-stage compressor, 2-stage turbine. Singled breech cartridge starter.
102	R.A.3	T.17 only	6,500	As Mk1, but with extra air tapped from compressor outlet casing to drive Godfrey turbo alternators, producing power for electronic equipment used in T.17 ECM role.
109	R.A.7	E.15, PR.7	7,400	Compressor similar to Mk1, but new turbine. Anti-icing added to air intake and IGVs. Air bleed now totally separate in operation from IGVs, controlled by a pneumatic unit. Triple-breech starter.
206	R.A.24	PR.9 only	11,250	200-series Avons have nothing in common with Mk1 and 1000-series except the name. Principal differences are 15-stage compressor, proportional-flow fuel-control system integrated into a single unit, the RTCU (range temperature control unit). Air bleed controlled by hydraulic connection from IGV ram. Flame tubes in an annulus surrounded by a single air casing, instead of being in separate chambers. IPN starter.

It is also possible with a very clean aircraft to cruise with little thrust at low and medium altitudes, so the pilot might be tempted to cruise with the bleed valves open. This involves a 10 per cent increase in fuel consumption, due to some of the turbine power being used to compress the air that is spilled overboard through the bleed valves.

The overspeed governors hold the engine very closely to the maximum permitted rpm at all altitudes. The jet pipe temperature at full throttle also remains constant up to about 35,000 ft (10,668 m), but above this altitude it begins to increase. This is known as JPT creep.

During a climb at intermediate throttle setting the rpm increases slightly with altitude and will necessitate throttling back if constant operating conditions are required. The following fuel map shows how aircraft range increases with altitude.

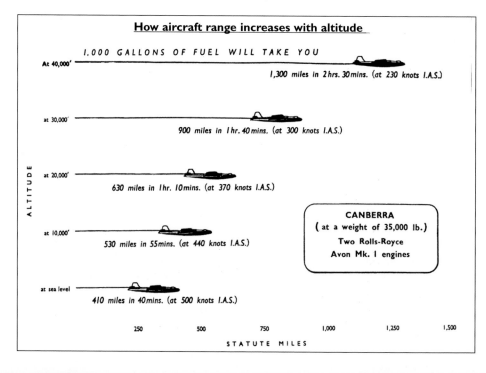

THE AVON FAMILY TREE
A summary of the progress and achievements of the Rolls-Royce Avon family of turbojet engines.

The relationship between the various R.A. versions of the Avon is shown in the family tree below. The broken line joining the two main branches indicates the point at which the new, more powerful design of Avon came into being – there is no constructional similarity between the two series of engines other than use of approximately the same maximum diameter.

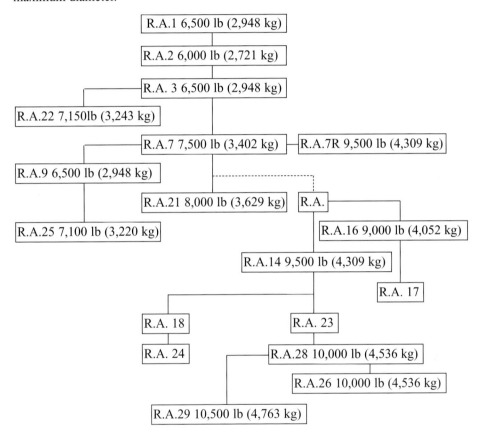

Avons, aircraft and records
The following is an impressive list of outstanding flights by Avon-powered aircraft, most of which were Canberras. The first jet aircraft non-stop flight of the Atlantic to be made without refuelling was made by a Canberra in 1951. Canberras of the Royal Air Force played their part in the Speed Section of the New Zealand Air Race in 1953. Between 1951 and 1958 the Canberra set up twenty-two world records, including eighteen record-breaking trans-world flights and three world altitude records.

World speed records *
Over 3 km course, 7 September 1953, by Hunter F.1 with R.A.7R – 727.6 mph.
Over 3 km course, 28 September 1953, by Swift F.4 with R.A.7R – 737.3 mph,
Over 100 km closed circuit, 19 September 1953, by Hunter F.1 with R.A.7R – 709.2 mph.

World class records *

Feminine, Class C Record

Over 15-25 km course, 31 May, 1955, Mystère IVN with R.A.7R – 715.2 mph.

Point to point records

Belfast – Gander, Newfoundland, in 4 hr 18 min on 31 August 1951, by Canberra B.2 with R.A.3s, 481.1 mph.

Belfast – Gander – Belfast in 10 hr 3 min on 26 August 1952, by Canberra B.5 (R.A.7s, 412.0 mph).

Gander – Belfast in 3 hr 25 min on 26 August 1952, by Canberra B.5 (R.A.7s), 605.5 mph.

Cape – London in 13 hr 16 min on 19 December 1953, by Canberra B.2 with R.A.3s, 452.8 mph.

London – Baghdad in 4 hr 51 min on 31 July 1955, by Valiant B.2 with R.A.14s, 523.5 mph.

London – Basra in 5 hr 11 min on 8 October 1953, by Canberra P.R.3 with R.A.3s, 544.3 mph (England – New Zealand Air Race).

London – Brussels in 18 min 3.3 sec on 10 July 1952, by Swift F.1 with R.A.7, 665.9 mph.

London – Cape in 12 hr 21 min on 17 December 1953, by Canberra B.2 with R.A.3s, 486.6 mph.

London – Christchurch in 23 hr 51 min on 8/9 October 1953, by Canberra PR.3 with R.A.3s, 494.5 mph (England – New Zealand Air Race).

London – Colombo in 10 hr 25 min on 8/9 October 1953 by Canberra PR.7 with R.A.7s, 519.5 mph (England – New Zealand Air Race).

Winner of the United Kingdom – New Zealand Air Race, 1953.

London – Darwin in 22 hr 0 min on 27/28 January 1953, by Canberra PR.3 with
R.A.3s, 391.2 mph.
London – Karachi in 8 hr 52 min on 27 January 1953, by Canberra PR.3 with
R.A.3s, 441.8 mph.
London – Khartoum in 6 hr 22 min on 22 January 1954, by Comet 2 with R.A.25s,
481.1 mph.
London – Nairobi in 9 hr 55 min on 22 September 1952, by Canberra B.2 with
R.A.3s, 427.3 mph.
London – New York in 7 hr 30 min on 23 August 1955, by Canberra PR.7 with
R.A.7s, 461.1 mph.
London – New York – London in 14 hr 22 min on 23 August 1955, by Canberra
PR.7 with R.A.7s, 481.52 mph.
London – Paris in 19 min 14.0 sec on 5 July 1953, by Swift F.4 with R.A.7,
669.3 mph.
London – Tripoli in 2 hr 42 min on 18 February 1952, by Canberra B.2 with
R.A.3s, 538.1 mph.
New York – London in 6 hr 17 min on 23 August 1955, by Canberra PR.7 with
R.A.7s, 550.4 mph.
Ottawa – London in 6 hr 42 min on 27/28 June 1955 by Canberra B.2, Aries IV
with R.A.3s, 469.8 mph.
Paris – London in 19 min 14.2 sec on 5 July 1953, by Swift F.4 with R.A.7,
664.5 mph.
Paris – Nice in 41 min 55.8 sec on 18 June 1955, by Mystère IVN with R.A.7R,
610.5 mph.
Singapore – Darwin in 4 hr 1 min on 7 August 1955, by Valiant B.2 with R.A.14s,
518.4 mph.

First polar inter-continental jet flight
Bardufoss, Norway – Fairbanks, Alaska, 3,210 miles in 6 hr 20 min in June 1955, by
Canberra, 507.1 mph.

Atlantic jet crossing
Aldergrove, Northern Ireland – Gander, Newfoundland in 4 hr 37 min on 21 February
1951, by Canberra B. Mk2 WD932 with R.A.3s, 450 mph (first non-stop,
direct jet crossing of the Atlantic without refuelling). On 21 December
1951, WD932 crashed in USA on flight from Baltimore.

* Information based on published records of the Fédération Aéronautique Internationale.

CHAPTER THREE

Canberra Marks and Production

During a production run of more than ten years 1,233 Canberras were built. English Electric built 488; daughter firm production was 294; forty-eight were built under licence in Australia for the Royal Australian Air Force by the Department of Defence Production; and 403 were built under licence in the United States of America for the United States Air Force, by the Martin Company in Baltimore, Maryland.

There were a total of forty marks of Canberra, including thirteen for the United States Air Force. Usually, it was the engine that called for the mark to be changed, for it changed the profile of the aircraft; but with the Canberra that was not always the case, for the mark was also changed when the role of the aircraft was changed. Therefore, I have included in my total of forty marks the seven B.15s and B.16s that were given the mark of E.15; and the sole one that was given, because of its role change, the mark PR.16.

Canberra B. Mk1

Four prototypes, designed to Air Ministry specification B3/45, were produced, serial numbers VN799, VN813, VN828 and VN850. These were given the designation B. Mk1. They were medium bombers with a 'solid' nose and a crew of two, the intention being to

Four Canberra prototypes – nearest the camera is WN467, the T. Mk4 prototype; then VX185, the B. Mk5 prototype; WE135, the PR. Mk3 prototype; and VX169, the B. Mk2 prototype.

Canberra B. Mk1 VN799 seen here on an early test flight. Painted blue overall.

bomb-aim by means of a radar sight. The bombers were unarmed, relying on their speed.

First prototype, VN799, first flew 13 May, 1949. Fitted with fin fillets and initially had a rounded fin tip. Powered by two Rolls-Royce Avon R.A.2 engines. In October 1949 it was transferred to A&AEE Boscombe Down for initial trials, and during this period was flown by Squadron Leader Saxelby, Flight Lieutenant Callard and Wing Commander Davies. On 14 November 1949 it returned to Warton, and the following month the 100th flight was completed. From March 1951 to November 1952 it was at RAE Farnborough for Mark 9 Autopilot trials. A Smith's Autopilot Mark 10 was installed by June 1953 and testing continued. During these trials an engine failure occurred and the aircraft was written off, crashing at 15.30 hours on 18 August 1953, 1½ miles south-east of Sutton Heath, near Woodbridge, Suffolk. Both crew members were killed.

Second prototype, VN813, ff 9 November 1949. Fitted with fin fillets. Top of rudder squared off after the first flight of VN799. The aircraft was fitted with Rolls-Royce Nene 5,000 lb static thrust (st) engines as an insurance against the failure of the Rolls-Royce Avon engines specified for the basic design. The Nene engines were later used as the de Havilland Spectre test-bed. VN813 was used at Warton for development flying until November 1950, when it was then delivered to Rolls-Royce for Nene development until September 1951. The aircraft was then transferred from Rolls-Royce to TRE Pershore for development work. In June 1953 it was transferred to de Havilland for development work. By 1956 it was at Follands and became the first aircraft flown with a fully controllable rocket motor (D.H. Spectre) in Great Britain.

Third prototype, VN828, ff 22 November 1949. After its initial flight take-off from Samlesbury, VN828 landed at Warton and remained on development flying until 1955. Aircraft fitted with fin fillets and powered by two Rolls-Royce Avon R.A.2 engines, small dorsal stroke removed. The aircraft was in the prevailing Bomber Command colours of grey top and black underside. VN828 was converted by Boulton Paul Aircraft in 1955 with a Mk8-type canopy for trials at RRE Defford of the Canberra T. Mk11 radar installation. Changes listed as being carried out by Boulton Paul Aircraft included B(I).8 nose, which was modified to take three crew – pilot, navigator and A.I.18 operator. The navigator was at the rear. Instruments were installed on starboard wall with a stowable table; B. Mk2-type wings, Rolls-Royce R.A.3 engines, installation of de Havilland scanner, etc. forward of Frame 1. A.I.18 in bomb-bay. Standard B. Mk2 rudder, gun pack and modified bomb-doors. Type-512 generators. Cooling system for A.I.18 Mk5 gunsight.

Fourth prototype, VN850, ff 20 December 1949. On 14 March 1950, first flight of a Canberra fitted with wing-tip tanks. On 31 July 1950, first jettison of wing-tip tanks. The first overseas display of the Canberra was carried out by VN850 in June, first in Paris and then in Antwerp. In September 1950 it was at the Farnborough Show with the B. Mk2 prototype (VX165). In October 1950 it was delivered to Rolls-Royce for Avon engine development. On 13 June 1951, while with Rolls-Royce on engine trials at Hucknall, it crashed at Bulwell Common, near Nottingham.

Canberra B. Mk2

This was the main production variant, and 418 were built. The prototypes were VX165 and VX169, and the former first flew on 23 April 1950.

The first production batch of Canberra B. Mk2s totalled seventy aircraft, serial numbers WD929-966, WD980-999, WE111-122, and were built by English Electric at Preston against Contract 3520. WD929 ff 8 October 1950. Several B. Mk2s were later converted to T.4, T.17 and TT.18 standard.

The second production batch of Canberra B.2s totalled eighteen aircraft, serials WF886 – WF892, WF907 – WF917, and were built by English Electric at Preston against Contract 3520. WF914 went to the Venezuelan Air Force, WF915 went to the Royal New Zealand Air Force and WF916 was later converted by British Aircraft Corporation to T. Mk17.

Serial numbers WG788 – WG789 were built by English Electric at Preston against Contract 3520, and both were released to service on 11 August 1952. The fourth

Engine start test on Short Brothers' first production Canberra B.2, WH853, at Belfast.

First prototype Canberra B. Mk2 VX165 painted in the early black and grey livery.

production batch of Canberra B. Mk2s totalled eighty-six aircraft, serial numbers WH637 – WH674, WH695 – WH742, and were built by English Electric at Preston against Contract 5786. Deliveries took place between August 1952 and July 1953. Some aircraft were later converted by BAC to T. Mk4, U. Mk10, T.11, T. Mk17 and TT.18 standard.

The first production order for Canberra B. Mk2s placed with Short Brothers and Harland Ltd totalled 100 aircraft, serial numbers WH853 – WH887, WH902 – WH925, WH944 – WH984, to be built at Sydenham against Contract 5790. WH853 ff 30 October, 1952, and they were delivered between November 1952 and October 1954. A revision of the contract in April 1953 resulted in the last forty aircraft, serials WH945 – WH984, being completed as Canberra B. Mk6s. Many aircraft were subsequently converted to various marks for high-level calibration duties (E.15s); electronic countermeasures training (T.17s); and for target-towing duties (TT.18s) (see Chapter Four).

The first production order for Canberra B. Mk2s placed with Handley Page Ltd totalled 100 aircraft, serial numbers WJ564 – WJ582, WJ603 – WJ649, WJ674 – WJ707, to be built at Cricklewood and Radlett against Contract 5943. Twenty-five aircraft, serial numbers WJ683 – WJ707, were subsequently cancelled. WJ564 ff 5 January 1953; WJ682 ff 18 April 1955. Deliveries took place between April 1953 and May 1955. Several aircraft were later modified by BAC to T. Mk4, T. Mk17 and TT.18 standard. WJ622 crashed in February 1954 before delivery.

The fifth production batch of Canberra B. Mk2s built by English Electric totalled fifty-seven aircraft, serial numbers WJ712 – WJ734, WJ751 – WJ784, against Contract 5786, but only twenty-six were built, as B. Mk2s. From WJ754 onwards, thirty-one aircraft were completed as B. Mk6s. All aircraft were built at Preston and they were released to service between August 1953 and January 1954. Serial numbers WJ715, WJ717, WJ718 and WJ721 were converted to TT.18 standard.

Canberra WV787, the 90th B.Mk2 produced by English Electric.

The first production order for Canberra B. Mk2s, placed with A.V. Roe & Co Ltd, totalled 100 aircraft, serial numbers WJ971 – WJ995, WK102 – WK146, WK161 – WK190, to be built at Woodford against Contract 5990. The order was subsequently reduced to seventy-five aircraft with the cancellation of serials WK166 – WK190, WJ971 ff 25 November 1952, and deliveries took place between March 1953 and March 1955.

WK141 and WK163 were modified for trials work. Subsequent conversions by BAC included WJ987, WK107, WK165 to U. Mk10; WJ975, WK106 to T. Mk11 and T. Mk19; WJ984 to B. Mk15; WJ971, 977, 981, 986, 988, WK102, WK111 to T. Mk17; WK118, 122 – 4, 126 – 7, 142 to TT.18; WJ974, WJ976, WK112 to Peru; WJ980 to Venezuela; WJ981, WJ988 to RNZAF; WK108 to Rhodesia; WK130, WK137, WK138 to Germany.

Two Canberra B. Mk2s, serial numbers WP514 and WP515, were built by English Electric against Contract 3520 as replacements for aircraft diverted off contract to meet export requirements. WP514 was listed as the 11th B. Mk2 and was released to service on 1 August 1951. WP515 was listed as the 41st B. Mk2 and was released to service on 2 March 1952.

One Canberra B. Mk2, serial WV787, was built by English Electric against Contract 3520 as an experimental model with Sapphire engines. It was delivered in August 1952.

One Canberra B. Mk2, serial XA536, was built by English Electric at Preston as a replacement for WD991 (which had crashed prior to delivery). It was released to service on 1 May 1953, and it was subsequently converted by the manufacturer to T. Mk11 and T. Mk19 standard.

The B. Mk2 was similar to the B. Mk1, but with a visual bomb-aiming position in a transparent nose-cone, which had an optical flat panel for the bomb-aimer. Classed as a light tactical bomber, it was powered by two 6,500 lb st Rolls-Royce Avon 101 engines (6,500 lb = 2,950 kg st), with cartridge-operated turbo-starters. Internal fuel capacity was 1,377 imp gal (6,260 litres). There were provision for auxiliary wing-tip tanks, each with a capacity of 244 imp gal (1,110 litres). The cabin was pressurized from engine compressors in place of the two-stage blower on the Mk1.

The Canberra B. Mk2 carried a three-man crew. The side-by-side seating of the B. Mk1 gave way to a seat on the port side and two seats for the navigators behind this in the B. Mk2.

Many redundant B. Mk2s were converted to later marks for a variety of other specialist duties. For example, take WD944. It was released to service on 9 October 1951. In 1957 it was converted to T. Mk4. In late 1970 it was purchased from the RAF and the nose fuselage was taken off and the rest of the aircraft was scrapped. The nose fuselage was then joined on to another fuselage and became a T. Mk84 (FAV 0619) of the Venezuelan Air Force.

This mark was supplied to Argentina, Australia, Ethiopia, Peru, Rhodesia, Sweden, the United Kingdom, the USA, Venezuela and West Germany.

Canberra P.R. Mk3

The prototype P.R. Mk3 was VX181, and it was completed to Specification PR. 31/46. It first flew on 19 March 1950. Only thirty-five production Canberra PR.3s were built, and the mark was superseded by the more powerful and longer-range PR.7.

Twenty-seven aircraft, serial numbers WE135 – WE151, WE166 – WE175, were built by English Electric as Canberra PR.3s, serials WE171 – WE172, for the Venezuelan Air Force. Then followed a further seven aircraft, serials WF922 – WF928, which were built by English Electric. The initial production Canberra WE135 made its first flight on 31 July 1952, and it was released to service on 11 November 1952. The others were released to service between November 1952 and January 1954.

The second production batch of Canberra PR.3s totalled twenty-four, but only WH772 was built as a PR.3, the other twenty-three being completed as PR.7s. This was against Contract 5786 and built by English Electric. WH772 was released to service on 27 February 1954.

Canberra VX181, the prototype PR. Mk3 on an early test flight.

Canberra PR. Mk3 WE135, the first production aircraft.

The PR.3 had a crew of two, pilot and navigator, and was the photo-reconnaissance version of the B.2. It was fitted with seven cameras for high-altitude photographic reconnaissance. The fuselage was extended by fourteen inches, forward of the mainplane, and it was fitted with additional fuel tanks, which gave a fuel capacity of 1,917 imperial gallons (8,715 litres).

The PR. Mk3 was supplied to the RAF, and when the PR. Mk7 came into service the aircraft were moved to the photo-reconnaissance element of No. 231 OCU at Bassingbourn. They were also supplied to Venezuela.

Canberra T. Mk4

The Canberra T. Mk4 was developed from the B.2 aircraft and designed to meet the requirements of Specification T2/49, which called for an operational trainer with side-by-side seating and dual controls for the pilot and student. The navigator's position was retained on the port side aft of the pupil. With so many B.2 aircraft entering service it was obvious that a dual-controlled training version would be required. The contract was signed in February 1951 and the prototype, WN467, flew for the first time on 6 June 1952. Including the prototype WN467, a total of sixty-six were produced.

The first production batch of T. Mk4s consisted of eight aircraft, serial numbers WE188 – WE195, and were built by English Electric. They were released to service between September 1953 and February 1954.

The second production batch of Canberra T. Mk4s totalled twelve aircraft, serial numbers WH839 – WH850, and were built by English Electric at Warton against Contract 5786. Deliveries took place between February and May 1954.

The third production batch of Canberra T.4s built by English Electric totalled twenty-five aircraft. Serial numbers WJ857 – WJ881, against Contract 5786. Deliveries took place between June 1954 and February 1955. WJ860 went to Peru.

The fourth production order for Canberra T.4s totalled twenty aircraft, serial numbers WT475 – WT494, to be built by English Electric at Preston against Contract 6445. But only eighteen were built, and serials WT493 and WT494 were subsequently cancelled. Delivery took place between February 1955 and September 1955. WT491 and WT492 went to the Royal Australian Air Force.

Canberra T. Mk4 prototype, clearly showing second clear-view panel on starboard side.

Canberra B. Mk2 WJ566, which was released to service on 1 April 1953 and later converted to T. Mk4 standard as seen here.

Two Canberra T.4 aircraft, serial numbers XH583 and XH584, were built by English Electric at Preston against Contract 11313. Deliveries took place early in 1955. Canberras XK647 and XK650 were built at Preston against Contract 12265 and were subsequently diverted to the Indian Air Force with serial IQ994 and IQ995 respectively.

Subsequently seventeen B.2 aircraft were converted to T.4 standard, some being complete conversions, others retaining the bomber's glazed nose, and they were identified from the original sixty-five T.4 aircraft as they had only one clear vision panel in the canopy. The T.4 was the training variant of the B. Mk2 with a 'solid' nose that hinged on the port side, giving access to instrument panel. The bulk of the T.4s were used by the Operational Conversion Units, Nos 230, 231 and 232, and they were also issued to most Canberra squadrons for continuation training. It is interesting to note that WJ863 was purchased from the RAF and the nose fuselage was fitted to a new fuselage to become a T. Mk84, serial FAV0621, for Venezuela.

The mark was supplied to Argentina, Australia, India, Peru, Rhodesia and Zimbabwe, South Africa, the United Kingdom and Venezuela.

Canberra B. Mk5

The B. Mk5 variant of the Canberra was designed to meet Specification B22/48. One of the original B.2 prototypes, VX185, was converted to this standard. It was basically a B.2 with a 'wet wing' incorporating leading-edge fuel tanks extending back to the main spar, and was the first Canberra to incorporate integral fuel tanks in the wings, features which were included in all subsequent production variants.

The B.5 was intended as a target marker, carrying radar in a solid nose with a large optically flat bomb-aimer's panel beneath nose. It was fitted with uprated Rolls-Royce Avon R.A. 7 engines of 7,500 lb (3,402 kg) thrust.

The B.5 was finished in dark grey and dark green/black, and was not put in production. VX185 was eventually converted to become the prototype B(I).8.

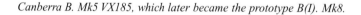

Canberra B. Mk5 VX185, which later became the prototype B(I). Mk8.

Canberra B. Mk6 WH952, which was built by Short Brothers and released to service on 29 January 1955.

Canberra B. Mk6

There was no B. Mk6 prototype, the English Electric production line introducing this mark from WJ754 which first flew on 26 January 1954, while Short Brothers and Harland did the same from WH945. A total of ninety-nine B. Mk6s were built, fifty at English Electric and forty-nine at Shorts.

Serial numbers WH754 – WJ784 were part of Contract 5786 that started out as Canberra B.2s but were completed as B.6 by English Electric. They were released to service between March 1954 and November 1954. Serials WJ761, 762, 764, 766, 770, 771, 773, 774, 776 – 778 and 781 – 784 were later converted to B.16 standard (see Chapter Four).

Six aircraft, WT301 – WT306, were built as B.6s by English Electric against Contract 6445, and were delivered between November 1954 and May 1955. Serials WT302 and WT303 were later converted to B.16s.

Six aircraft, serial numbers WT369 – WT374, were built as Canberra B.6s by English Electric and were released to service between December 1954 and February 1955. Serials WT369, WT372-374 were later converted to B.16s.

Four Canberra B.6s, serial numbers XH567 – XH570, were built by English Electric at Preston against Contract 11313. Deliveries took place between January 1955 and March 1955. XH570 later converted to a B.16. A single aircraft, XK641, was built by English Electric against Contact 12265, and it was released to service in May 1956. It was later converted to the B.15 standard.

Two Canberra B.6s, serial numbers XJ249 and XJ257, built by English Electric at Preston against Contract 5786 to replace WJ779 and WJ784 were diverted to France, and serialled F779 and F784 respectively. Deliveries took place during April/May 1956. XJ249 and XJ257 both crashed in 1957; the former hit a tree in low cloud, and XJ257 was listed as Category 5 damage after the undercarriage failed to lower.

Forty aircraft, serial numbers WH945 – WH984, were completed as Canberra B. Mk6s by Short Brothers and Harland against Contract 5790, which was for a hundred Canberra B.2 aircraft. Deliveries of the B.6 took place between November 1954 and October 1955.

Canberra B. Mk6 WJ764 was released to service on 20 May 1954. It was later converted to a B. Mk16.

A further nine aircraft, serial numbers WT205 – WT213, were built as Canberra B.6 aircraft by Short Brothers and Harland, against Contract No. 6/ACFT/6448. They were delivered between November 1955 and April 1956. This made a total of forty-nine aircraft built by Shorts, and thirty-three of them were later converted to B.15 standard.

Similar to the B.5 but with the glazed nose of the B.2, and produced in smaller numbers than the B2, the B. Mk6 was powered by Avon 109 engines, each 7,400 lb st (3,356 kg), and had additional fuel capacity. The B.6 usually had provision for the Low-Altitude Bombing System (LABS). Certain B.6s converted to 'Blue Shadow' aircraft and had special equipment installed by the RAF. Blue Shadow aircraft had a crew of two.

The mark was supplied to Ecuador, France, India, Peru and the United Kingdom.

Canberra B. Mk6 high-altitude medium bomber. Seen here is WJ755, which was the second one off the production line from English Electric and released to service on 22 March 1954.

Canberra B(I). Mk6

This was an interim night interdictor version of the B.Mk6, and a total of twenty B(I). Mk6s were built.

The principal production batch comprised only nineteen aircraft, serial numbers WT307 – WT325, and were built as Canberra B(I).6 by English Electric. They were delivered between April 1955 and February 1956. One Canberra B(I).6, XG554, originally ordered against Contract 5786 and subsequently transferred to Contract 6445, was built by English Electric at Preston as a replacement aircraft for the RAF. It was delivered on 29 February 1956.

The B(I).6 was an interim interdictor aircraft pending availability of the definitive B(I).8. The B(I).6 was a sub-variant, and the first one, WT307, first flew on 31 March 1955. The aircraft were equipped with a pack of four 20 mm cannon in the rear part of the bomb bay. Underwing pylons were also provided for carrying two 1,000 lb (454 kg) bombs or packs of 2 in. (6 cm) rockets.

The B(I).6 was supplied to the RAF and served exclusively with No. 213 Squadron in Germany.

Canberra PR. Mk7

The PR. Mk7 was the photo-reconnaissance version of the B.6, and a total of seventy-four were built.

The second production batch of the photo-reconnaissance Canberras totalled twenty-four aircraft and were ordered as the PR.3 variant, but only the first example was built as such. The other twenty-three aircraft, serial numbers WH773 – WH780 and WH790 – WH804, were completed as PR.7s. All were built by English Electric at Warton against Contract 5786. WH773 first flew on 28 October 1953, and deliveries took place between November 1953 and July 1954 – some Canberra PR.7s were later converted to T.22 standard by BAC at Samlesbury.

The second production batch of Canberra PR.7s, serial numbers WJ815 – WJ825,

Canberra PR. Mk7 WH774 was the second production aircraft, and was released to service on 19 November 1953.

totalled eleven aircraft, and were built by English Electric against Contract 5786. Deliveries were between July 1954 and October 1954. From this small batch of eleven, four aircraft, serial numbers WJ818, WJ820, WJ823 and WJ824, received Category 5 damage.

The third production batch of Canberra PR.7s totalled forty aircraft, serial numbers WT503 – WT542, and were built by English Electric at Preston against Contract 6445. Deliveries took place between October 1954 and March 1956. Serials WT510, WT525 and WT535 were subsequently converted by BAC to T.22 standard. WT528 was Aries V.

The Canberra PR.7 had basically the same fuselage as the PR.3, but with uprated Avon 109 engines – each 7,400 lb st (3,356 kg st) – and integral wings of the B.6. Normal equipment for the PR.7 was one vertical 6-inch camera plus either four 20-inch or six 36-inch cameras.

This mark was supplied to India and the United Kingdom.

Canberra B(I). Mk8

This aircraft was a long-range night interdictor or high-altitude bomber and target marker, and readily convertible from one role to the other.

A total of fifty-seven aircraft were built and the first production order was for thirty aircraft, serial numbers WT326 – WT348 and WT362 – WT368. These were released to service between July 1955 and July 1956. From this first batch three received Category 5 damage; these were serial numbers WT331, WT334 and WT335, and were the sixth, ninth and tenth produced. The serial numbers were then a bit erratic, with XH204, XH207 – XH209, XH228, XH231 and XH234. Canberra XH207 received Category 5 damage. The others were released to service between October 1956 and May 1957. XK951 was the twenty-fourth aircraft built by English Electric and was released to service on 21 September 1956. XK952 was the twenty-sixth built by English Electric and was released to service on 15 October 1956. XK953 was built but never delivered and was converted to Interim B(I). Mk58 aircraft, serial number IF895, and was delivered to the Indian Air Force and later returned for full conversion. XK959 was also built but not delivered and converted to Interim B(I). Mk58 aircraft, serial number IF898, for the Indian Air Force.

Canberra B(I). Mk8 taking off from Short's Belfast airfield. This was the first B(I). Mk8, WT337, built by Shorts, and it was released to service on 2 August 1956, being the first of twelve to roll out of the Belfast factory.

A batch of twenty aircraft, serial numbers XM244 and XM245 and XM262 – XM279, were built by English Electric at Preston and ordered to replace those diverted to overseas customers. They were released to service between September 1958 and April 1959. A single aircraft, serial number XM936, was built for the RAF by English Electric at Preston and was released to service on 6 April 1959. Twelve aircraft, serial numbers WT337, WT340, WT342, WT345, WT347, WT363, WT366, XH204, XH208, XH228, XH231 and XH234, were sub-contracted to Short Brothers and Harland at Belfast.

The B(I).8 flew in prototype form on 23 July 1954, as a conversion of the unique B.5, VX185. The first production B(I).8, WT326, first flew on 8 June 1955, and was released to service on 21 July 1955.

The Canberra B(I).8 was similar to the B(I).6, but with a completely revised nose, which was a transparent nose-cone for low-level navigation and visual bombing, including nuclear strike. A crew of two was carried, with the pilot sitting further back on the port side under a fighter-type bubble canopy. The navigator/bomb aimer sat below and to the right of the pilot.

The following details apply particularly to the B(I).8, but are generally applicable to all versions.

Wings
Cantilever mid-wing monoplane. Symmetrical high-speed aerofoil. Dihedral, inner wing (to engine nacelle) 2°, outer wing 4° 21'. Root chord 19 ft (5.8 m). Tip chord 7 ft 8 in (2.34 m). All-metal single-spar structure. Irving-Westland pressure-balanced ailerons with spring-tabs in each. Four hydraulically operated split trailing-edge flaps. Air-brakes consist of drag channels which could be extended from top and bottom wing surfaces. Gross wing area 960 sq ft (89 m²).

Fuselage
All-metal semi-monocoque structure.

Tail unit
Cantilever monoplane tailplane with dihedral and single fin and rudder. All-metal structure, except for forward portion of fin, which was of wood construction, with plywood covering. Variable-incidence tailplane hinged at its leading edge and operated by an English Electric actuator in the rear fuselage. Spring trim-tabs in both elevators. Mass-balanced rudder with spring trim-tab. Area of horizontal tail surfaces 190.8 sq ft (17.72 m²). Area of vertical tail surfaces 66.53 sq ft (6.18 m²). Tailplane span 27 ft 4.9 in. (8.35 m). Tailplane dihedral 10°.

Landing gear
Retractable nose-wheel type. Each main unit, of English Electric design, was an oleo-pneumatic shock-absorber strut carrying a single wheel inboard on a cantilever stub axle. Dowty levered-suspension liquid-spring fully castoring nose unit with twin wheels. Hydraulic retraction. Dunlop wheels, tyres and plate brakes. Track 15 ft 9 in. (4.79 m).

Power-plant
Two Rolls-Royce Avon 109 axial-flow turbojet engines. Oil-cooled radiator buried in wings outboard of nacelles. Flame detectors and a fire extinguishing system were fitted. Cartridge-fired turbine starter. Fuel in three main tanks in upper part of fuselage above bomb-bay and in wing tanks, total capacity 2,756 imp gal (12,570 litres). Provision for auxiliary wingtip tanks, each with capacity of 244 imp gal (1,110 litres).

Accommodation
Pilot on Martin-Baker Type-1C ejection seat under fighter-type canopy offset to port side of fuselage. Navigator's seat totally enclosed in nose. Cabin pressurization by air supply from engine compressors.

Armament
In bomber role could carry 6 x 1,000 lb (454 kg), or 1 x 4,000 lb (1,815 kg) and 2 x 1,000 lb, or 8 x 500 lb (227 kg) bombs internally, plus up to 2,000 lb (907 kg) of stores on under-wing pylons. In interdictor role, a pack of four 20 mm Hispano cannon was installed in rear of weapons bay, leaving room in forward part for 16 x 4.5 in (11.5 cm) flares or 3 x 1,000 lb bombs. Also equipped to carry Nord (later Aérospatiale) AS.30 air-to-surface missiles; two packs of 37 rockets externally. Also had LABS gear for nuclear weapons.

This aircraft was supplied to Peru, the United Kingdom and Venezuela.

Canberra PR. Mk9
This was a high-altitude photographic reconnaissance aircraft.

A total of thirty-two Canberra PR. Mk9s were ordered, serial numbers XH129 – XH137 and XH164 – XH186. But only twenty-three were built; serial numbers XH178 – XH186 were cancelled. Canberra WH793 began life as a PR. Mk7, and it was released to service on 20 April 1954. The following month it was delivered to D. Napier and Son at Luton, for development work on the PR.9 variant. On 8 July 1955, WH793 made its first flight as a PR.9 prototype.

All the Canberra PR.9s were built by Short Brothers and Harland at Belfast, and the first production PR.9, XH129, flew for the first time on 27 July 1958. This aircraft crashed in the Irish sea on 9 October 1958, while still on manufacturer's trials. The pilot, Don Knight, ejected at low level, but the navigator, Peter Durrant, was lost. XH177 – the last to be built – first flew on 18 November 1960. It was delivered to service on 13 June 1961 and was scrapped on 12 April 1966. The Canberra PR.9s were delivered between September 1958 and December 1960. XH132 was converted by Short Brothers to an SC.9.

At the time of the PR.9 order, Shorts had, in fact, been engaged almost continuously on Canberra production for some six years. More than a hundred Canberras had been built at the Queen's Island factory, and all were test-flown by the company's test pilots. Mr Roberts, then marketing director of Short Brothers, was in fact the project test pilot on the PR.9 Canberra, and also on the high-altitude U. Mk10.

As in the case of major contracts, Shorts made extensive use of its subsidiary factories in order to speed the supply of components to the main production lines at Belfast. All detail press-work, for example, was carried out at the Hawlmark factory, in Newtownards; drop tanks were made at the neighbouring Glen works; various machine shop details were manufactured by the Precision Engineering Division at Castlereagh, while other units assisted in the production of rear fuselages, flight components, frames and tailplanes.

Assembly of major structural components was undertaken at the Queen's Island factory. Shorts' contribution to the PR.9 was by no means confined to production, for the company had also undertaken a considerable amount of design work, including structural modifications, layout of hydraulic and air systems and installation of electrical, photographic, and radio equipment. A particularly important task was the provision of an automatic ejector seat for the navigator, which was installed in production PR.9s.

Canberra PR.9 XH130 high-altitude photographic reconnaissance aircraft taking-off from Sydenham.

This entailed a complete redesign of the nose section and the redistribution of all navigational and photographic control equipment. It is a tribute to Shorts' technical team that a mock-up of the redesigned nose was completed in less than two months by the Experimental Department at Queen's Island.

The main problems posed by the decision to provide an ejector seat arose from the fact that, in the original design of the PR.9, the navigator's seat was in the form of a swivel chair mounted on rails. This meant that it could readily be moved back and forward and could turn from side to side, thus giving the navigator quick access to the various instruments distributed throughout the nose. As a safeguard in the event of crash landing, a separate strengthened seat was provided against the rear bulkhead of the cabin. When required to take photographs, the navigator moved forward and lay prone in the nose of the aircraft.

With the installation of a fixed ejector seat, however, it had to be possible for the navigator to operate from one position, and it was thus necessary to group all instruments, including those for camera sighting and control, within a comparatively short radius.

This requirement created a number of difficulties. The area of the fuselage that could be utilized was reduced by approximately half, and within this it was necessary to provide a completely unobstructed ejection path, as well as accommodating controls and instruments. In fact, not only was all necessary equipment repositioned but, in addition, a number of new instruments were installed.

In the revised layout all photographic controls were concentrated on the port side of the fuselage. Main navigational equipment was positioned immediately forward of the operator,

Canberra PR. Mk9 high-altitude photographic reconnaissance aircraft on the production line at Short Brothers' Belfast factory. Nearest the camera is XH133, which was the fifth one on the production line.

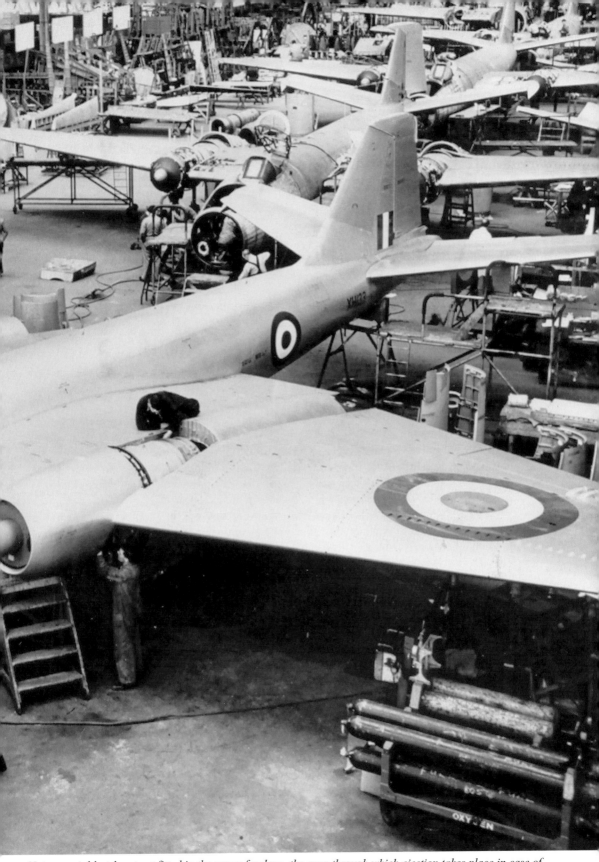

Note: special hatch not yet fitted in the upper fuselage, the area through which ejection takes place in case of emergency for the navigator. In the second aircraft a man is working in the nose section, and even without the instruments it can be seen how tight it is for room.

The last production Canberra PR. Mk9, XH177, taking off from Shorts' Belfast airfield.

together with a tail-warning indicator, while subsidiary navigation instruments, oxygen regulator, intercom controls and lighting switches were mounted to starboard. Emergency equipment, including fire extinguisher and first-aid kit, were distributed within easy reach.

To replace the camera sighting position in the nose, an easily adjustable periscopic sight was mounted immediately in front of the navigator. Additional photographic equipment was also installed.

A hinged chart table was provided. When in use this rested on the navigator's knees, and in the event of an emergency it automatically folded clear.

The lightweight Martin Baker Mk IV ejector seat was fully automatic, and was slightly modified to requirements. Ejection was through a specially designed frangible hatch in the upper fuselage. This hatch could also be partly opened, by operating a lever, in the event of an emergency landing. Checks were carried out on the mock-up built by Shorts to ensure that the ejection envelope was sufficient for the largest navigators.

Considerable modifications to the original nose structure were, of course, necessary. These included lowering the aircraft floor to provide additional space, and the elimination of the Perspex forward window, the port window and the entrance and windbreak doors to starboard. The entrance door was replaced by hinging the front portion of the nose to open just forward of the navigator's seat, and two windows were introduced, one on either side, above the port and starboard control consoles.

The project throughout called for considerable design ingenuity. Not only were the overall dimensions of the aircraft preserved, but the centre of gravity remained almost unaltered, and no major structural modification was made aft of the original navigator's cabin.

The PR.9 had the same basic fuselage as the PR.7, but with a revised nose. Also, broader wings extended in span to 67 ft 11½ in. (20.7 m), and there were increased wing chord inboard of engines, further uprated Rolls-Royce Avon Mk206 turbojets and Fairey powered flying controls. The pilot's canopy on production aircraft was similar to B(I). Mk8, but opened for access.

The Canberra PR.9 was designed to carry out strategic reconnaissance at high altitude.

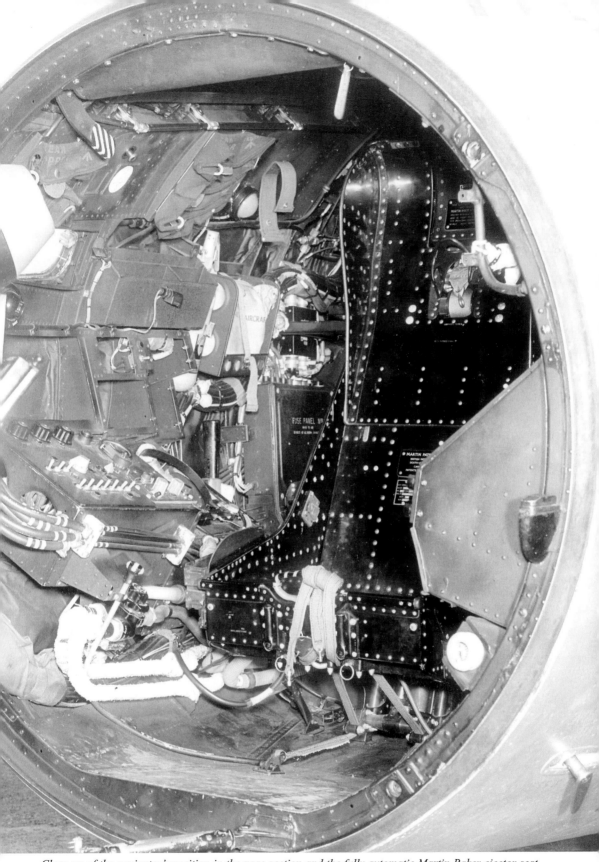

Close-up of the navigator's position in the nose section and the fully automatic Martin Baker ejector seat on the right and instruments on the left. Note the special rails at the top, which are part of the special hatch.

Canberra XH132 'Red Top' Canberra conversion SC.9.

Red Top Canberra Conversion – SC.9

This was a single Canberra PR.9, serial number XH132, converted by Shorts, under Ministry of Aviation contract, for use in conducting field trials with the de Havilland Red Top missile guidance system. It was modified to accept the Red Top homing head and various components of the missile's guidance system. The role for the SC.9 was to gather infra-red data on target characteristics and to evaluate target detection systems. The SC.9 first flew in May 1961 and was later delivered to Turnhouse for use by Ferranti.

The model was supplied to the Royal Air Force (all except XH132), and served with the Royal Air Force in Cyprus and Malta.

Three Canberra PR.9 aircraft, serial numbers XH166 (341), XH167 (342) and XH173 (343), were supplied to Chile.

Close-up of Canberra conversion SC.9 showing 'Red Top' homing head.

BASIC DATA

Dimensions

B. Mk2	Span 63ft 11½ in. (19.5 m)
	Length 65 ft 6in. (20 m)
	Height over fin 15 ft 7 in (4.75 m)
PR. Mk3	Span 63 ft 11½ in. (19.5 m)
	Length 66 ft 8 in. (20.3 m)
	Height over fin 15 ft 7 in (4.75 m)
T. Mk4	Span 63 ft 11½ in. (19.5 m)
	Length 65 ft 6 in. (20 m)
B. Mk6	Span 63 ft 11½ in. (19.5 m)
	Length 65 ft 6 in. (20 m)
	Height 15 ft 7 in. (4.75 m)
PR. Mk7	Span 63 ft 11½ in. (19.5 m)
	Length 66 ft 8 in. (20.3 m)
	Height 15 ft 7 in. (4.75 m)
B(1). Mk8	Span 63 ft 11½ in. (19.5 m)
	Length 65 ft 6 in. (20 m)
	Height 15 ft 7 in. (4.75 m)
PR. Mk9	Span 67 ft 11½ in. (20.7 m)
	Length 66 ft 8 in. (20.3 m)
	Height 15 ft 7 in. (4.75 m)

Weights

B. Mk2	Bomb load 6,000 lb (2,725 kg)
	Normal loaded weight 40,500 lb (18,390 kg)
	Max. loaded weight 46,000 lb (20,885 kg)
	Max. landing weight 40,000 lb (18,160 kg)
PR. Mk3	Normal loaded weight 40,000 lb (18,160 kg)
	Normal landing weight (with tip tanks) 44,000 lb (19,976 kg)
T. Mk4	Max. loaded weight 38,000 lb (17,240 kg)
	Normal loaded weight 33,000 lb (14,980 kg)
	Normal loaded weight (with tip tanks) 37,000 lb (16,800 kg)
	Max. landing weight 31,500 lb (14,300 kg)
B. Mk6	Weight empty 21,679 lb (9,833 kg)
	Basic operating weight 22,950 lb (10,410 kg)
	Max. military load 8,000 lb (3,630 kg)
	Max. take-off weight 55,000 lb (24,950 kg)
	Max. landing weight 40,000 lb (18,145 kg)
PR. Mk7	Max. loaded weight 55,000 lb (24,950 kg)
	Normal loaded weight 49,000 lb (22,246 kg)
	Normal loaded weight (with tip tanks) 53,000 lb (24,060 kg)
	Max. landing weight 40,000 lb (18,160 kg)
B(1).Mk8	Weight empty 23,173 lb (10,511 kg)
	Basic operating weight 26,396 lb (11,973 kg)
	Max. military load 5,318 lb (2,412 kg)
	Max. take-off weight 56,250 lb (25,515 kg)
	Max. landing weight 40,000 lb (18,145 kg)

Performance

B. Mk2   Max. speed at sea level 517 mph (M 0.68 (827 kph))
Max. speed above 30,000 ft (9,150 m) 570 mph (M 0.82 (912 kph))
Rate of climb at sea level at full load 3,800 ft/min (1,160 m/min)
Limiting altitude determined by pressure breathing system 48,000 ft (14,640 m)
Take-off distance to 50 ft (15.25 m) at max. weight (zero wind) 4,590 ft (1,400 m)
    or 3,540 ft (1,080 m) without tip tanks
Landing distance from 50 ft (15.25 m) at max. landing weight 4,500 ft (1,372 m)
Landing distance from 50 ft (15.25 m) with only 250 imp gal (1,138 litres)
    fuel 2,520 ft (770 m)
Max. still-air range with full bomb load 2,656 miles (4,250 km)
Ferrying range 2,986 miles (4,780 km)

PR. Mk3   As for B. Mk2 except:
Take-off distance to 50 ft (15.25 m) 4,410 ft (1,345 m) or 3,450 ft (1,050 m)
    without tip tanks
Max. still-air range 3,580 miles (5,730 km)
Ferrying range 3,660 miles (5,856 km)

T. Mk4   As for B. Mk2 except:
Rate of climb at sea level, 4,300 ft/min (1,310 m/min)
Take-off distance to 50 ft (15.25 m) 3,120 ft (950 m), or 2,370 ft (725 m)
    without tip tanks
Landing distance from 50 ft (15.25 m) at max. landing weight 3,450 ft (1,050 m)
Max. still-air range 3,110 miles (5,000 km)

B. Mk6   Max. speed at 40,000 ft (12,200 m) at 44,000 lb (19,760 kg) AUW: 541 mph
    (871 kmh)
Rate of climb at sea level 3,500 ft/min (1,065 m)
Service ceiling 48,000 ft (14,630 m)
Take-off distance to 50 ft (15.25 m) 5,800 ft (1,768 m)
Landing distance from 50 ft (15.25 m) 3,900 ft (1,190 m)
Range with max. fuel, no reserves, 3,790 miles (6,100 km)
Range with max. load, no reserves, 3,400 miles (5,470 km)

PR. Mk7   Max. speed at sea level 517 mph (M 0.68 (827 kmh))
Max. speed at 40,000 ft (12,200 m)
At 44,000 lb (19,760 kg) AUW: 541 mph (871 kmh)
Rate of climb at sea level 3,500 ft/min (1,065 m)
Take-off distance to 50 ft (15.25 m) zero wind, 5,650 ft (1,720 m), or 3,960 ft
    (1,210 m) without tip tanks
Landing distance from 50 ft (15.25 m) at max. landing weight 3,900 ft (1,190 m)
    or 2,320 ft (710 m) with only 250 imp gal (1,138 litres) of fuel
Max. range with operational equipment 4,340 miles (6,985 km)
Ferrying range 4,400 miles (7,080 km)

B(I).Mk8   Max. speed at sea level 517 mph (827 kmh) (M 0.68)
Max. speed at 40,000 ft (12,200 m) at 44,000 lb (19,760 kg) AUW: 541 mph (871 kmh)
Rate of climb at sea level 3,400 ft/min (1,035 m)
Service ceiling 48,000 ft (14,630 m)
Take-off distance to 50 ft (15.25 m) 6,000 ft (1,830 m)
Landing distance from 50 ft (15.25 m) 3,900 ft (1,190 m)
Range with max. fuel, no reserves, 3,630 miles (5,840 km)
Range with max. load, no reserves, at 2,000 ft (600 m) with 10 min over
    target at full power 805 miles (1,295 km).

CHAPTER FOUR

Conversion Variants

All Canberra variants that followed the PR. Mk9 into service with the Royal Air Force and Royal Navy were conversions of earlier production versions, usually surplus B. Mk2s, but in one case the PR. Mk7 was also used.

Marshall of Cambridge (Engineering) Ltd was involved in the major design and trial installation modification programmes that resulted in its undertaking substantial crash production programmes which proved its awareness of Ministry time-scale requirements and the firm's capability to react accordingly.

Marshalls had been engaged in the design and trial installation of several major radio/radar fits for Canberra aircraft. The most significant of these was the revised radio fit for the B. Mk6 aircraft. This project, together with a number of armament modifications, was considered to be sufficiently radical to warrant the introduction of the new marks of Canberra, the B. Mk15 and B. Mk16 (Blue Shadow aircraft). These new marks covered the introduction of UHF/VHF, HF radio compass, Blue Silk, roller map and Decca Navigator. Marshall's Technical Publications Department was responsible for the provision of user and technical handbooks for the new marks of aircraft.

Marshalls accomplished the complete design for these new marks and steered their development through various stages to the finalized production version. The firm was then engaged in the production, which entailed a vigorous 'Return to Works' programme at Cambridge.

Marshalls was associated with RRE in design work for a limited ECM fit for B. Mk2 aircraft.

Canberra U. Mk10

First of the new variants was the U. Mk10, an unmanned target aircraft for guided-weapon firing trials, and it was converted from a B. Mk2. All design work for the U. Mk10 conversion was carried out by Short Brothers at Belfast. With the U. Mk10 Shorts had placed Britain ahead of the USA and other countries, and it was safe to say that it was the most advanced aircraft of its kind in the world. Unlike other aircraft targets, the U. Mk10 needed no shepherd aircraft to accompany it on its sorties. But the true importance of Shorts' achievement lies in the advance which it made possible in the technique of checking guided-weapon performance by the use of pilotless targets. The new Canberra conversion extended considerably the potential scope of such trials, its main advantages for the target role being its high-altitude performance, large reflecting surface – which means a missile could home on a target of representative size – high speed and endurance at height. Thus, the U. Mk10 provided a means of testing the most highly developed missiles of the day and catering for those of the future.

During the high-altitude phase of flight-testing the Canberra U. Mk10, it was flown at heights well in excess of 50,000 feet (15,240 m) under automatic control – a remarkable performance. It was capable of fully automatic operation in all phases of flight. Optimum performance was ensured by limiting control of the aircraft to a given

Canberra U. Mk10 WH733 high-speed target drone.

Canberra WJ987, the seventeenth production B. Mk2 from A.V. Roe, seen here after being converted to U. Mk10 pilotless target aircraft for use in guided-weapon development.

number of fixed attitudes. These were climb, slow level, fast level (a variable airspeed facility was provided for selecting any airspeed over most of the speed range), overshoot, fast glide and land glide.

Remote control of the U. Mk10 during normal flight was maintained from the ground master control position. For landing and take-off the master controller could transfer control to two operators who controlled, respectively, pitch and azimuth, but the ground master controller could override these positions.

The master controller could select any of the drone's fixed attitudes, and within these attitudes further manoeuvres were available, permitting turns and height adjustments to be made.

The ground controller's commands were transmitted via a VHF radio link to an airborne receiver. The signals passed from the receiver to a Relay Set Receiving (RSR) through a selector filter and relay unit. The commands selected operated appropriate relays in the RSR and initiated the required autopilot airspeed and the aircraft control or ancillary function. Some ancillary functions were automatically initiated other than by radio link; for example, landing gear UP was initiated at 160 knots if gear was not already retracted.

The U. Mk10 had a destroy system built in, and a signal could be received in the aircraft by an additional receiver supplied from a separate battery. The additional receiver was virtually self-contained, and the output signal detonated an explosive charge that was positioned to sever the tail unit.

A control supervisory unit for pilot presentation was installed in the cockpit. This consisted of a series of control buttons with associated indicator lamps, generally similar to those available to the Ground Master Controller. Operation of those buttons produced the same effect on the aircraft as the corresponding ground control without use of the radio link.

Another remarkable feature of the Canberra U. Mk10 was the fact that it was fitted with a system which automatically recorded missile miss distance for later analysis. This was a result of collaboration between Shorts and the Weapon Research Establishment, South Australia. Timing sequences for operating the equipment in co-ordination with missile firings were initiated by the ground control system.

Canberra U. Mk10 conversions carried out by Shorts – 26 aircraft in all

Canberra U. Mk10 (for RAAF)	Serial numbers WD961, WD929, WJ987, WD951 and WJ624. Delivered between November 1958 and mid-1959. Serial numbers WH733, WH742, WH729, WJ609, WJ604, WH710, WJ621, WJ623 and WK110. Delivered between 16 September 1959 and 30 May 1960. Serial numbers WK107, WH652, WH705, WH860 and WH885. Delivered between 23 February 1962 and 3 July 1962.
Canberra U. Mk10 (for RAF, Malta)	Serial numbers WJ638, WH704, WH720, WH876, WH921 and WD941.

Canberra T. Mk11

Following a requirement by Fighter Command for an advanced navigation and radar operator trainer, a small number of B. Mk2 aircraft were modified to T. Mk11 standard.

The T. Mk11 was the first of the RAF conversions, and the first initial example, WJ734, was flown on 29 March 1958. Prototype conversion was undertaken on VN828,

Canberra WH903 converted to T. Mk11 and later to T. Mk19, in the markings of No. 85 Squadron at RAF Binbrook. Aircraft in natural metal finish.

which had been the third prototype B. Mk1.

The T. Mk11 had Ferranti Airpass interception radar equipment housed in an extended, sharply pointed nose radome, and carried a crew of four, including two pupils. Boulton Paul Aircraft were responsible for designing and producing the modification. It was used for training pilots and navigators of all-weather fighters in the use of AI (Airborne Interception) radar, particularly by the Javelin OCU, No. 228, and the first T.11 entered service with the OCU at Leeming in 1959. The Canberra T.11s were fitted with the same AI 17E interception radar as the Javelin FAW.5s When the OCU disbanded in January 1967, the T.11s were transferred to No. 85 Squadron at Binbrook, whose role was target towing for air-to-air firing and radar interceptions. With the re-forming of 85 Squadron as a Bloodhound air-defence missile unit, the remaining T. Mk11s were passed on to No. 100 Squadron, although by this time they had the AI radar removed and in this form were known as the T.19.

The T.11 was supplied to the RAF, and two similar aircraft were supplied to the Royal Swedish Air Force, where they were designated Tp52, and these were given an attractive alternative colour scheme.

Ten aircraft were scheduled to be converted to T.11 standard, but only nine were converted: serial numbers XA536, WH714, WH904, WH903, WJ610, WH724, WJ975, WK106 and WJ734.

Canberra WJ643, a conversion from a Handley-Page-built B.2, was used by Ferranti as a test-bed for its Airpass radar installed in the Canberra T.11.

Canberra B(I). Mk12

This was the last new production Canberra and was outwardly similar to the B(I).8. The conversion was designed and effected by Boulton Paul. A total of sixteen B(I).12s was produced. It was the export version of the B(I).8 for the Royal New Zealand Air Force and the South African Air Force.

Canberra T. Mk13

This was the export version of the T.4 for the Royal New Zealand Air Force, conversion designed and effected by Boulton Paul. Only two were produced, serial numbers NZ6151 and NZ6152 – one being converted from a T.4.

Canberra U. Mk14

Following the use of the U.10s, a further small batch of B.2s were converted as pilotless targets, which were known as U.14 or B.14, and were a modified and improved version of the U.10. Improvements included the fitting of PR.9-type powered flying controls.

Only six U.14s were built; these were WD941, WH704, WH720, WH876, WH921 and WJ638. In early 1961 these aircraft were delivered to No. 728(B) Squadron Fleet Air Arm at Hal Far, Malta, where they operated alongside the Meteor U.15s and U.16s of this unit. The purpose of this Royal Navy squadron was to provide targets for the operational trials of the Sea Slug surface-to-air missile being operated from the trials ship HMS *Girdle Ness*. During these trials one Canberra, WH921 (590), was destroyed by a missile. At the end of the trials the remaining aircraft were flown home and put into storage.

Canberra B. Mk15

The first B. Mk15 – WH961 – first flew on 4 October 1960, and it was a modified B.6 with additional radio and radar equipment. A total of thirty-nine, of which thirty-three were from those built by Short Brothers and Harland, were modified for the tactical nuclear or conventional bombing role or as ground-attack aircraft. New equipment included UHF and HF communications sets, Secca roller map with feed-in from Doppler navigation system, forward-facing F.95 camera in the nose and a G.45 camera in the starboard wing leading-edge, as well as the existing F.24 camera in the rear fuselage.

The Canberra B.15 could carry 6,000 lb (2,722 kg) of bombs internally with underwing strongpoints. Nord extra wing pylons were added at Rib 5 – this being done at Warton – for two 1,000 lb (454 kg) bombs, two Nord AS.30 missiles or two Microcell packs, each containing 37 x 2 inch (5 cm) unguided rockets for ground attack.

The B.15 remained in service until early 1969 with the Akrotiri Canberra Strike Wing, and when the wing disbanded the Canberras were flown back to the UK, some being sold to BAC at Warton for possible refurbishment in lieu of export orders.

The prototype B. Mk15 conversion aircraft was Canberra B. Mk6 WH967, which was released to service in February 1955.

Canberra B. Mk16

The B.16 was a two-seat aircraft converted from the B.6 (BS) Blue Shadow aircraft, and was similar to the B.15 but retained some radar aids of the B.6. Here again pylons were fitted, but the B.16 did not have Nord. Eighteen B.6s, all from the English Electric batch, were converted to B.16 standard.

The B.15 and the B.16 were used operationally only in the Middle and Far East. The Akrotiri Strike Wing, Cyprus, comprising Nos 32, 73 and 249 Squadrons, was equipped, in the main, with B.15s. Nos 32 and 73 Squadrons only had B.15s; No. 249 Squadron had B.15s and B.16s; so too did No. 6 Squadron. No. 45 Squadron in Malaya was equipped with B.15s.

In 1971, seven B.15/16s, under the revised designation E.15, were issued to No.98 Squadron at Cottesmore to be used as interception targets for air-defence training. In 1976, No. 98 Squadron disbanded and handed its aircraft over to No. 100 Squadron at Marham. While with No. 73 Squadron in the Sixties, WH961 had been equipped with extra cameras as the sole PR.16.

Canberra T. Mk17

The T.17 was the electronic countermeasure (ECM) aircraft, and was in fact an extensively modified B.2. The work was done in packages on three aircraft, but only one, WJ977, got the full package.

The T.17 radar nose had numerous 'blisters', and it was used to provide electronic countermeasure and radar jamming training to members of all three services. It was a most ugly aircraft, with its bulbous nose and various protrusions having a somewhat sinister fascination. The T.17 has a variety of aerials sprouting from its fuselage and also two on the fin. Apart from its extensive range of radio and radar jamming devices, the

Close-up of nose of Canberra T. Mk17 WJ625 at Abingdon, in July 1968. Note serial in stencil form on nose-wheel door and stencil details on nose.

A typical B. Mk2 conversion with a new lease of life as a trainer. Canberra T. Mk17 (ex-B.Mk2) WH664, in the old 360 Squadron markings of a lightning flash through the number. Note underwing scoop.

T.17 could also carry and release large quantities of window from its wing-tip dispensers. Normal crew consisted of pilot, navigator and electronic warfare officer.

The T.17 equipped only No. 360 Squadron, a joint RAF/RN electronic warfare training unit that formed at Warton out of B Flight of No. 97 Squadron and the Royal Navy's ECM unit, No. 831 Squadron, on 23 September 1966.

WJ988 first flew in October 1966, and was the first to be delivered to No. 360 Squadron on 1 December 1966. It was shown publicly for the first time at the Royal Review of the Royal Air Force at Abingdon in July 1968.

A total of twenty-four T.17s were produced, the last, WH872, being in March 1968. Several T.17s were held in storage for the intended formation of No. 361 Squadron in the Mediterranean area, but the rundown in the Middle East made this unnecessary, and No. 361 Squadron disbanded in July 1967, its crews and equipment joining No. 360 Squadron.

Canberra TT. Mk18

The Canberra TT.18 was the result of a requirement by both the Royal Air Force and the Royal Navy for an aircraft to replace the ageing Meteor TT.20s, in service with the GAACUs and the Fleet Requirements Unit at Hurn. As in all earlier conversions, low-time B.2s were selected from storage and completely refurbished by BAC to 'as new' condition for towing spooled wire targets. Externally they were similar to the B2 apart from the two Rushton target-towing winches, designed by Flight Refuelling, one under each wing mounted on a pylon. Each winch was able to carry either one Rushton target with up to five miles of wire or two sleeve targets on shorter wires. The Rushton target provided a general-purpose towed-target facility for the British armed services. It was launched, towed from and recovered into a winch system fitted to the tug aircraft.

Canberra TT. Mk18.

Close-up of Rushton winch on Canberra TT. Mk18 WJ639 of No. 7 Squadron.

The tow cable was attached via a tow swivel to the target tow lug, which was positioned such that the line of the tow cable passed close to the centre of gravity of the target. Stabilization was effected by vertical and horizontal fins mounted at the rear of the target body, which trimmed it to give approximately zero incidence in both yaw and pitch. Thus a stable non-rotating equipment platform was provided which could be manoeuvred freely throughout the design speed range. Visual augmentation was obtained by the use of tracking flares or smoke generators fitted in a carrier, capable of containing six units, attached to the bottom vertical fin. Each single flare or smoke generator had a duration of 60-70 seconds and was visible over a range of 10,000 yards (9,144 m). Infra-red augmentation could be obtained by fitting IR flares, which had a duration of 20 – 30 seconds, dependent upon altitude. The number of flares fired together was under the control of the operator and depended upon the weapon and mode of attack. Radar augmentation was by use of Luneberg lenses contained within the target body. Results indicated that at X Band radar frequency an average echoing area of 65 sq ft (6 m^2) was obtained. Monostatic and bi-static lenses were available.

A large cargo space was provided for carrying miss distance indicators or other instrumentation as required. A radio command system was used to remotely ignite the flares in predetermined sequences, and also to switch on or off any instrumentation that was carried.

The target was compatible with all known gun directors, its radar image being roughly equivalent to that of a fighter aircraft. It could be equipped to suit a variety of practice applications, ranging from gunnery to guided missiles for both ground-to-air and air-to-air interceptions. Some of the missiles for which the Rushton had been proved to be satisfactory were the Rapier, Sea Cat, Tiger Cat, Sidewinder, Red Top, Matra R.530, Firestreak and Blowpipe.

The TT.18 was the only Canberra variant to have a window on the starboard as well as the port side. It was added to allow the navigator a view of the starboard winch. This variant also had fin aerials and a UHF aerial behind the nose-wheel doors. The prototype, WJ632, equipped with Flight Refuelling drogue-towing equipment beneath the wings, made its first flight on 21 March 1966, followed two years later by the initial 'production' conversion, WK122. Of the eighteen built, nine went to the Fleet Requirements Unit.

The RAF unit chosen to operator the Canberra TT.18 was No. 7 Squadron. Although one of the most famous bomber squadrons, it had not operated the Canberra before, having flown Stirlings and Lancasters during the Second World War, and then Lincolns and Valiants. The first Canberra TT.18s were delivered to the squadron in May 1970. No. 7 Squadron, which had re-formed as part of No. 18 Group at St Mawgan, Cornwall, soon took over from the old Meteor-equipped CAACUs and provided targets for the Army's gunners and ships of the Royal Navy. The TT.18s were painted with black and yellow target-towing identity stripes.

Canberra T. Mk19

In the early 1960s eight Canberra T.11s, which had already been converted from B.2s were modified, and with their change of role were redesignated T.19s.

Nine T.11s had been selected for conversion, but because one had been on the ground for such a long time, having been used for TI work and installations at Boulton Paul, it was decided not to bring it to a flying state, so only eight were converted.

To convert from a T.11 to a T.19 was a very simple modification, which involved the removal of the AI radar equipment from the black needle-nose radome and replacing

Canberra B. Mk2 WH903, built by Short Brothers and Harland. Released to service on 31 January 1954. Converted to T. Mk11, then to T. Mk19, as seen here. Note port wingtip – mounted pitot head that prevented this mark from carrying tip tanks.

it with a block of concrete to maintain equilibrium. This device was wittily dubbed Blue Circle radar by some of the aircrew. Blue Circle being a well known brand of cement.

The port-wingtip-mounted pitot head on the T.19 prevented this mark from carrying tip tanks, and some of these aircraft were fitted with an auxiliary fuel tank in the bomb-bay, giving up to 200 miles (322 km) additional range.

The crew of the T.19 consisted of a pilot and navigator, both with ejection seats, and there was provision for a third crew member, who was accommodated on the rumble seat to the right of the pilot.

Canberra B. Mk20

This was the licence-built version produced in Australia, a tactical bomber modified to meet RAAF operational requirements. The first twenty-eight had similar engines to the B.2, with which they were roughly comparable, although they carried the integral fuel tanks of the B.5. The remaining twenty had the more powerful Avons of the B.6 (see Chapter Five).

Canberra T. Mk21

This designation was given to the training version of the B.20 (see Chapter Five).

Canberra T. Mk22

On 28 June 1973, yet another new version of the Canberra made its first flight. This was the T.22, WT510, a much modified PR.7, the first of seven to be converted for use by the Royal Navy Fleet Requirements and Air Direction Unit (FRADU) at RNAS Yeovilton. The role for this small number of specialized Canberras for the Royal Navy was radar operator training, replacing Sea Vixens, and it was difficult to understand why such a training conversion came into being so late in the life of the Navy's Buccaneers.

Marshalls of Cambridge was responsible for all the design on the T.22 Blue Parrot Canberras, but was not involved on the conversion itself, which was done at British Aerospace.

To cater for the installation of equipment required for the Blue Parrot role, certain basic design changes to the Canberra PR.7 were necessary, one of the major changes being the replacement of the fuselage nose with a radome-type nose similar to that already fitted to certain Buccaneer aircraft having a Blue Parrot installation, which was normally used for the detection of surface vessels in any weather. Other changes included a revised layout at the pilot's and navigator's stations and the abolition of the navigator's forward station in the nose of the aircraft; adaptation of the flare bay to accommodate the master reference gyro; modifications to the air-conditioning system to supply pressurization and cooling air to the radar; installation of a pitot/static pressure head to the port wingtip in a manner similar to that fitted to Canberra T.19 aircraft; modifications to the demand-oxygen system of the Canberra PR.7 layout by transferring the oxygen bottles from the upper equipment bay to the wings; a new inverter layout (4 inverters) to cater for the necessary a.c. power supplies to various systems. New AR.1 systems were also fitted to the aircraft: PTR 175, UHF standby, Tacan, radio compass AD 722, VOR/ILS. IFF Cossor 1520, Blue Parrot and height encoding system. The first T.22 conversion delivered was WH801. These aircraft were operated by Airwork Services for the Royal Navy.

Canberra B. Mk20 A84-245 of No. 2 Squadron Royal Australian Air Force.

Canberra T. Mk22 WT510, which shows well the Buccaneer nose. Note serial duplicated on fuselage.

American Canberras – USAF designation B-57
The six American built B-57 variants were B-57A, eight built; RB57A, sixty-seven built; B-57B, 202 built; B-57C, thirty-eight built; RB-57D, twenty built; B-57E, sixty-eight built, making a total of 403. (see Chapter Five)

Canberra PR. Mk57
This was a modified version of the Canberra PR.7 for the Indian Air Force. The conversion was designed by Boulton & Paul. A total of ten aircraft were modified to PR.57 standard. Eight were new aircraft and the other two were converted from existing RAF PR.7s. (see Chapter Five.)

Canberra B(I). Mk58
This was a modified version of B(I).8 for the Indian Air Force. The conversion was designed by Boulton & Paul. A total of seventy-one were produced. (see Chapter Five.)

First flight for Canberra T. Mk22 WT510, on 28 June 1973. This aircraft was released to service on 29 December 1954 as a PR. Mk7. Note the extensive markings beneath the canopy.

Overseas Orders and Production

T he Canberra was exported to fifteen countries, earning more than £90 million for the UK, and was the first post-war-designed British aircraft to be built under licence in America for the US Air Force and the first foreign design built for US combat deployment since the end of the First World War.

Interest from overseas came early in the history of the Canberra. It soon proved to be a winner, and its versatility to adapt to various needs and climates was proved by its wide range of customers, the bulk of whom ordered aircraft from the parent company, though Australia and the United States set up their own production lines. The Canberra was to feature in the front-line strength of air forces of many nations.

United States of America – B-57
Following trials in the USA at Andrews Air Force Base, in which a Canberra (WD932) competed against a number of American aircraft, including the Martin B-51, North American B-45 Tornado and Douglas A-26 Invader, an agreement was reached in which the Glenn L. Martin Company at Baltimore would build the Canberra under licence for the United States Air Force as the B-57 night intruder. Once the agreement was signed on 19 April 1951, the Martin Corporation prepared for quantity production. Canberra

American Canberra B.57 variant for the USAF. Seen here is No. 54263 of the USAF during a visit to Germany in 1977.

Martin RB-57A 0-21475 of the Kansas Air National Guard at its home base in the early 1970s.

WD940 flew out on 31 August 1951, as part of the delivery flight of first Canberra B.2s to the USA as pattern aircraft. It became bureau number 51-17352.

The initial production version of the Martin B-57 was the B-57A, which, apart from the use of licence-built Armstrong-Siddeley Sapphires, Wright J65-W-1 turbojet engines (7,220 lb st (3,280 kg st)) each as the powerplants, was the equivalent to the RAF B.2. Only eight of this version were built, serialled 52-1418 to 52-1425, the first one making its maiden flight on 20 July 1953. The B-57A had a crew of two – pilot and navigator-radar operator/bombardier.

The next sixty-seven aircraft were for photographic reconnaissance use, with cameras installed aft of the bomb-bay, and were designated RB-57A. The first entered service with the 363rd Tactical Reconnaissance Wing in late 1954.

The first major redesign of the B-57 came with the B-57B, the aim being to produce an aircraft more suitable to the night intruder role. Modifications included the fitting of a completely new forward fuselage with tandem seating for the two crew members, pilot and radar operator/navigator/bombardier, beneath a continuous jettisonable canopy; ejector-type seats; and improved bullet-proof windscreen with anti-icing and demisting. Hydraulically operated speed brakes were added to the rear fuselage which moved in co-ordination with finger-type brakes on each wing. Other improvements included the fitting of a rotary bomb door, which rotated through 180 degrees just before the bombs were released, leaving no excrescences to reduce speed on the bombing run, and the provision of either eight 0.5 in. machine-guns or 20 mm cannon in the wings. Weapon pylons were also fitted below the outer wing for four Napalm tanks, in addition to eight 5 in. HVAR rockets. Gross weight was more than 50,000 lb (22,700 kg). Maximum speed exceeded 600 mph (960 kmh), the ceiling was more than 45,000 ft (13,725 m), and the range was more than 2,300 miles (3,700 km). The first B-57B flew for the first time on 28 June 1954. Some 202 B-57Bs were built, the first aircraft entering service with the 461st Bombardment Wing of the Tactical Air Command in January 1955. The 345th Wing also converted to the type during 1956.

Following on from the B-57B came the B-57C, which was basically a B-57B with dual controls, its role being that of a transition trainer with the B-57-equipped wings. The B-57C was also used for instrument training, for giving piston-engine pilots experience in jet operation or for giving single-engine fighter pilots multi-engine experience. The first aircraft, 53-3825, flew on 30 December 1954, and a total of thirty-eight Canberra Cs were built.

Only twenty of an extensively modified reconnaissance aircraft were built: this was the RB-57D, and it was far removed from the original Canberra design. Although the fuselage remained basically that of the B-57B, it was mated to a completely new wing of 106 ft (32.3 m) span. Its length was 65 ft 6 in. (20 m) and height 14ft 10 in. (4.5 m), with power being supplied by two Pratt and Whitney J57 turbojet engines of 10,000 lb (4,536 kg) thrust. Two versions of the aircraft were built, six as two-seat reconnaissance aircraft (RB-57D2) and the remaining fourteen having single seat layout. The RB-57D had a maximum speed of 632 mph (1,017 km/h) at 40,000 ft (12,190 m) and a service ceiling of 60,000 ft (18,290 m). Six of the single-seaters were modified for electronic countermeasures work, being then designated as the RB-57D(C), having an enlarged bulbous nose and tail radomes, increasing the length by 2 ft 4 in. (71 cm), and wingtip fairings that, together with a completely new wing, raised the span to 107 ft 6 in. (32.76 m). The type entered service with USAF Tactical Air Command, Pacific Air Forces, MATS (MAC) for air sampling, and the Aerospace Defense Command, calibrating the NORAD radar network. All RB-57Ds were grounded during 1967 because of structural problems.

The final production variant of the B-57 was the B-57E, a multi-purpose aircraft that was able to carry out tactical bomber reconnaissance as the RB-57E and transition training as the TB-57E, and was also equipped for towing a wide variety of targets, four of which were normally carried on each flight in external containers carried beneath the fuselage. Its role was to provide both air-to-air and ground-to-air firing practice at high altitudes. A total of sixty-eight B-57Es were produced, the last being completed in 1959. Dimensions: span 64 ft (19.5 m), length 65 ft 6 in. (19.9 m), height 16 ft (4.88 m).

Two further versions of the B-57 were to be built, but these were converted by General Dynamics from existing B-57B airframes. The first of these was the RB-57F, a very extensively modified aircraft for strategic reconnaissance at extreme altitudes. A completely new wing of 122 ft 5 in. (37.32 m) span and 2,000 ft² (185.8 m²), almost twice the original 64 ft (19.5 m) wing, was designed. A new vertical tail increased the height to 19 ft (5.7 m), and the length became 69 ft (21.03 m), so that the aircraft looked grotesque. Two Pratt and Whitney TF33-P-11, 18,000 lb (8,165 kg) thrust turbofans supplied the power, which could be supplemented by two 3,300 lb (1,360 kg) thrust Pratt and Whitney J60-P-9 turbojets mounted below the wings, a two-man crew being carried. Endurance of more than ten hours was possible with altitudes of 90,000 – 100,000 ft (27,436 – 30,480 m) being attainable. The first RB-57F was delivered on 18 June 1964.

Eighteen aircraft were converted to RB-57F standard, three being converted from B-57A and 11 B-57B airframes, while the last four were built on RB-57D airframes. A number of aircraft operated with the 58th Weather Reconnaissance Squadron at Kirkland Air Base in New Mexico.

The final B-57 modification programme was that for the B-57G night intruder, which produced an aircraft capable of detecting, tracking and striking at moving targets in total darkness. Fifteen aircraft were converted from B-57B airframes by the Martin Aircraft Corporation and the Westinghouse Electric Corporation. A new modified nose section housed forward-looking radar and infra-red detection systems. Their chief role was as standard early-warning platforms for tasks such as threat-evaluation and

Martin B57 N1005 at the G.T. Baker Aviation School.

simulation, fighter affiliation and jamming tests on NORAD.

Eleven of the fifteen aircraft served with the 13th Bomb Squadron at Ubon Air Force Base in Thailand from September 1970 for night operations, and they carried the code 'FK'. The remaining four were operated by the 4424th Combat Crew Training Squadron of the 1st TFW at MacDill Air Force Base, Florida, and were coded 'FS'. After less than two years the B-57Gs were withdrawn and assigned to the 190th Tactical Reconnaissance Group of the Kansas Air National Guard. In the early 1980s the B-57 saw service as the RB-57 with a number of National Guard units and with the 5041st TOS (Tactical Operations Squadron) and a number of other second-line units.

During 1959 Pakistan received twenty-two B-57B aircraft and three B-57Cs, making a total of twenty-five aircraft under the United States Military Assistance Program (MAP). Taiwan, Republic of China, had some Martin-built Canberra RB-57D aircraft from America, but whether actually on loan or purchased it is not known. These Canberras were used in the Vietnam War in 1965.

Australia – Canberra B. Mk20; T. Mk21

Australia was the first Commonwealth country to standardize on the English Electric Canberra as its primary all-jet bomber. Unlike others, however, it decided to produce its own aircraft for the Royal Australian Air Force under licence from English Electric, at the Government Aircraft Factory at Fisherman's Bend near Melbourne.

On 20 December 1950, a contract was signed by the Australian Government for two Canberra B. Mk2 aircraft.

The following aircraft are listed as pattern aircraft for Australian Canberra production: WD935-A84/1; WD942-A84/2; WH710-A84/3; WD983-A84/125; WD939-A84/307.

A84/1 (it is believed this aircraft never actually went). A84/2 and A84/3 came back to the United Kingdom.

WD935 (ex-A84/1) was later used for AI.18 trials and is in the Royal Air Force Museum at St Athan.

WD942 (ex-A84/2) returned from Australia on 6 December 1956, and was used for AI.18 development. It ended its days at Shoeburyness.

WD983 was diverted as pattern aircraft; flown out from Lyneham. It was later converted to a T.21 aircraft.

WD939. On 27 June 1951, Canberra WD939 (later A84-307) made the initial flight of the first B.2 for Australia. On 1 August 1951, it departed from Lyneham for delivery to the Royal Australian Air Force. The aircraft reached Darwin in 22 hours 5 minutes flying time, a total of 10,249 miles (16,493 km). It was piloted by Wg Cdr D.R. Cuming, chief test pilot of the RAAF. WD939 was used as a pattern aircraft and was later converted to a T.21.

The Australian production version, known as the Canberra B.20, was different only in minor details from the British-built B.2. It was a high-speed tactical bomber modified to meet RAAF operational requirements, and a total of forty-eight were built. The first twenty-eight production B.20s were powered by the 6,500 lb (2,948 kg) thrust Rolls-Royce Avon Mk.101, the remaining twenty having the 7,500 lb (3,402 kg) thrust Avon Mk. 109 engine. Like the airframe, the Rolls-Royce Avon engines were also licence-built, by the Commonwealth Aircraft Corporation.

The B.20 weighed 24,700 lb (11,203 kg) empty, and had an AUW of 57,000 lb (25,855 kg). Its maximum speed was 580 mph (933 km/h), and its rate of climb was some 3,800 ft/min (1,158 m/min). It had a service ceiling of 48,000 feet (14,630 m).

The all-metal fuselage was semi-monocoque in construction and was designed to facilitate disassembly into three major sections. All controls, hydraulics, wiring, etc. were designed to meet this end (a condition required mostly because the testing facilities were located some distance from the factory). In front of the fuselage a pressurized cabin was provided for the crew and was sealed off from the remainder of the fuselage by a diagonal bulkhead. Entry was gained via a hatch on the starboard side of the canopy, and the hatch could be jettisoned in an emergency. The pilot's canopy and the navigator's

Canberra B. Mk20 A84-237 of No. 2 Squadron RAAF.

hatch could also be jettisoned. Martin Baker Mk. II or Mk. III ejection seats were used for both pilot and navigator. The centre fuselage divided horizontally, with the bomb-bay in the lower compartment. Bomb doors, hydraulically operated with remote selection were fitted with rollers that slid in curved tracks to retract into the fuselage. The maximum fuselage diameter was 6 ft (1.83 m). The three Canberra sections were then transported to Avalon, where they were assembled and flight tested.

The first Canberra B.20 built by the Government Aircraft Factory, A84-201, made its maiden flight on 29 May 1953, at the Avalon testing establishment. Three squadrons were to operate the Canberra, Nos 1, 2 and 6.

The final production B.20 was delivered in September 1958 (A84-248). Five further RAF Canberras, three B.2s and two T.4s were sent to Australia. The British-built B.2s and five B.20s were later converted from bombers to dual-control trainers by the Government Aircraft Factory at Fisherman's Bend, Melbourne. The dual-control trainers were then designated as T.21s and they retained the glazed nose. The T.21s served with No. 1 Operational Conversion Unit at Amberley and were almost the same as the B.20, except for the power-plant (Avon Mk101 engine) and the obvious cockpit redesigned to accommodate the instructor. The first flight in the T.21 configuration took place in June 1958 at Avalon, and the first aircraft was delivered in September 1958. The last T.21 (A84-125) was delivered in June 1959.

The Australian Canberras were to see some action overseas. No. 2 Squadron was deployed to Butterworth in Malaya in 1958, and during its stay flew some combat missions. In 1967 No. 2 Squadron moved to Phan Rang, South Vietnam, as part of the 35th Tactical Fighter Wing of the US 7th Air Force, and its Canberras again saw action. The radio callsign for the squadron was 'Magpie', after its insignia, and the squadron flew its first combat missions in the latter part of April 1967. The first US bombing of North Vietnam was in August 1964, when President Johnson ordered MTB bases and oil storages bombed in reprisal for alleged attacks by North Vietnamese torpedo boats on US destroyers on 2 and 4 August. In the first two months of operations No. 2 Squadron dropped more than 1,000 tons (454 kg) of bombs on numerous targets in North Vietnam during high-and low-level day and night strikes. The RAAF armed its Canberras with 500 lb (227 kg) Australian-made bombs, and later switched to 750 lb (340 kg) American-made bombs, which were more streamlined.

The Canberras operated in many roles in the Vietnam War and during the Khe San and Hue sieges. Canberra A84-231 (callsign Magpie 91) was the first Canberra lost in Vietnam. On the night of 3 November 1970, the Canberra, piloted by F/O Michael Herbert and navigated by F/O Robert Carver, took off from Phan Rang Air Base, and after releasing his bombs at 22,000 feet in the Da Nang area, the pilot reported that he was turning away, but was not heard from again and did not return to base. Despite extensive searches over the next four days, no sign was found of either the crew or Canberra A84-231. It had vanished without trace, and has never been found to this day. On 14 March 1971, another Canberra was brought down by a surface-to-air missile. The crew ejected safely and were picked up by an American helicopter. The Canberras flew their last mission on 31 May 1971, and in four years of war they had dropped 76,389 bombs. Just days after their last support mission, No. 2 Squadron returned home to Australia after spending thirteen years overseas. The ceasefire agreement was signed in January 1973.

In 1963 Australia decided to replace the Canberra with the F111, but delays led to the Canberras of Nos 1 and 6 Squadrons being replaced by Phantoms loaned from America. No. 2 Squadron was the last unit to operate the Canberra, eight B.20s and four T. 21s, continuing until June 1982.

Venezuela – Canberra B(I).82, B. Mk82, PR. Mk83, T. Mk84, B(I).88

Even before the first Canberra had been delivered to the RAF the type was receiving considerable interest from a number of overseas air forces. The first true export order from an overseas air force came in 1952, when Venezuela ordered six B.2s. On delivery they carried the serials 1A-39 (WH708), 2A-39 (WH709), 3A-39 (WH721), 1B-39 (WH722), 2B-39 (WH736) and 3B-39 (WH737), and were finished in a grey/blue colour scheme. But they took time to settle in their new mounts, and three Canberras, WH708, WH722 and WH737, received Category 5 damage. During 1957 a further order for Canberras was received from Venezuela, this time for eight B. Mk2 aircraft, making a total of fourteen B.2 aircraft supplied to Venezuela. Eleven of those B.2 aircraft were later converted to B.82s, with revised radio and armament fit. During 1957 two new T.4 aircraft were ordered, and when converted with new radio and armament fitment became T.84s. Venezuela also ordered eight new B.8s, and when converted with revised radio and armament fit they were designated B(I).88.

In 1965 a further six aircraft were ordered, though this time they were to be refurbished ex-RAF aircraft, as production of new airframes had ceased in 1962. The order called for four ex-RAF B.2 aircraft, which were converted to carry gun pack and wing pylons and by so doing became B(I).82 aircraft. The other two aircraft were PR.3s and both were converted PR.83s with revised radio and armament fit. At the time of writing one aircraft is still flying and being operated more intensively than when it was first delivered. In service they replaced the aged B-25 Mitchells of the 40th Escuadron de Bombardeo. By mid-1978 all the remaining Canberras had joined Escuadron 39, based at Maracay. In 1980 some of the Canberras underwent a refurbishment programme by BAe in the UK. Venezuela was the first country to deploy Canberras overseas, and that was not to Argentina.

English Electric Canberra B.82, No. 1131 of the Venezuelan Air Force awaiting delivery at Warton.

France – Canberra B. Mk6

During 1954 France ordered six production Canberra B.6s, which were to be used mainly for experimental purposes by the French Air Force at the Centre d'Essais en Vol at Bretigny until at least 1978. Supplied direct from the production line, they were F763 (ex-WJ763), F784 (ex-WJ784), F316 (ex-WT316), F779 (ex-WJ779), F304 (ex-WT304) and F318 (ex-WT318). The colour scheme was silver overall with standard French markings. The Canberras were retired in 1979.

Ecuador – Canberra B. Mk6

Ecuador was the third overseas country to order the Canberra, when in 1955 it took delivery of six new Canberra B.6 aircraft to form one squadron of the Fuerza Aerea Ecuatoriana. The aircraft received the serials FAE 71390, FAE 71391, FAE 71402, FAE 71405, FAE 71411 and FAE 71509. In 1962 Canberra FAE 71405 crashed in Ireland, but was sent back to BAC at Warton for refurbishment and then returned to Ecuador.

Peru – Canberra B(I). Mk56, B(I). Mk68, B. Mk72, T. Mk74, B(I). Mk78

In 1955 Peru became the first export customer for the Canberra B(I).8, the order being for nine new aircraft. They were delivered with the serials 474-482 and designated B(I) 78. They served with Grupo 21 of the Fuerza Aerea Del Peru. These aircraft were later converted to B.78 with revised radio fit, and renumbered 206-212. During 1966 Peru ordered a further batch of Canberras. This time they were rebuilt ex-RAF aircraft and consisted of six B.2 aircraft, serial numbers 233 (ex-WJ974), 234 (ex-WJ976), 235 (ex-WK112), 236) ex-WH726), 237 (ex-WH868) and 238 (ex-WE120). With a revised radio fit they became B.72 aircraft. Three ex-RAF T.4s were also ordered, and with a revised radio and armament fit they became T.74s.

In later years Peru ordered six B.6 aircraft, which became B(I).56s and brought the total of Canberras then in service to twenty-four. The year 1974 saw a further order for

Canberra B. Mk6 for the Ecuador Air Force.

Canberra B(I). Mk68 for the Peruvian Air Force seen here at Marshall's of Cambridge.

Canberras from Peru. This time twelve aircraft were ordered, and eleven were delivered via Marshalls of Cambridge, which was completely responsible for the design and conversion of the ex-RAF B(I).8 interdictor aircraft into B(I).68 aircraft for the Peruvian Air Force. English Electric converted one to make the total twelve. They were fitted with gun packs (four 20 mm Hispano guns) and wing pylons for carrying bombs or Matra rocket launchers (eighteen SNEB 2.7 in. (68 mm) rockets). Avro triple carriers carrying six 1,000 lb (454 kg) bombs could be fitted in the bomb-bay, or practice bomb carriers each carrying twenty-four 25 lb (11 kg) practice bombs. The radio fit was updated and consisted of VHF communication (Marconi AD170), VOR/ILS (Marconi AD260), radio compass (Marconi AD370), HF (Collins 618T-3), UHF (Collins AN/ARC159) and intercom (Ultra UA60).

India – Canberra PR. Mk57; B(I). Mk58; T. Mk4; B(I). Mk66; PR. Mk67

Orders received for Canberras from India in 1958 were to make the B(I).8 the most successful variant in the export market. The first sixteen aircraft were diverted from RAF contracts and were serialled IF895 to IF910. Designated B(I).58, the conversion was designed and executed by Boulton Paul. Although RAF serials were allocated, these were only marked on in chalk for test-flying purposes. Further batches of B(I).8s sold to India were serialled IF911-933 and IF960-984, bringing the total of this mark sold to India to sixty-five aircraft. Other aircraft ordered during the same period included six modified T.4 aircraft, serialled IQ994-999, a number of these being ex-RAF aircraft. The T.4s were not given another number. In spite of the fact that many people have referred to them as T. Mk54s, this is an unofficial designation. Because they were identical to standard RAF T.4s, apart from a new ventilation scoop, they were never allocated a new mark number. A total of eight PR.57s, a modified version of the PR.7, again converted by Boulton Paul, were also ordered at the same time, these being IP986-993. During 1963 a further batch of B(I).58s were ordered. This was six aircraft, serials BF595-600, and it brought the total of B(I).58s to seventy-one. In the following year two ex-RAF PR.7 aircraft were ordered,

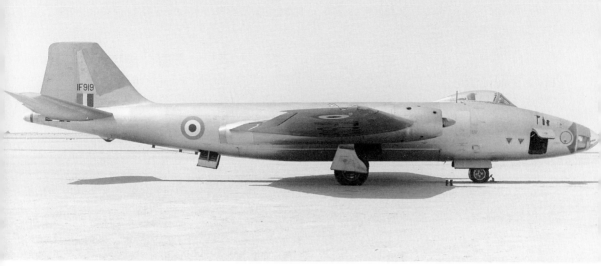

Canberra B.58 IF919 in service with No. 35 Squadron Indian Air Force.

and these were designated PR.67. A T.4 (later BQ944) was also ordered at the same time. In 1966 and 1967 a number of Indian Canberras visited the United Kingdom to act as navigation aircraft for the Hawker Hunters then being delivered. Examples included B.58s IF900 and IF976 of No. 5 Squadron, IF923 of No. 16 Squadron, along with IF919 and IF960 of No. 35 Squadron. India also had six more T.4 aircraft, which they converted themselves in Bangalore for a target-towing role, and they were designated TT.4-18.

India was also one of the countries to use its Canberras in action, this being during the war with Pakistan, between 3 and 17 December 1971. Canberras were used for low-level attacks on Pakistan's airfields, armoured columns and gun positions. Night interdiction and photographic reconnaissance missions were also carried out by Canberras. Some six aircraft were lost in action during this short war; this compared

Canberra T. Mk4 IF1021 of the Indian Air Force.

favourably with other, later types flown by the Indian Air Force.

In 1970, when the Royal New Zealand Air Force declared its remaining Canberra B(I).12s surplus to its requirements, these were obtained by India, the ten aircraft being delivered in 1971, to serve alongside the B(I).58s. Ten B(I). Mk66 Canberras – modified B.Mk6 aircraft – were ordered from BAC during the early 1970s. By the end of the 1970s some eighty-six Canberra aircraft were still in service, mostly in the strike role with Nos 5, 16, 35 and 106 Squadrons, the latter in the photo-reconnaissance role.

As at December 2003, one squadron, No. 106, of the Indian Air Force (IAF), still operates the Canberra aircraft in the reconnaissance and target-towing roles; and when I asked a senior official at the High Commission of India, at India House in London, on 23 December 2003, what aircraft would replace the Canberra, he said, '*We have not yet identified a successor aircraft, and staff work is presently under way to define the air staff requirements for the successor aircraft.*'

For the Indian Air Force – Bharatiya Vayu Sena – whose motto is '*Nabha Sparasham Deeptam*' ('Touching the Sky With Glory'), the Canberra has done that faithfully for the IAF for many decades; and the old lady is still 'Touching the Sky with Glory' for the aircrews of the Indian Air Force.

New Zealand – Canberra B(I).12, T. Mk13

During 1958 the New Zealand government ordered thirteen Canberras from Britain. These were eleven B(I). Mk12 aircraft (modified version of B(I). Mk8) and two T. Mk13 aircraft (modified version of the T. Mk14), the conversion being designed and effected by Boulton and Paul. The prototype for the B(I).12s was WT329 (became NZ6101), and the B(I).12s were serially NZ6101 – NZ6111 and the two T.13s NZ6151 and NZ6152. It was a direct ministry-to-ministry sale, and they all entered service with No. 14 Squadron at Ohakea. When No. 14 Squadron's role was changed to that of a light bomber unit, it took part in regular exercises with the Far East Air Force. In September 1964, the squadron deployed to Singapore on a permanent basis until November 1966.

The squadron then returned to New Zealand, and once again became based at Ohakea, until the Canberras were phased out of service in 1970, and all sold to the Indian

Canberra B(I). Mk12 NZ6104 of the Royal New Zealand Air Force.

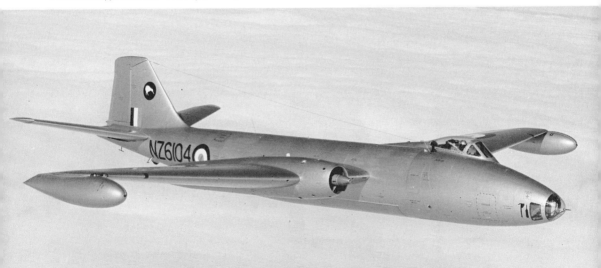

Canberra T. Mk13 NZ6151 of No. 14 Squadron RNZAF.

Air Force, except one B(I). Mk12. During service with the RNZAF, three Canberras were lost, one of these being an RAF Canberra B.2 (WF915) in service with 75 Squadron. On 26 October 1961, the Canberra hit severe turbulence and spun out of control. The pilot ejected but the navigator was killed. Canberra NZ6101 crashed on 2 November 1960 when on approach to Christchurch airport. The crew were shaken, but not stirred. Their aircraft was a write-off. In November 1964, NZ6104 crashed into the sea off Singapore, killing the two crew.

Rhodesia Zimbabwe – Canberra B. Mk2 and T. Mk4

Another Commonwealth country ordered the Canberra in 1959. This was Rhodesia, which received fifteen ex-RAF B. Mk2 aircraft. Three T. Mk4s that had been converted from B. Mk2s by English Electric were also acquired. These had the serials RRAF174 to 176. After the name change of the country, one B. Mk2 and one ex-RAF T. Mk4 were supplied to Zimbabwe.

Canberra B. Mk2 of the Rhodesian Air Force.

Canberra B. Mk2 with T. Mk11 nose awaiting delivery to Sweden, and seen here at Warton in its new livery.

Sweden – Canberra B. Mk2

A rather unusual order was placed for two Canberras in 1960 by Sweden. These were for two ex-RAF B. Mk2s with a T. Mk11 nose fitted, but they did not have T. Mk11 equipment fitted and so were officially B. Mk2s. They were the only two of this mark to be exported. Once in service with Sweden they were designated as Tp.52 with the serials 52001 (ex-WH711) and 52002 (ex-WH905). The two Canberras were used for special duties, radar trials being one, and were retired in 1973.

South Africa – Canberra B(I). Mk12; T. Mk4

The ever-popular interdictor version of the Canberra found new orders in 1962 when South Africa ordered six new B(I).12 aircraft. To produce them the production line was reopened (it had closed in 1961 after the delivery of the RNZAF aircraft), and the last B(I).12 serial number 456, was the last new production Canberra. Three ex-RAF T. Mk4 aircraft were also supplied in 1963. These did not become T. Mk13 aircraft, and they carried the serials 457 – 459, while the B(I).12s were 451 – 456. All served with No. 12 Squadron SAAF.

Canberra B(I). Mk12 '456' – South African Air Force with its blue turtle badge. This was the last new production Canberra. Aircraft silver overall finish – triangles on wing tanks and fuselage in red. Red, white, blue fin badge.

Canberra B. Mk2 YA-153 (ex-WK138), West German Air Force.

West Germany – Canberra B. Mk2

During 1966 another European country ordered a small number of ex-RAF B.2s. This time it was the West German government, and a total of three aircraft were delivered for experimental work; they were coded YA-151 (ex-WK130), YA-152 (ex-WK137) and YA-153 (ex-WK138). The three B.2s were initially operated by *Erprobungstelle 61* based at Oberpfaffenhofen, near Munich, but were later transferred to the Defence Ministry for special military photographic duties, with special cameras fitted in the bomb-bay. The three Canberras then carried German civil markings and were painted a bright orange. During 1977 they reverted to military markings, retaining their orange livery, and were then retired from service. One is preserved in its orange livery and military markings, at the Auto and Technik Museum, Sinsheim, Germany – well worth a visit, if only to see this lovely orange Canberra, which is in the colour section.

Ethiopia – Canberra B. Mk52

Overseas orders continued to be received long after production had ceased. Most were fulfilled with refurbishment ex-RAF aircraft as suitable airframes were released from service. In 1969 Ethiopia ordered four B.52s for service with the Imperial Ethiopian Air Force. These were converted from B. Mk2s and saw action in 1977 during the Ogaden war. During an attack on Asmara airfield by Eritrean separatists, the remaining two Canberras were destroyed, the other two Canberras having been destroyed by accidents in 1976.

Canberra B. Mk52 of the Imperial Ethiopian Air Force. Badge red and yellow with dark surround.

Ethiopian AF Canberra B. Mk52 with underwing rockets.

Group photo taken in March 1982, showing part of Grupo II, just before the Falklands War. Comodoro Segat, second from right kneeling.

Argentina – Canberra B. Mk62; T. Mk64

In mid-1969 Argentina ordered a number of refurbished ex-RAF B. Mk2 Canberras to replace its ancient Avro Lincoln piston-engined bombers that had given faithful service to the Fuerza Aerea Argentina. Canberra B-101 (ex-RAF WJ616/G-27-111/G-AYHO) was the first of ten B. Mk62s, and was handed over to Argentina on 16 November 1970, in its original factory paint of grey and green topsides with light grey undersurfaces. The Canberras had standard NATO symbols on the airframe but lettering in Spanish. They were delivered to Argentina during 1970-71. Two trainers, B-111 (ex-RAF WT476/G-27-121) and B-112 (ex-RAF WJ875/G-27-122), designated T. Mk64, were also purchased from Britain during mid-1969, and both were delivered on 26 February 1971. The T. Mk64 and B. Mk62 equipped one squadron, No. 1 Escuadron de Bombardeo, at their home base at General Urquiza in Parana.

The Canberras of the Fuerza Aerea Argentina saw action during the Falklands War in May/June 1982. The Canberras' first mission was on 1 May, when six aircraft took off from Trelejo in two flights of three. The pilots flew a Hi-Lo-Hi profile, and Captain Alberto Baigorri recalls:

> We began our descent around 250 miles before Puerto Argentino (Port Stanley) until we reached an altitude of fifteen to twenty metres above the water, and we were intercepted 150 miles before Puerto Argentino. The No. 3 in my flight called a missile headed my way – I looked towards the right and saw the missile hit the No. 2 aircraft, flown by pilot Teniente Eduardo de Ibañez and navigator Lieutenant Mario Gonzalez. The Canberra continued to fly off my right wing with an engine in flames as it started to go down – I saw de Ibañez and Gonzalez eject before it hit the water. Above us I saw a Sea Harrier looking to see whose turn it was next! I broke right and called my No.3 to break

The first of the magnificent five, Canberra PR. Mk9 HX131, the third production PR.9, but now back as good as new, makes a low pass over Shorts' Airfield Road production complex on 22 August 1986.

Canberra T. Mk22 WH803 in the markings of the FRADU – Royal Navy.

Sgt Griff Williams (standing) and Junior Tech Martin Alderson of No. 231 OCU, RAF Wyton, May 1984.

Canberra T.17 that shows clearly the markings and camouflage.

Lovely view of Canberra B-102 (G-AYHP), 1st Lieutenant Jorge Segat's aircraft, showing the bomb-doors open, the FAA roundel on the left wing only, with the serial on the right wing, topside, and is reversed underside, which you see here. Note its livery, the original factory paint of grey and green topsides with light grey undersurfaces. Under both wings are twin Matra 155 rocket launchers, with a total of thirty-six SNEB 68 mm rockets.

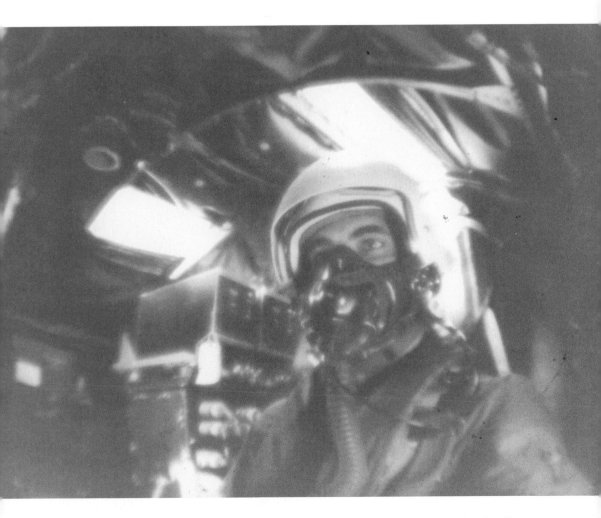

A unique photograph of Captain (later Comodoro) Jorge Segat, navigator bombardier-CME in Canberra B-102, en route for its baptism of fire on 1 May 1982. The steel, gun-metal eyes show no fear, only confidence for the major task ahead.

Canberra B(I). Mk56 '242' supplied to the Fuerza Aerea del Peru. Shown on a test flight before delivery and still carrying the British Class B registration G27-99. Note later-type starter breech fairings.

Canberra B. Mk2 in the markings of the Venezuelan Air Force awaiting delivery at Warton.

The four unique pictures depict the sad demise of Canberra WJ753 'L' of No. 100 Squadron, which crashed at RAF Marham on 19 June 1978. WJ753 was released to service on 8 January 1954.

It was the last B. Mk2, the 203rd built by the English Electric Company.

The Canberra B. Mk2, in its orange livery and German military markings, proudly displayed at the Auto and Technik Museum Sinsheim, Germany. It still looks good today. Truly well preserved, with dignity, and proves that the Grand Old Lady can fly for ever.

Canberra B(I). Mk66 of the Indian Air Force.

Close-up of Canberra WH793.

Close-up of West German B. Mk2 showing nose markings.

Lt Jerry Millward, F/Off Bob Webb and Flt/Lt Gordon Walker with a 360 Squadron Canberra T.17 (WH646) at RAF Wyton, May 1984.

The Author and Wing Commander Wallis talking over the Canberra book in the hangar of *Little Nellie* – the yellow one as seen in the James Bond film, *You Only Live Twice* – and her sisters at Reymerston Hall.

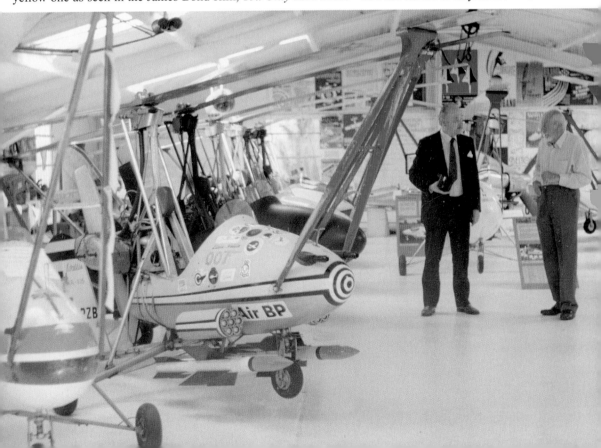

Canberra of the night: B-109 ready and waiting. A beautiful night for love, but for the warm-blooded crew-men of the Fuerza Aerea Argentina it is for war, not love. Note the starting cylinders are poised and ready. B-109 was former RAF WH875/G-27-163, and was delivered on 8 September 1971.

XH134 of No. 39 (1 PRU) Squadron banks for nice undershot and to say *'Arrivederci'*.

Canberra WT338 of No. 100 Squadron, in Cyprus in 1983 on detachment from RAF Wyton, was being prepared for flight and was being checked-out under the nose, when suddenly, someone touched a switch, and it collapsed. It would have been in the wheel-well, the wheels could not have been locked and when it tripped a micro-switch, the front collapsed. A very unique photograph, indeed, the only known such photograph, and published here for the first time.

Above the clouds: Canberra PR. Mk9 of No. 39 (1 PRU) Squadron. One of the magnificent five. Looks good – is good.

Canberra T. Mk64 B-111 on the ready line at Parana near Santa Fé. The trainer version of the Canberra is also fully equipped for the bomber role.

Canberra B-109 stands at the ready with starting cylinders on hand near the nose. Note the ECM pod in the shadow under the left wing and the close-fitting tropical 'umbrella' that helps keep the cockpit cool while reducing chances of defects in avionics caused by extreme heat. ECM units were rushed into service after it was realized that the Canberras had little chance of survival when encountering Sea Harriers or advanced guided missiles.

An Argentine pilot suits up for a mission in English Electric Canberra B-101,
which carries the name 'Pelicano 1'.

Close-up view of one of the locally produced external tanks (manufactured June 1982, according to the stencilling on the tank) for the Canberra. These tanks served just as well as the originals.

> *left – I saw the Sea Harrier still above us, but apparently it could not see us on its radar screen so we got out of there. After making sure the Sea Harrier was not around, we turned about and tried to locate the pilot and navigator, but we could not find them – they were lost.*

Another who saw the incident was Captain (later Comodoro) Jorge Julio Segat, navigator of Canberra B. Mk62 B-102 (WJ713/G-27-112/G-AYHP), who takes up the story:

> *My role on board the Canberra was that of navigator bombardier-CME, and my pilot during the war was Captain Eduardo Garcia Puebla, the flight leader, an excellent officer, a great pilot. With him we took part in the baptism of fire of the Argentine Air Force on 1 May 1982, and we saw how the first Canberra was brought down by a missile fired from a Harrier. The plane followed its line of flight without exploding, and gave time for Lieutenant de Ibañez and First Lieutenant Gonzalez to eject over the Atlantic, the first to die in our group... I can assure you that the Canberra Mark 62 and Mark 64 are wonderful. It has been a matter of great satisfaction and pride to fly the Canberra, and experiment with it; not only for its dignity, but also for its efficiency in the roles for which it was constructed. I say fly it since at present I belong to the First Squadron of Air Transport, and I am flying C130 and KC130 Hercules, another plane which saw significant action in the Guerra de Las Malvinas.*

When interviewed in June 1984, Captain Segat was flying Hercules, hence his reference to them. The Guerra de Las Malvinas is the Falklands War. I would just like to add that Captain Segat was also navigator bombardier-CME of Canberra B. Mk62 B-105 (WH702/G-27-127). After that interview in 1984, he was duly promoted, having led a full and active life (he flew very few desks) with the FAA, and on 1 May 2004 – 1 May was significant, for on this date in 1982 was his baptism of fire – he retired from active service with the rank of comodoro (colonel): a great man that I am proud to call a close friend. May God and the Virgin Mary be with him and look after him as he *'fumare de pipa'*, an old Argentina saying that means to chew over old times with a good friend and a good bottle of vino.

Special crew photograph taken just before the Falklands War ('Guerra de Las Malvinas'). The original photograph was given to me by Captain Jorge Julio Segat, and is much treasured. They are, looking from right to left: 1st Lt Pagano (flew various missions day and night) 2nd from rt; 1st Lt Jorge Segat (various missions day and night) 3rd from rt; 2nd Lt Daniel Gonzalez (disappeared in combat) 6th from rt; 2nd Lt Coke (died in an air accident September 1982. A participant in the battle of 1 May) 8th from rt; Lt de Ibanez (disappeared in combat) 9th from rt; 1st Lt Mario Gonzalez (bombarded San Carlos Bay several times) 11th from rt.

1st Lieutenant Jorge Julio Segat points to the plaque that commemorates the Canberra crewmen who failed to return from the 'Guerra de Las Malvinas' (Falklands War). Each Argentine station carries such a rollcall of honour.

The B. Mk62 can carry a maximum disposable weapons load of 6,000 lb (2,720 kg), and the squadron mainly used 1,000 lb (454 kg) bombs for their attacks on British positions. The Canberras also used chaff and flares to a limited extent, but it is thought that these measures did little to deter British attacks against the bombers, and the pilots quickly realized the need for some sort of electronic countermeasures, but it took the Argentine government fifteen days to obtain ECM pods, the military being naïve enough to think that sophisticated equipment such as ECM would not be needed. After the disastrous daylight raid of 1 May, the Canberras of No. 1 Escuadron de Bombardeo quickly switched to night bombing. The night missions had limited results, as Captain Alberto Baigorri recalls:

> *Our second mission was to San Carlos, and since we were so vulnerable we shifted to night missions against those ships that were the farthest away from the islands. We went in at 500 ft after the normal Hi-Lo-Hi profile, and this became our standard attack altitude, using radar altimeter to hold it. We hit San Carlos, Darwin, Mt Kent and other targets at various times in this manner. Our mission was fairly limited considering the lack of proper training for this type of attack, the stress on the pilots, the weather conditions of the South Atlantic with ice visible on the cockpit canopy and the rest of it. After the San Carlos attack we made a few night missions that were conducted at high altitude – 40,000 ft.*

The Canberras are very well maintained, but Argentine officers admit that there was considerable worry over spares for the aircraft since their main source of supply was, of course, Britain. Canberra pilots also complained that their tactics were very outdated, being mainly what they were taught by British instructors during the Lincoln period.

During the Falklands War, two Canberras were lost in the attacks against the British, one on 1 May and another on 13 June, when Captain Roberto Pastran and his navigator Captain Fernando Casado were hit by a Sea Dart while flying the unit's last mission. Captain Pastran managed to eject, but his navigator, Captain Casado, was disabled by the explosion and was killed in the crash. Captain Pastran was captured by the British Forces.

An interesting footnote to the Falklands War is that before April 1982, Argentina had ordered, and paid for, two Canberras – B. Mk62 WH914 and T. Mk64 XH583, and a spare wing for an aircraft that had been involved in an accident – from the then British Aerospace, but the 'paid in full' order was never fulfilled. The aircraft were being overhauled in the factory, and after the Falklands War, 'Great Britain decided to keep them', said the Argentine Air Attaché. And he added,

Comodoro Jorge Segat in the 'Room of The Heroes' in September 2003. They are remembered.

> ...we can also let you know that afterwards Great Britain gave them to Chile
> so as to recognize their support during the conflict. The last information we
> could trace was that one of them was destroyed in an accident a few years later.

When I contacted British Aerospace in 1984, I was told that WH914 and XH583 were still in pieces, and with only a deposit paid, the order was never completed. I asked again in 1987, and was told they were still there, and still in pieces. In January 2004, when I asked BAE Systems about the Canberras for Argentina, Jon Bonnick, the Communications Manager, said,

> As for WH914 and XH583, these aircraft that were going to go to the
> Argentine Air Force until the Falklands War intervened, these were recorded
> still at Samlesbury in 1987, but we believe they were later scrapped.

They were not scrapped, and the truth of the matter is as told by the Argentine Air Attaché, Group Captain Daniel Paredi: Great Britain kept them and gave them to Chile.

The Canberra was withdrawn from service with the Fuerza Aerea Argentina (FAA) on 5 April 2000 in Parana, Province of Entre Rios, and quite naturally now has pride of place in their museum.

The Canberra Demonstration Team just before departing for the Le Bourget Air Show on 4/5 July. 1953. S/Ldr John Crampton is the tallest in the rear row. On his left, wearing a beret, is F/Lt Tony Caillard (later Air Vice-Marshal), No. 101 Squadron, RAF Binbrook.

CHAPTER SIX

Canberra Squadrons

No. 3 SQUADRON

English Electric Canberra B(I). Mk8   **January 1961 to December 1971**

Formed on 13 April 1912, from No. 2 (Aeroplane) Company of Air Battalion, Royal Engineers, and based at Larkhill, Wiltshire, No. 3 (F) Fighter Squadron is the oldest aeroplane unit in the service, a feat duly recorded in its motto: *Tertius Primus Erit* (The third shall be first).

During the First World War it pioneered aerial gunnery and photo-reconnaissance, and was the first squadron to make a photo map of battle lines on the Western Front. It was a general-duties unit until 1917, when it was equipped with Camel aircraft and took over a fighter role. The squadron took part in the first massed air-to-ground attacks in support of Allied troops.

In 1938 it was the second RAF squadron to receive the new Hurricane fighter, and in 1940 it was in action in France. Equipped with Tempests in 1944, the squadron formed part of the air defence against the V-1 offensive on Britain, and shot down 288 flying bombs. In 1948 it received its first jets – Vampires.

A fighter squadron for thirty-seven years, No. 3 became a bomber unit on 4 January 1961, when No. 59 Squadron was renumbered 3 at RAF Geilenkirchen in Germany. It was equipped with English Electric Canberra B(I). Mk8 aircraft in the strike/interdictor role.

As soon as the squadron was settled with its new mounts, detachments to RAF Idris, Libya, commenced in May 1961, on a monthly basis. Aircraft used Tarhuna Range for bombing practice while at Idris.

Canberra B(I). Mk8s of No. 3 Squadron, Geilenkirchen, in 1968

No. 3 Squadron at RAF Laarbruch, Germany, in 1969.

Canberra of No. 3 Squadron makes a pass for the camera in Cyprus.

Canberra B(I)8 of No. 3 Squadron with a pair of Gloster Javelines from No. 11 Squadron. This gives some idea of the Canberra size with the fighters and a chance to compare the Canberra fighter style canopy.

Nos 1, 2, 3 and 4 Squadrons together at Gibraltar.

In May 1962 the Canberras were detached to Akrotiri for interdictor training, and on their return from Cyprus the following month, No. 3 Squadron used Wildenrath as its operating base because runway extensions were being carried out at Geilenkirchen. Quick Reaction Alert (QRA) commitment was maintained at Geilenkirchen, where the squadron returned in August.

Over the next three years the Canberras were deployed to Malta, Kuantan, Malaya and Cyprus. August 1965 saw the first squadron exchange with Canberras 3/34 FBW German Air Force with F-84s from Memmingen. The following month, the monthly bombing practice detachments to Idris were moved to RAF Luqa, Malta.

February 1966 brought news that No. 3 Squadron had won the Salmond Trophy, awarded to the squadron with the best results in the Command Bombing and Navigation Competitions run throughout the year. The Canberras had a very busy summer, with participation in the 5th Air Cent Tactical Weapons Meet at Chaumont in June 1966, and the following month four aircraft were deployed to Rimini, Italy.

During November and December 1966 the Canberras were detached to Cyprus, on exercise Citrus Grove, for bombing training. Other exchanges followed, and the squadron retained the Salmond Trophy for the second year running. During December 1967/January 1968 No. 3 Squadron moved to RAF Laarbruch prior to the closure of Geilenkirchen.

Over the next few years the squadron continued with exercises and exchanges, and during August/September 1971 the squadron had its first detachment to Decimomannu, Sardinia, to use Cape Frasca weapons range. But this was to be the last time for the Canberras. On 3 December, 1971, the Canberra Disbandment Parade took place, reviewed by Air Marshal Sir Harold Martin KCB, DSO, DFC, AFC, C-in-C RAF Germany. Meanwhile at RAF Wildenrath, No. 3 (F) Squadron was re-forming in its traditional fighter role with Harrier vertical-take-off jet fighters.

No. 6 SQUADRON

English Electric Canberra B. Mk2	**July 1957 to January 1960**
B. Mk6	**December 1959 to December 1962**
B. Mk15	**January 1962 to January 1969**
B. Mk16	**January 1962 to January 1969**

No. 6 Squadron RFC came into being at Farnborough in the spring of 1914, and in October moved to Belgium. It is interesting to note that No. 6 Squadron was commanded by Captain H.C.T. Dowding, who in the Second World War was AOC-in-C Fighter Command during the Battle of Britain. In July 1915, Captain Hawker, for almost a year of continuous aerial combat, was awarded the Victoria Cross. Between the wars the squadron was in Iraq, Egypt and Palestine; and at the start of the Second World War it was in Shandur on the Suez canal, equipped with Lysanders. It had detachments in the Western Desert; and in 1942 re-equipped with the Hurricane IId 'Tankbuster', one of only two squadrons to do so. They became known as the 'tin-openers' and their emblem was a 'flying tin opener'. In 1944 the squadron moved to Italy, where it remained for the duration of the war. At Cyprus in 1948 the squadron traded in its Tempests for Vampires, which in turn were traded in for Venoms.

No. 6 Squadron reverted to the bomber role when its Venoms gave way to Canberras in July 1957. With a change of role the squadron flew Canberras as part of the Near East Air Force Strike Wing at Akrotiri, Cyprus, in support of the CENTO countries. It first flew Canberra B. Mk2s from July 1957, and then B. Mk6s, and finally B. Mk15s and B. Mk16s, with which it used underwing rockets as well as bombs. During the Canberra period the squadron colours returned to the aircraft. The 'flying tin opener', the proud emblem of the squadron, which was a legacy of tank-busting operations in the Western Desert with special Hurricanes, reappeared on the tip tanks, and the Gunner's Stripe (dark blue and red) was reintroduced. The squadron remained in Cyprus; and, after twelve years the Canberra era came to an end when the squadron disbanded in 1969 and re-formed in the UK as the first of the RAF's Phantom squadrons.

Canberra B. Mk16 XH570 of No. 6 Squadron comes in to land at Luqa, Malta, August 1968. Note the 'flying tin opener' badge on the fin, a legacy of the squadron's tank-busting days in the Western Desert during the Second World War.

No. 9 SQUADRON

English Electric Canberra B. Mk2   **May 1952 to June 1956 and**
and   **June 1957 to November 1958**
B. Mk6   **September 1955 to July 1961**

No. 9 Squadron saw the Second World War out with Lancasters, trading these in for Lincolns, which in turn were traded in for Canberras. It was one of the first squadrons to be equipped with the new jet bomber, and received the first B. Mk2s in May 1952.

The year 1956 began with a visit to Nigeria, coinciding with the tour by the Queen and the Duke of Edinburgh. During the tour the squadron gave flying demonstrations and made ceremonial flypasts over Lagos and the Nigerian regional capitals. Visits were made to Nigeria, Gold Coast (Ghana), Sierra Leone and Gambia. The squadron returned to Binbrook in February 1956, and the following month it was detached to Butterworth, Malaya, and the Canberras were in action against the terrorists. In April 1956 No. 9 Squadron was detached from Malaya to Manila in the Philippines. After a few weeks the squadron returned to Binbrook, and it now had on strength a few B. Mk6s that had arrived on the squadron in 1955. Soon after its return to the UK, the squadron took the lead in the flypasts for Her Majesty the Queen's Review of Bomber Command at Marham on 23 July 1956. After many other events No. 9 Squadron was detached to Malta during the latter part of 1956 to take part in operations during the Suez crisis. Other tasks included attacks on Malayan terrorists.

The squadron returned to England in December 1956. Its days with the Canberras were now numbered, and on 13 July 1961 No. 9 Squadron disbanded at Coningsby, Lincolnshire, where it re-formed in 1962 as a V-Force squadron.

No. 10 SQUADRON

English Electric Canberra B. Mk2   **January 1953 to January 1957**

No. 10 Squadron re-formed at Scampton as a light-bomber squadron with Canberra B. Mk2s in January 1953. The squadron conducted tests of pressure and air-ventilated suits on long-range flights. In April 1955, No. 10 Squadron moved to Honington when Scampton closed for reconstruction, transferring in the move from No. 1 to No. 3 Group. That same year it won the Armament Officer's Trophy in the annual bombing competition.

During October and November 1956 the squadron was detached to Nicosia, Cyprus, and at the end of October opened the operations against military objectives in Egypt by leading a bombing raid against Almaza airfield, Cairo. WH853 dropped the RAF's first bombs on Egyptian soil in the Suez campaign.

After its duty in the Suez operation the squadron returned to the UK, and on 15 January it disbanded. It re-formed on 15 April 1958 as a V-Force squadron at Cottesmore.

No. 12 SQUADRON

English Electric Canberra B. Mk2   **April 1952 to June 1955 and**
and   **August 1957 to March 1959**
B. Mk6   **May 1955 to July 1961**

No. 12 Squadron dates back to 1915, when it flew BE2cs and RE8s in the First World War. Between the wars it had a variety of aircraft, de Havilland 9A, Fairey Fawn and Fox, Hawker Hind and Hart. It entered the Second World War with Fairey Battles, having armed up with these in 1938, and until June 1940 it flew from airfields in France. With the Fairey Battles, the squadron won the first RAF VCs of the Second World War. These were

Canberra B. Mk6 WH960 of No. 12 Squadron. The fox on the fin is red.

awarded posthumously to Flying Officer D.E. Garland, pilot, and Sergeant T. Gray, his observer, after a low-level attack on a metal bridge at Veldwezelt, over the Albert Canal.

In November 1940 the squadron traded in its Battles for Vickers Wellingtons. But it flew these for only a year before converting to the four-engined Avro Lancaster, which it flew for the remainder of the war. The squadron had one famous Lancaster, and in the eleven months from May 1944 to April 1945, Lancaster I ME758 N-Nuts flew 108 operational sorties. In August 1946 the Lancasters gave way to Lincolns.

No. 12 Squadron traded in its Avro Lincolns for Canberra B. Mk2s early in 1952, and that same year four Canberras, WD987, WD990, WD993 and WD996, made a 24,000-mile (38,625 km) goodwill tour of South America (Operation Round Trip). Leader of the flight and himself pilot of one of the Canberras was AVM D.A. Boyle (later MRAF Sir Dermot Boyle). In mid-1955 the squadron took on strength some B. Mk6s and in October of that year was detached to Butterworth, Malaya, to take part in the air war against the terrorists. It returned in March 1956, having made twenty-four successful strikes. After only a few months back in the UK the squadron was again on the move, when it was detached to Malta in September 1956, and it Canberras were again in action, this time against military objectives in Egypt during the Suez War. The squadron disbanded on 13 July 1961 at Coningsby, where it re-formed in 1962 as a V-Force squadron.

No. 14 SQUADRON

English Electric Canberra B(I). Mk8   **December 1962 to June 1970**

No. 14 Squadron formed at Shoreham, Sussex, on 3 February 1915, and in November moved to the Middle East. The squadron served in the Sinai Desert and the Western Desert. It returned to the UK in January 1919 and disbanded.

It re-formed in February 1919, when No. 111 Squadron at Ramleh, Palestine, was renumbered No. 14. At the outbreak of the Second World War it was at Ismailia, Egypt, flying Vickers Wellesleys. Throughout the war the squadron remained based in Sudan, Iraq and Egypt, and its primary role from December 1942 was as a torpedo-bomber squadron.

Canberra T. Mk4 WT478 of No. 14 Squadron.

On 1 June 1945, the squadron disbanded, but on the same day its number plate was transferred to No. 143 (Fighter Reconnaissance) Squadron based at Banff, Scotland. It reverted to a bomber role when No. 128 Squadron was renumbered 14 at Wahn, Germany. It was equipped with Mosquitoes, and when it re-equipped with Vampire jets in 1951 it assumed a day-fighter role.

No. 14 Squadron, the only day-fighter unit in RAF Germany, disbanded on 17 December 1962, but on the same day began a new career as a Canberra light-bomber/night-intruder unit when No. 8 Squadron at Wildenrath was renumbered 14. Disbanded at Wildenrath on 30 June 1970, it re-formed on the same date at Bruggen as a Phantom fighter strike squadron.

No. 15 SQUADRON

English Electric Canberra B. Mk2   **May 1953 to April 1957**

No. 15 Squadron formed on 1 March 1915, at South Farnborough, Hampshire. The squadron carried out photographic and artillery co-operation duties in the First World War.

It disbanded in December 1919. In March 1924 it re-formed as a bomber squadron and became part of the A & AEE for the next ten years. In June 1934 it re-formed at Abingdon as a day-bomber squadron equipped with Harts, and at the outbreak of war was flying Battles. These gave way to Blenheims, and in August 1942 the squadron moved to Bourn. Four months later it re-equipped with four-engined Lancasters, which it flew for the duration of the war. The squadron had one of the most famous Lancasters in Bomber Command – this was Lancaster 1 LL806 J-Jig, which flew 134 operational sorties.

No. 15 Squadron re-equipped with Lincolns in 1947, and three years later had Washingtons, which it traded in for Canberras in 1953. While flying Canberras the squadron was detached to Libya in June 1956, Cyprus in October/November 1956 and Malta in December 1956/January 1957. It disbanded at Honington, Suffolk on 15 April 1957. It was re-formed on 1 September 1958 as a V-Force squadron at Cottesmore.

Canberra B(I). Mk8 WT346 of No. 16 Squadron. Shark-mouth decoration and 'The Saint' on the fin. This aircraft was later preserved at RAF Cosford as 8197M.

No. 16 SQUADRON

English Electric Canberra B(I). Mk8   **March 1958 to June 1972**

Although dating back to 1915 – the squadron formed at St Omer in France on 10 February 1915 – it did not become a bomber squadron until 1958. No. 16 Squadron re-formed on 1 March 1958, at Laarbruch in Germany, as a Canberra light-bomber/night-intruder squadron. With Canberra B(I). Mk8s, the squadron soon worked up to operational pitch in the attack role, training with the Low-Altitude Bombing System (LABS) for nuclear bombing attacks, as well as the more conventional attack methods. It is interesting to note that the Canberras carried the black band round the fuselage that dated back to pre-war days, when it was seen on the squadron's Atlases and Audaxes. The squadron flew the Canberra B(I). Mk8s for a period of fourteen years, on the same task, at the same base, longer than any other squadron.

During that period, as one of the three squadrons of the 2nd Tactical Air Force Canberra Strike Wing – the other two being 59 and 88 Squadrons – one Canberra was always at ten minutes readiness to carry out a nuclear attack, had the order been given.

No. 16 Squadron disbanded at Laarbruch, Germany, on 6 June 1972, the last remnant of the Canberra bomber force to be operational. It re-formed at Laarbruch on 16 October 1972, with Buccaneers.

Canberra B(I). Mk8 XM271 of No. 16 Squadron flies low over Malta, November 1971. Note the shark-mouth decoration and the 'Saint' badge on the fin.

Canberra B. Mk2 WJ605, which was built by Handley Page and released to service on 18 September 1953. Seen here with No. 18 Squadron. (Black speedbird insignia.)

No. 18 (BURMA) SQUADRON

English Electric Canberra B. Mk2   **August 1953 to January 1957**

No. 18 Squadron RFC formed at Northolt on 11 May 1915, saw service in France during the First World War, and at the end of the war disbanded in September 1919. It re-formed in October 1931; and throughout the Second World War 18 Squadron had two main types of aircraft. These were Bristol Blenheims, for the first half of the war, and then Douglas Bostons. No. 18 Squadron's claim to fame is the fact that it was one of its Blenheims, the one in question being R3843 'F-Freddy', whose crew, on 19 August 1941, while *en route* to a target in northern France, dropped by parachute, over Saint Omer aerodrome, just to the east of Calais, a spare right artificial leg for Wing Commander Douglas Bader, who had been shot down in France ten days earlier. Just after the end of the Second World War, 18 Squadron disbanded in 1946. In December 1947 it re-formed and its Dakotas took part in the Berlin Air Lift. When that came to an end it disbanded.

In keeping with the expansion of the Canberra Force, 18 Squadron re-formed on 1 August 1953 at RAF Scampton. The Squadron's Canberras were detached to Libya and Cyprus, and were in action during the Suez War. The Suez War was short, and so, too, were the Canberra days for No. 18 Squadron, for they quickly came to an end when it disbanded on 1 February 1957, its Canberra days now in the history books. On 16 December 1958, it re-formed as a V-Force Squadron.

No. 21 SQUADRON

English Electric Canberra B. Mk2		**September 1953 to June 1957**
after re-formed	**B. Mk2**	**October 1958 to January 1959**
Laverton detachment	**B. Mk6**	**October 1958 to January 1959**

No. 21 Squadron formed at Netheravon on 23 July 1915, and is one of the senior squadrons of the Royal Air Force. It served in France throughout the First World War and operated with RE7s. BE12s and RE8s.

The outbreak of the Second World War found the squadron equipped with Bristol Blenheims, stationed in East Anglia. The squadron carried out sweeps into Heligoland Bight to attack shipping, and penetrated deep into Germany photographing airfields.

When the invasion of Norway started, 21 Squadron was stationed at Lossiemouth in the north of Scotland, from which base the Blenheims made shipping sweeps and bombed Stavanger airfield.

During the withdrawal at Dunkirk, 21 Squadron operated from Norfolk at high pressure, bombing bridges, attacking tank columns and holding up the advancing panzers to give Allied soldiers the breathing space to extricate themselves.

The squadron moved to Malta in January 1942 and carried out attacks against enemy targets on land and sea during January. It was disbanded overseas on 14 March 1942, and re-formed on the same date at Bodney, the satellite station to RAF Watton. The squadron was equipped with Blenheim IVs and was to operate as a medium-bomber squadron in No. 2 Group. During the summer of 1942 the squadron began to re-equip with Lockheed Venturas, and on 6 December, operating from Methwold, was one of the squadrons which made the daring low-level raid on the Philips radio component factory at Eindhoven. It contained daylight operations with the Venturas until early September 1943.

From September 1943 until it disbanded in Germany in November 1947, No. 21 Squadron operated the de Havilland Mosquito – the famous 'Wooden Wonder'. With the Mosquito it bombed V-weapon sites, railways and other targets. After the war it operated a courier service between Furth airfield (Nuremberg) and Blackbushe during the period of the Nazi war criminals' trials.

It re-formed on 21 September 1953 as a Canberra medium-bomber squadron at Scampton. It was detached to Cyprus in February/March 1955, and then carried out a goodwill tour to the Sudan, Kenya, Aden and Bahrain with its Canberras. When the squadron returned to the UK it was based at Waddington from June 1955. That same year it was detached to Cyprus during October. It disbanded in June 1957, but on 1 October 1958 was revived as a Canberra bomber squadron when No. 542 Squadron, which had been on detachment at Laverton, Australia, was renumbered 21. C Flight, equipped with B. Mk6s, never operated in the UK, and was detached to Laverton, Australia, until disbanded on 1 January 1959. The squadron finally disbanded as a Canberra unit on 15 January 1959.

No. 27 SQUADRON

English Electric Canberra B. Mk2　　　　　　　**June 1953 to December 1957**

On 5 November 1915, No. 27 Squadron formed at Hounslow (near the present Heathrow Airport) with a few Martinsydes, and before the end of the year had moved to Dover. The squadron saw service in France before disbanding in January 1920. Between the wars it saw service in India on the North-West Frontier; and at the outbreak of the Second World War it was in Malaya. It fought Japanese forces, and after suffering heavy losses it disbanded in early 1942. It re-formed in India before the end of 1942 and then saw service in Burma. The squadron disbanded in 1946. At the end of 1947 it re-formed as a transport squadron, and played a major role in the Berlin Air Lift before disbanding in late 1950.

The squadron reverted to the bomber role when it re-formed on 15 June 1953 at RAF Scampton in Lincolnshire as a Canberra medium-bomber unit. In June 1954, six of the squadron's Canberras were on Operation Med. Trip, and were detached on a goodwill tour of France, Italy, Greece, Turkey, Yugoslavia and Portugal. During October, November and December 1956, No. 27 Squadron was detached to Cyprus, because of the Middle East crisis, and subsequently took part in Operation Musketeer. The squadron's Canberras went into action against military targets in Egypt, and all was well for the squadron.

No. 27 Squadron disbanded on 31 December 1957, and on 1 April 1961 re-formed at RAF Scampton with the Vulcan bomber, as part of the V-Force.

2

Canberra B. Mk2 WH638, which was released to service on 27 August 1952. Here in the markings of No. 32 Squadron. Squadron marking on fin in blue and white.

No. 32 SQUADRON

English Electric Canberra B. Mk2   **January 1957 to July 1961**
B. Mk15   **July 1961 to February 1969**

No. 32 Squadron formed at Netheravon, Wiltshire, on 12 January 1916, and in May moved to France with DH2 fighters. The squadron CO, Major L. Rees, won the Victoria Cross during the Somme offensive. During the Second World War the squadron flew Hurricanes in the Battle of Britain and then saw action in North Africa and Italy. In 1944, No. 32 Squadron became part of the Balkan Air Force. In the post-war years it was based in Palestine and in the Mediterranean area.

In January 1957 No. 32 Squadron became a Canberra light-bomber squadron when it moved from Mafraq, Jordan, to Nicosia in Cyprus, disposed of its Venom aircraft (having for some time previously been a Venom fighter/ground-attack unit) and began to

Canberra B. Mk15 WH966 of No. 32 Squadron at Malta in September 1968. Note the squadron markings have again changed.

re-arm in the UK. The first flight of Canberra-trained aircrew assembled at Weston Zoyland on 15 January 1957, and a few days later the Canberra arrived. No. 32 Squadron worked up to operational status with 542 Squadron, which was then based at Weston Zoyland. The first Canberra flight flew out to Cyprus in February, followed by the second flight the following month. This event marked a change from the fighter to the bomber role for the first time in the squadron's history. No. 32 Squadron formed part of the Akrotiri Strike Wing, tasked with taking the offensive to any trouble spot in the Eastern Mediterranean area. From its Cyprus base the squadron flew many detachments, principally to Africa and Malaysia, during the Indonesian confrontation. On 6 June 1957, the squadron was presented with its standard, an award created by King George VI to mark the 25th anniversary of the Royal Air Force in 1943, and which signifies twenty-five years' service by a squadron.

In July 1961 the Canberra B. Mk2s were replaced by Canberra B. Mk15s, with which the squadron carried out operational training locally, interspersed with various detachments to Near Eastern, Middle Eastern and South East Asia countries. In 1965 the squadron became operational with the Nord AS.30 under-wing-mounted missile, and continued as part of the Akrotiri Strike Wing until disbanding at Akrotiri on 3 February 1969. On the same day it was re-formed at Northolt as a short-range communications squadron.

No. 35 (MADRAS PRESIDENCY) SQUADRON

English Electric Canberra B. Mk2   **April 1954 to September 1961**

No. 35 Squadron formed on 1 February 1916 at Thetford, Norfolk, and a year later moved to France. It returned to England in March 1919 and disbanded the following June.

It re-formed on 1 March 1929 at Bircham Newton, Norfolk, as a bomber squadron, first with DH9As and then Fairey 111Fs. In October 1935 it moved to the Sudan, but after only ten months returned to England.

At the outbreak of the Second World War No. 35 Squadron was employed as a training unit, and in April 1940 lost its identity on being absorbed into No. 17 OTU. In November 1940 the squadron re-formed for the express purpose of introducing the new four-engined Handley Page Halifax into operational service. The squadron flew Halifaxes until March 1944, when they were replaced by Lancasters, and flew these until 1949; they

Canberra B. Mk2 WH911 of No. 35 Squadron with revised insignia – introduced in 1960 – on base of fin. White shield superimposed on yellow lightning flash outlined in black, black horse's head, yellow wings and black 'XXXV'. Note insignia also on tip tanks.

in turn were replaced by Lincolns. In February 1950, No. 35 Squadron disbanded. It re-formed with Washington aircraft at Marham, Norfolk, on 1 September 1951.

After two and a half years with Boeing Washingtons, No. 35 Squadron replaced them with Canberras in April 1954, and was the final Canberra bomber unit stationed in Britain (Marham and Upwood). During the Middle East crisis several 35 Squadron Canberras were detached to Nicosia, Cyprus, in October/November 1956 to reinforce the Canberras of Nos 18 and 61 Squadrons. No. 35 Squadron disbanded on 11 September 1961, and re-formed in 1962 as a V-Force squadron at Coningsby.

No. 40 SQUADRON

English Electric Canberra B. Mk2   **October 1953 to December 1956**

After its wartime role flying Vickers Wellingtons from bases in the Middle East, No. 40 Squadron then flew Liberators and Lancasters until it disbanded in Egypt in April 1947. At the end of that year it was re-formed as a transport squadron with Avro Yorks until it disbanded in March 1950.

No. 40 Squadron then re-formed at Coningsby on 28 October 1953, commanded by Squadron Leader K.B. Rogers DFC, AFC, a New Zealander. It was once again in Bomber Command, this time equipped with English Electric Canberra B.2 light-bomber aircraft. This marked the transfer of the squadron to jet aircraft, and the new problems of speed and high-altitude bombing operations had to be mastered. Ground servicing, too, had to be revised, but the squadron was soon back to operational status and the usual bombing practice and training flights continued.

On 24 February 1954, the squadron moved to Wittering, and all crews soon became categorized under the Bomber Command efficiency assessment scheme. The first crews in No. 3 Group to become 'Select' on Canberra were on 40 Squadron, which also became the second squadron in the Group to be fully categorized. Categorized crews are permitted to fly overseas individually on 'Lone Ranger' exercises, and most crews have visited Idris, Gibraltar and bases in Germany. Some 'Select' crews have travelled to Khartoum, Nairobi, Aden and Sharjah.

At the end of July 1955 the squadron was detached to Malta to join the air – sea manoeuvres in the Ionian Sea. Units of the American Sixth Fleet were the targets, and all attacks were successful, culminating in a very-low level dummy raid on two aircraft-carriers. More exercises followed, and the period from September 1955 to 3 April 1956 was fully occupied with routine training, including Group and Command bombing exercises, a great deal of flying being done in this period. Some aircraft landed in Norway after simulated raids to test Norwegian defences, and others were detached to Wahn in Germany to practice their operational roles under NATO command. This, however, was the normal daily routine of a Canberra squadron in peacetime.

On 3 April 1956, all Canberra B.2 aircraft were grounded as a result of many fatal and near-fatal accidents attributed to the failure of the electrically operated tailplane actuator. As Squadron Leader Wallis knew, there were many problems. Out of the first 203 B. Mk2s, fifty-eight were Category 5.

On 5 May 1956, Squadron Leader E.L. Wallane took command of the squadron. He found all the aircraft still grounded. The period from this date was a very trying one, as the squadron did not have all its aircraft modified to fly again until mid-August 1956. The problem of maintenance of morale of the air and ground crews was very real, and diverse activities were organized to keep everyone occupied. Sports and visits to industry and breweries were liberally arranged. The aircrews were kept in flying practice in the

T.4 Canberra Trainer. The average flying time per crew per month fell to the low figure of six hours.

It was not until 22 June 1956 that the first B.2 was modified and cleared to fly; even then, certain performance restrictions were enforced. The modification programme continued very slowly, two aircraft being completed by the end of June and a total of four by 13 July.

These four aircraft were modified in time to allow the squadron to take part in the formation flypast in honour of HM the Queen at RAF Marham on 27 July. It was not until mid-August that all the aircraft were fit to fly.

The impending crisis in the Middle East of the Suez War affected the squadron in that on 2 August such B.2s as had been modified to fly again commenced flying sorties on Exercise Accumulate. This involved the uplift of 1,000 lb (454 kg) bombs to the Middle East theatre. Twenty-three sorties to Malta were flown in seven days.

Routine training and command exercises followed until 1 November 1956, when after thirty-two months at RAF Wittering, the squadron moved to RAF Upwood. On 15 December 1956, No. 40 Squadron amalgamated with No. 50 Squadron. The disbandment of the squadron from an administrative standpoint took effect from 1 February 1957.

No. 44 (RHODESIA) SQUADRON

English Electric Canberra B. Mk2   **April 1953 to July 1957**

No. 44 Squadron formed at Hainault Farm, Essex, on 24 July 1917, as a home defence squadron, and it became the first squadron to use the single-seat Sopwith Camel for night operations. It disbanded in 1919. In March 1937 it re-formed at Wyton as a bomber squadron with Hawker Hinds, and at the outbreak of the Second World War it was based at Waddington, Lincolnshire, flying Hampdens. Its early duties were sweeps over the North Sea, and the squadron bombed the invasion barges in the Channel and North Sea ports.

In December 1941, No. 44 became the first squadron to convert to all Lancasters. To show the enemy their new mounts the squadron made a low-level unescorted daylight raid on the Maschinenfabrik Augsburg-Nürnberg Aktiengesellschaft, a diesel factory at Augsburg in

Canberra B. Mk2 WD965, which was released for service on 4 February 1952. It was the 36th off the production line. Seen here with No. 44 Squadron sporting the white pheasant of RAF Honington on its fin. On its nose is a red speedbird, the mark of RAF Scampton, where it once served with No. 10 Squadron.

southern Bavaria. On this raid Squadron Leader J.D. Nettleton won the Victoria Cross.

The squadron remained with Lancasters throughout the Second World War and right up until June 1947. It then flew Avro Lincolns and Boeing Washingtons. It traded in the latter for Canberras in the early part of 1953. In October 1956 the Canberras were on active service during the Suez War and were detached to Cyprus, from where the squadron made bombing attacks on the Egyptian airfields. After this, training was resumed and overseas flights were made until 16 July 1957, when the squadron disbanded after more than twenty years' continuous existence.

The squadron was re-formed in September 1960 at Waddington, equipped with Vulcan B.1 aircraft.

No. 45 SQUADRON

English Electric Canberra B. Mk2   **December 1957 to December 1962**
                    B. Mk15   **September 1962 to November 1970**

No. 45 Squadron formed at Gosport, Hampshire, on 1 March 1916, and operated in France with Sopwith 1½ Strutters on reconnaissance duties. After the war it returned to England and disbanded at the end of 1919.

It re-formed at Helwan, Egypt, in April 1921, and after a period in Iraq the squadron moved back to Egypt in 1927, to be absorbed into No. 47 Squadron at Helwan. No. 45 re-formed at Heliopolis, Egypt, on 25 April 1927 as a bomber squadron, and at the outbreak of the Second World War was based at Fuka and equipped with Blenheims. After serving in Egypt, Libya, Palestine and India during the war, the squadron moved to Negombo, Ceylon, in 1946.

From Kuala Lumpur, Malaya, the squadron made day and night bombing attacks on the Communist terrorists.

After a period in the fighter-bomber role, flying Meteors and Vampires, then Venoms, No. 45 eventually became a bomber squadron again in November 1957 at Tengah, Singapore.

The squadron was detached to Coningsby, where No. 45's crews converted to Canberra light bombers in late 1957. Having re-equipped with B. Mk2s the squadron returned to Tengah, and with their new mounts continued the anti-terrorist campaign until the conclusion of Operation Firedog and the Malaya Emergency in 1960. Initially

Canberra B. Mk2 WH667 of No. 45 Squadron. On the tail the squadron marking – a red camel with blue wings on a white disc. Aircraft silver overall with light grey fin panel. Serial numbers and anti-glare panel are black.

the Canberra B. Mk2s were silver overall with a light grey fin panel, black serials on the fuselage and underwing plus type-D markings with the squadron insignia on the fin – a red camel with blue wings on a white disc. The Canberras then received grey and green camouflaged upper surfaces, with the fuselage serials in white.

In 1962 the squadron re-equipped with Canberra B. Mk15s, and with this improved version remained as Malaya's resident bomber squadron. The Canberras were soon into action, for 1963 saw the start of the 'Confrontation' with Indonesia. During the confrontation detachments were maintained in Borneo, at Labuan and Kutchings, and border patrols were flown. The Canberras provided part of an effective deterrent strike force against Indonesian attacks, right up until the end of hostilities in 1966. The squadron then continued at Tengah in a peacetime role. The camouflage on the Canberra B. Mk15s consisted of light grey undersides instead of the silver adopted on the B. Mk2s. All serials were black, with the Camel insignia being reduced in size and losing the white surround.

With the withdrawal of British forces from Malaysia, No. 45 Squadron disbanded at Tengah on 13 January 1970.

In September 1972, No. 45 Squadron re-formed at Wittering as a strike fighter squadron with Hunters to provide operational training for future Jaguar ground-attack pilots.

No. 50 SQUADRON

English Electric Canberra B. Mk2   **August 1952 to October 1959**

No. 50 Squadron formed at Dover, Kent, on 15 May 1916, as a home defence squadron. After disbanding in 1919 it re-formed at Waddington, Lincolnshire, on 3 May 1937, as a bomber squadron equipped with Hawker Hinds. At the outbreak of the Second World War the squadron was flying Hampdens, with which it attacked many enemy targets in the early days.

In 1942, No. 50 Squadron converted to Manchesters, then to Lancasters, and took part in almost all the major raids, including the one on the German V-weapons experimental establishment at Peenemünde.

At peace once again, No. 50 Squadron converted to Lincolns in 1947 and continued

Canberra B. Mk2 WH725, which was released to service on 16 May 1953, here with No. 50 Squadron. On the fin the lion rampant motif from RAF Upwood's badge. The marking on its tip tank comprises a light blue sword with yellow handle, and '50' in red (all trim in black). This aircraft is preserved at Duxford.

with these until it disbanded in January 1951. It re-formed in August 1952 at Binbrook with Canberra B. Mk2s, and resumed exercises and long-distance flights, some of which took its Canberras to distant parts of the world. The squadron moved to Upwood in January 1956 and remained there until disbanding in October 1959.

The squadron re-formed again on 1 August 1961, and was stationed at Waddington, equipped with Vulcan B.1s.

No. 57 SQUADRON

English Electric Canberra B. Mk2   **May 1953 to December 1957**

No. 57 Squadron formed at Copmanthorpe on 8 June 1916, as a home defence squadron, and the following December moved to France as a fighter-reconnaissance unit. In May 1917, the squadron re-equipped with de Havilland 4s. It returned to England in August 1919 and disbanded in the following December.

In October 1931, No. 57 Squadron re-formed at Netheravon as a day-bomber squadron equipped with Hawker Harts. At the outbreak of the Second World War the squadron was flying Blenheims. In November 1940 it rearmed with Vickers Wellingtons and flew these for almost two years before trading them in for Avro Lancasters. It flew the Lancaster for the remainder of the war, and the squadron took part in all the major raids.

Disbanded on 25 November 1945, No. 57 Squadron re-formed the next day at Elsham Wolds, Lincolnshire. With its Lincolns, the squadron operated against the Malayan terrorists in 1950.

In 1953 the squadron converted to Canberras, and in November of that year six Canberras flew from Cottesmore on a goodwill tour of the Middle East, giving flying displays in Iraq, Jordan and Libya. During October and November 1956, several aircrews were detached to Nos 15 and 44 Squadrons in Cyprus to take part in the Suez War.

1957 was a very busy year, with detachment in Singapore in January and February,

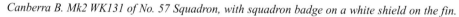

Canberra B. Mk2 WK131 of No. 57 Squadron, with squadron badge on a white shield on the fin.

Canberra B. Mk2 WH920 – the 54th built by Short Brothers, and released to service on 25 May 1954 – seen here with No. 57 Squadron, bearing the Cottesmore fin marking, which incorporated the main features of the station badge.

and Italy in June and July. The end of 1957 brought to an end the Canberra era, when the squadron disbanded on 9 December. It re-formed as a V-Force squadron at RAF Honington on 1 January 1959.

No. 59 SQUADRON

English Electric Canberra B. Mk2	**August 1956 to March 1957**
B(I). Mk8	**February 1957 to January 1961**

No. 59 Squadron formed at Narborough, Norfolk, on 1 August 1916, and was employed in France on army co-operation duties. During the Second World War it was on similar duties in France before being transferred to Coastal Command in July 1940. It remained a GR unit for the rest of the European war. After the war it served as a transport unit, flying York and Hastings aircraft.

It became a Canberra light-bomber squadron of 2nd Tactical Air Force on 20 August 1956, when No. 102(B) Squadron was renumbered 59 at Guterslöh, Germany. In 1957 it rearmed with Canberra B(I). Mk8s and moved to Geilenkirchen. Part of the unit was detached to Akrotiri, Cyprus, between July and November 1958. On 4 January 1961, No. 59 was renumbered No.3 Squadron.

Canberra B(I). Mk8 XH231 of No. 59 Squadron. Fin marking is a continental road 'danger' sign (white triangle outlined red and black exclamation mark).

No. 61 SQUADRON

English Electric Canberra B. Mk2   **August 1954 to March 1958**

No. 61 Squadron formed on 2 August 1917 at Rochford, Essex, equipped with Sopwith Pups. After the Armistice the squadron disbanded in 1919. It re-formed at Hemswell, Lincolnshire, on 8 March 1937, as a bomber squadron within No.5 Group, Bomber Command. It was equipped with Ansons, later Blenheims, and at the outbreak of the Second World War flew Hampdens. After a few months with Manchesters the squadron re-equipped with Lancasters in April 1942, and it remained a Lancaster squadron for the remainder of the war.

Post-war the squadron flew Avro Lincolns, which it traded in for Canberras during the summer of 1954 while at Wittering. In June 1955 the squadron moved to Upwood, Hants. The Canberras carried the RAF Upwood badge on their fin and No. 61's red Lincoln Imp badge on the wingtip tanks. From October 1956 to January 1957 the squadron was detached to Nicosia, Cyprus, and operated against the Egyptian forces during the Suez War.

On 31 March 1958, No. 61 Squadron disbanded.

No. 73 SQUADRON

English Electric Canberra B. Mk2   **March 1957 to August 1962**
B. Mk15   **June 1962 to March 1969**

No. 73 Squadron formed at Upavon, Wiltshire, on 1 July 1917, and was in action on the Western Front with Sopwith Camel fighters in support of the Tank Corps. During the Second World War the squadron flew Hurricanes up until 1943 and then rearmed with Spitfires. It served on the Western Front, North Africa, Italy and Yugoslavia. After the war the squadron remained in the Mediterranean area and successively rearmed with Vampires and Venoms.

It became a Canberra light-bomber squadron in March 1957, with aircrews converting to Canberra B. Mk2s at Weston Zoyland in England and ferrying them that same month to their base at Akrotiri, Cyprus, where they formed part of the Akrotiri

Canberra B. Mk15 WH948 (fourth Short-built B. Mk6, which was released to service on 5 November 1954). Seen here in Malta with No. 73 Squadron. On the fin is a blue demi-talbot with red maple leaf on shoulder in a yellow circle.

Canberra B. Mk15 WH971 (ex-Short B. Mk6, which was released to service on 1 June 1955). Seen here with No. 73 Squadron as part of the Akrotiri Canberra Strike Wing. Note Matra rocket launcher underneath wing.

Strike Wing, tasked with policing the Eastern Mediterranean area.

One Canberra, B.2 WD988, was in experimental all-white finish, and it was dubbed 'Moby Dick'. Squadron markings were on the tip tanks in dark blue and light blue. Fin markings comprised blue demi-talbot with red maple leaf, all within a blue frame. During the First World War the squadron was commanded by Major T.O.B. Hubbard, who designed a badge for his Camel aircraft. This showed Old Mother Hubbard's dog looking into an empty cupboard. It decided to adopt a demi-talbot in order not altogether to lose the association with the old badge. The Talbot is charged with a maple leaf to commemorate its Canadian personnel in the First World War.

In 1962 the B. Mk2s were replaced by Canberra B. Mk15s, and the squadron continued in the same role. In 1969 the bombing task in Cyprus was taken over by Vulcans, and No. 73 Squadron disbanded in March 1969.

No. 76 SQUADRON

English Electric Canberra B. Mk6   **December 1953 to December 1960**

No. 76 Squadron formed on 15 September 1916 at Ripon, Yorkshire, as a home defence unit. After disbanding in June 1919 the squadron re-formed in April 1937 at Finningley, Yorkshire, as a bomber unit equipped with Wellesleys. By the start of the Second World War these had given way to Hampdens and Ansons, and in May 1941 the squadron re-equipped with four-engined Halifaxes. It was the second squadron to fly the Halifax, which it kept for the duration of the European war.

At the end of hostilities it was renumbered No. 62 Squadron in September 1946. But on 9 December 1953, No. 76 re-formed in Bomber Command as a Canberra unit at RAF Wittering. It underwent an extensive programme of training in instrument flying and radar and visual bombing. This programme involved participation in air-defence exercises, including those with NATO forces and also long-distance flights to Germany and the Mediterranean.

In November 1955 the air element of an Atomic Task Force began to form up at

Weston Zoyland, and seven Canberra B. Mk6s from No. 76 Squadron were part of the initial equipment. The Canberras, as part of the Nuclear Weapons Task Force aircraft, were detached in Australia in March 1956, and the Canberras were first based at an airfield near Perth in Western Australia. Later they moved to Edinburgh Field near Adelaide to take part in further nuclear tests at Maralinga. When these tests were complete the squadron remained in Australia and in 1957 gave its support in the experimental explosion of Britain's first hydrogen bomb at Christmas Island in the Pacific Ocean. The main role for the Canberras was atomic cloud sampling at all altitudes. For extreme altitudes, a few of the Canberra B. Mk6s were rocket assisted, one being WT207, and they had Napier Double Scorpion rocket motors installed in their bomb-bays.

On 9 April 1958, Canberra WT207 got into difficulties during a flight test from Hemswell, and blew up over Derbyshire. Flight Lieutenant J.P. De Salis and Flying Officer P. Lowe gained the doubtful distinction of making the highest recorded crew ejection – 56,000 ft (17,000 m).

No. 76 Squadron returned to England in December 1959 and was based at Upwood until it disbanded in December 1960.

No. 88 (HONG KONG) SQUADRON

English Electric Canberra B(I). Mk8   **January 1956 to December 1962**

No. 88 Squadron dates back to the First World War. It was formed at Gosport, Hampshire, on 24 July 1917, and it saw service in France as a fighter-reconnaissance squadron.

Disbanded in 1919, it re-formed at Waddington, Lincolnshire, on 7 June 1937, as a bomber squadron, equipped with Fairey Battles. After a few months with Bristol Blenheims in 1941 it rearmed with Douglas Bostons, and flew these from October 1941 until it disbanded in April 1945.

In September 1946, No. 88 Squadron re-formed for the third time, and for the next eight years served as a Sunderland flying-boat squadron in the Far East Flying-Boat Wing. The squadron disbanded in October 1954.

No. 88 then returned to a bomber role, when it re-formed in Germany, on 15 January 1956, as a light-bomber/night-intruder unit of the 2nd Tactical Air Force, and it became the first squadron to receive the Canberra B(I). Mk8. These were fitted out to carry four 20 mm Hispano cannon, or 'Big Bang', an American weapon, the fins on the bomb retracting down when in the bomb-bay, or three 100 lb (45 kg) bombs in the bomb-bay and one 1,000 lb (454 kg) bomb on each wing pylon plus 20 mm cannon. For the NATO role it was the conventional fit, and for the Middle East Police role it had guns and bombs. The Canberras were black underside with grey/green on top, with a yellow snake on the tail. The later-style fin decoration was a large yellow and black snake with red and white tongue on camouflaged aircraft. It is interesting to note that the squadron had a live snake as a mascot – Squadron Leader Fred Aldrevandi – and he ate guinea pigs and white mice.

The Canberras carried out their overseas firing at Malta, Cyprus, El-Adam, Sharjah and Gibraltar. Canberra WT331 crashed at Sharjah, on the Persian Gulf, and the navigator, Squadron Leader 'Boss' Brown, was shot out of the nose like a human cannon ball. He broke his arm and had many other injuries, but managed to crawl back to the aircraft . . . and there was the pilot putting on his jacket and hat. The Canberra is still in Khan Creek, along with a Pembroke.

In 1959, No. 88 Squadron's neighbours were No. 59 Squadron at Geilenkirchen with B(I).8s, No. 16 Squadron at Laarbruch with B(I).8s, and No. 213 Squadron at

Brüggen with B(I).6s. The aircraft rotated around the three Canberra B(I).8 Squadrons, after majors at Aldergrove. The Germans called the Canberra B(I).8 'Jaeger Bomber'.

No. 88 was a close-knit squadron, the first all-regular squadron in the RAF, after National Service. Like 16 and 59 Squadrons, No. 88 also had United States Air Force personnel on strength. The trips to Gibraltar were to fetch the booze for the monthly sherry party. Ground and air crews were very close.

The Headquarters UK/German 'Friendly Society' was at Hoichneukirch (Kermis village), between Rheydt and Köln; and, in the autumn of 1959, they were having their village fête with fairground. Canberra WT335 of 88 Squadron was to give a display, on its return from bombing at Noordhorn. The Canberra made a low pass over the fairground, and as it turned its wing touched the ground and it ended up spread across two fields. One thing that came out at the inquiry was that tools were found in the wreckage. The Station Commander assembled the whole technical aircraft workforce and told them that it was they who had killed the crew of WT335. However, it was later proved that the navigator – a one-time electrician – carried a tool kit. The tools were non-service, plus a bicycle lamp. But the story has a sadder ending, for the navigator's mother was picked up at Ostend by one of the pilots in a Jaguar car and they were hit by a truck in Belgium and the squadron buried four people in Rhinedalen cemetery.

In 1961, when the newly independent state of Kuwait requested help against a threatened Iraqi invasion – Iraq's General Cassim wanted Kuwait's oil – Great Britain, in less than a week, brought in a mixed force of about 7,500 troops with two fighter squadrons, a helicopter carrier and two fleet carriers, mostly from nearby bases, but in part from as far away as West Germany, the United Kingdom and Hong Kong. The Canberras from No. 88 Squadron went to war and gave support during the Iraqi threat.

No. 88 Squadron flew the Canberra B(I).Mk8 until 17 December 1962, when it was renumbered 14 Squadron at Wildenrath, Germany.

No. 90 SQUADRON

English Electric Canberra B. Mk2   **November 1954 to May 1956**

No. 90 Squadron formed at Shawbury, Shropshire, on 8 October 1917, only to disband on 3 August 1918. After eleven days it re-formed as a home defence unit, but again it was short lived, for it disbanded in June 1919.

With the war clouds gathering, No. 90 Squadron re-formed as a bomber unit in March 1937; but just after the outbreak of the Second World War in September 1939 it became a training squadron, and was eventually absorbed into No. 17 OTU.

In May 1941, it re-formed with Flying Fortresses and carried out high-altitude day-bombing missions. But, true to form, it was once again short lived, and the squadron disbanded in February 1942. However, it was not to be out of the lists for long, for in November 1942 it re-formed at RAF Bottesford as a heavy bomber unit equipped with Stirlings. The squadron exchanged its Stirlings for Lancasters in June 1944, and with the Lancaster continued to play a major part in Bomber Command's offensive until the end of the war.

No. 90 Squadron re-equipped with Avro Lincolns in 1947, and after several detachments overseas, disbanded on 1 September 1950, only to re-form the following month at RAF Marham in Norfolk, with Boeing Washingtons; and in 1954 it traded these in for Canberras, which it flew until it disbanded on 1 May 1956. Like so many of the squadrons, it flew the Canberra for only a very short period.

No. 90 Squadron re-formed (for the sixth time) on 1 January 1957 as a V-Force squadron at RAF Honington.

Close-up of fin marking on WH739 of No. 100 Squadron. It comprised yellow and blue (Wittering Canberra Wing) chequers with green discs in centre. (No. 40 Squadron at RAF Wittering used similar marking, but discs in red.)

No. 100 SQUADRON

English Electric Canberra B. Mk2	**April 1954 to August 1959**
B.MK6	**August 1954 to August 1959**
B(I). Mk8	**1956 to August 1959**
After re-formed: Canberra B. Mk2	
E. Mk15, T.19, TT.18, PR.7	**February 1972 to 1991**

No. 100 Squadron has the distinction of being the first British squadron to be formed specifically for night bombing. It formed at Hingham, Norfolk, in February 1917 and took part in the battles of Vimy Ridge and Arras.

After the First World War it returned to England, only to be reduced to a cadre unit and posted to Baldonnel, Ireland, where, on 31 January 1920, it re-formed as a fighter unit with Bristol Fighters. In February 1922, it moved to Spittlegate, Lincolnshire, and became a day-bomber squadron. In 1930 the squadron moved to Donibristle, Scotland, and converted to a torpedo-bomber role.

It re-formed at Waltham as No. 100 (Bomber) Squadron on 15 December 1942, with Lancasters, and flew these for the remainder of the Second World War. In May 1946 the Lancasters were traded in for Avro Lincolns, which the squadron operated against the Malayan terrorists in 1950 and against the Mau-Mau in Kenya in 1954.

In April of that year, shortly after A Flight's return from Kenya, the squadron finally bade farewell to the piston age and re-equipped with Canberra B.2 aircraft. The changeover led to a considerable reduction in personnel, with only selected pilots and navigators going on to the Bassingbourn OCU, but by the time the Duke of Edinburgh visited the squadron in July, it had become operational with the new aircraft.

The official records of January 1955 state that 'The Squadron is Main Force

Squadron of Bomber Command, selected, equipped, and manned for trials work with the Bomber Command Development Unit.' Despite the reference to Main Force operational status, No. 100 Squadron was now really a trials unit performing whatever Canberra test flying was required by the BCDU, which was also based at Wittering.

The CO of the time, Squadron Leader C.P.H. Kunkler wrote,

> *I regret that during my period of command, the Squadron did not achieve great heights. This was not because we did not have some first-class chaps doing an excellent job, but simply because the Squadron had the special role of the Bomber Command Development Unit and one did not compete with the glamour boys of the Command with high bombing scores, etc.*

The daily round of trials work, which covered everything from experimental paint to electronics equipment, was relieved on 21 October 1955, when the squadron was presented with its standard by the AOC-in-C Bomber Command, Air Marshal Sir George Mills KCB, DFC, who had himself served with No. 100 Squadron between 1927 and 1929. The squadron qualified for its standard, awarded after twenty-five years' service, in 1943, and the battle honours chosen to be represented on it were Ypres 1917, Somme 1918, Independent Force and Germany 1918, Malaya 1941-42, Fortress Europe 1943-44, Ruhr 1943-45, Berlin 1943-45 and Normandy 1944.

It was during their time at Wittering that No. 100 Squadron aircraft began carrying the blue and gold chequers of the Borough of Stamford on the fins. These chequers were markings of the Wittering Wing, with the skull and cross-bones overlaid within a green disc on No. 100 Squadron aircraft and a broom in a red disc for No. 40 Squadron.

Because of changes in BCDU policy and the arrival of Valiant bomber squadrons at RAF Wittering, No. 100 Squadron was then divided into a Trials Flight at Wittering and a Recce Flight at Wyton, the latter being established on 27 August 1956, with Canberra PR.7s and crews taken mainly from the disbanded No. 82 (PR) Squadron. While the Trials Flight soldiered on in the service of the BCDU with Canberra B.2s, B.6s and B(I).8s, the Recce Flight prepared to undertake high-level meteorological work for the forthcoming Christmas Island hydrogen bomb tests. In March 1957, four Canberra PR.7s were sent out to the Pacific, where they provided daily met. reports for the Senior Met. Officer. On D-Day, 15 May 1957, two met. sorties were launched at 03.30 and 04.30 hours, followed by a photo sortie at 07.30 hours to provide up-to-the-minute wind and weather data for the task force commander and the Valiant H-Bomb crew. During the drop itself, a 100 Squadron aircraft 'stood off' and took photographs of the developing mushroom cloud, and another aircraft went on a weather sortie at 15.00 hours to help track the progress of the radioactive particles.

On its return from Christmas Island, the 100 Squadron Recce Flight handed over its aircraft to No. 58 Squadron, leaving the Trials Flight to continue its development work with new equipment and techniques, until it too, was disbanded, on 31 August 1959. The squadron standard was not laid up for long, for on 1 May 1962 No. 100 Squadron re-formed at Wittering again, this time with Victor B.2 Strategic V-bombers. It operated with free-fall nuclear bombs for a time, interspersed by the old far-flung trip to air displays in Canada and New Zealand. At the beginning of 1964, its Victor V-bombers were converted to carry the Blue Steel stand-off weapons. In March 1967, squadron crews achieved the rare distinction of winning Bomber Command's bombing competition outright, for which they were given a unique silver trophy by Rolls-Royce, depicting their 'Winged Lady' surmounting a symbolic representation of a bomb and inscribed 'FOR EXCELLENCE'. Nonetheless, the squadron's days were still numbered, and when responsibility for the British strategic nuclear deterrent was handed over to the Royal Navy, the Victor 2s were phased out as strategic bombers, and No. 100 Squadron was disbanded again on 30 September 1968.

For a time it was hoped that No. 100 Squadron would reappear as a Buccaneer unit, but when it eventually re-emerged on 1 February 1972, it was a Target Facilities Squadron with Canberra B.2s and T.19s at West Raynham. The standard was symbolically returned to the squadron's safe keeping by Air Chief Marshal Sir Andrew Humphrey on 23 February, fifty-five years to the day since No. 100 Squadron first came into being. The squadron's main role now was to provide realistic opposition for the air-defence and radar units of the RAF, both at home and abroad. On 5 January 1976, the squadron moved to RAF Marham in Norfolk, where it absorbed the flying personnel of Nos 85 and 98 Squadrons.

In January 1982, No. 100 Squadron moved to RAF Wyton, in the process absorbing the Canberra TT.18s of the disbanded No. 7 Squadron from St Mawgan, and a few PR.7s from the defunct No. 13 Squadron. All marks of Canberra were equipped to tow sleeve and banner targets, the TT.18s being easily identified by their flight refuelling 'Rushton' winch pack beneath each wing proclaiming their specialized target-towing role. Typical targets were air-to-air IR missiles, Ack-ack gunnery and line-of-sight missiles.

The seemingly ageless Canberra soldiered on in its role of providing target-towing facilities for the RAF's fighter squadrons, and, in the latter years, specialist electronic warfare training, before it was retired in 1991 and replaced by the Hawk.

With the closure of RAF Wyton, No. 100 Squadron moved to RAF Finningley, but its days were numbered; and when that station closed, No. 100 Squadron and its Hawk T1As moved to RAF Leeming in Yorkshire in 1995, now far removed from its Canberra days but with them etched deep in its history.

No. 101 SQUADRON

English Electric Canberra B. Mk2   **May 1951 to June 1954**
B. Mk6   **June 1954 to January 1957**

No. 101 Squadron RFC was formed at South Farnborough, Hampshire, on 12 July 1917 as a night-bomber squadron, and flew FE2bs until the squadron returned to England in March 1919. It disbanded the following December. The squadron re-formed in March 1928, and it became the only operational squadron to have Sidestrands and then Overstrands, the first RAF bombers with enclosed and power-operated nose-gun turrets.

During the Second World War No. 101 Squadron operated with Lancasters equipped with special equipment to confuse enemy R/T frequencies. Known by the code-name 'Airborne Cigar', it operated this special equipment from October 1943 until April 1945, and in all flew 2,477 sorties in support of the bomber force. After the war the squadron's Lancasters were replaced by Lincolns, and then, in May 1951, it became the first squadron to receive the new Canberra jet bomber, the first aircraft, WD936, arriving on 25 May. These were modern counterparts of the old Sidestrands – the squadron was back again with twin-engined bombers.

No. 101 Squadron re-equipped with Canberra B. Mk2s, and subsequently it became the first squadron to get Canberra B. Mk6s, and in 1955, when four of its aircraft took part in anti-terrorist strikes in Malaya, it became the first RAF jet bomber squadron to fly on war operations.

On 7 February 1955, a flight of four Canberra Mk6s from No. 101 Squadron took off from RAF Binbrook to begin a four-and-a-half-month detachment in Malaya. It had two assignments. One was tropical trials on the engines, airframe, electrical and bombing installations, the other to support the Security Forces by bombing the terrorists in their jungle camps.

Some months before the flight left for Malaya, a comprehensive training programme was devised, consisting mainly of formation flying, low-level bombing and practice in operating the radio compass, recently installed in the aircraft.

The day before departure, two Transport Command Hastings arrived at Binbrook to load spares; they were also to carry the ground crews, both first and second-line echelons. The plan was to send the first Hastings away some two to three hours before the Canberras, so that when they overflew it, it could pass, on R/T, an up-to-the-minute landing forecast, which it would have obtained by W/T. The second Hastings was to follow on after the Canberras had left, ready to deal with any unserviceability *en route*.

They flew the normal Transport Command trunk route – Idris, Habbaniya, Mauripur, Negombo and Changi – and made no attempt to break any speed records since no provision had been made for fast turn-rounds at the intermediate stops. It was decided to night-stop at each of the staging posts and repair overnight any defects that might have occurred, so as to be ready for take-off the following day.

In addition to its normal three-man crew, each of the four Canberras carried a ground crew NCO; collectively, these NCOs made up a team of aircraft, electrical, instrument and radio fitters. And a most successful provision this was, too, for, except for one occasion, the Canberras were turned round ready for the next day's flight before the first Hastings arrived.

On the outward flight the Canberras took off at ten-minute intervals, later reduced to five, and were in R/T contact all the time so that the leader could broadcast information on such things as weather and heights to fly.

The flight passed without incident as far as Mauripur, where the presence of a large number of kitehawks created a temporary hazard to the aircraft when, in box formation, they were making a low-level run past the control tower. Travelling at high speed, it was impossible to see these enormous birds until they were almost abreast of the aircraft. In view of the frequency with which they narrowly missed the formation, and the damage they could do on impact, it was decided to cut out low-level fly-pasts in this area.

The flight to Ceylon (Sri Lanka) and the crossing of the Bay of Bengal brought no difficulties, since the inter-tropical front was well to the south. Practising homing onto the Hastings on these flights, using the radio compass, was very successful. All aircraft arrived at Changi on time, with the exception of one of the Hastings, which was delayed at Butterworth for a few hours until an engine snag was rectified.

The four Canberras were based first at Changi on Singapore Island, and later at Butterworth. Because of the excellent help and co-operation given by the Far East Air Force, the tropical trials were begun almost immediately, and in a very short time the detachment was able to operate against the terrorists. The targets attacked were either pinpoint or area targets. 'Pinpoints' were terrorists' camps; these were built deep in the jungle but within easy reach of inhabited localities, because the terrorists were largely dependent on supplies from civilian sympathizers, or needed to be within striking distance of civilians who could be coerced into supplying food. Sited in small clearings, the camps consisted of a few roughly constructed bashas, housing anything between ten and sixty men; the large camps had small cultivated areas, parade grounds and even air raid shelters. The camps were sought out by Security Force patrols, the Intelligence organizations, photo-reconnaissance and by low-flying AOP Austers flown by Army pilots, who – in another direction – were an important link to all pinpoint strikes. Before an attack could be mounted, police clearance of the target area involved had to be obtained.

Area targets varied in size between 1,000 and 6,000 sq yds (836 and 5,000 m²). The area might be one in which it was considered camps existed, though their exact location was not known, or one through which terrorists were known to be moving. The aim of a strike was to harass the terrorists and lower their morale. Often air strikes were made in co-operation with ground troops, the object being to drive the terrorists by pattern bombing into the range of a line of troops. Different techniques were used for the two types of target.

Pinpoint targets were all attacked in vic formation. Having received the target position as a six-figure map reference and the time on target, all further operational planning was done at squadron level in conjunction with the ground liaison officer, who provided the Army background, explained the need for the strike, told them where the enemy had last been seen, and precisely where their own ground troops were positioned.

The target position was first plotted in terms of latitude and longitude on a one-inch map of the area, then replotted on a 1:1,000,000 topographical map. Next a circle was drawn, using the target as the centre point, the radius being the distance flown in ten minutes at an IAS of 200 knots (370 km/h) at 4,000 ft (1,220 m) above the target height. After a careful study of the map features within this area – augmented where necessary by mosaics – and taking account of the position of the sun at the planned time of attack, the position of the target in relation to high ground and any other relevant factors, such as the position of ground troops, a direction of attack was decided on.

The required track was plotted from a point on the edge of the ten-minute circle to the target, and at least three easily recognizable checkpoints were chosen for the run-in. On the one-inch map the selected track was then back-plotted from the target, enough one-inch scale being allowed to cover the last five minutes of the run-in to the bomb-release point. Two timing checkpoints were chosen as near as possible to the four-minute and two-minute points.

At this stage, it was essential that the time to run from these points to the target was absolutely accurate. The distances were measured in yards, the ground speed converted into yards per second, and from the computer the time to run was calculated in seconds.

At H-hour -10 an Auster marker aircraft was airborne at a gate position, four minutes' flying time from the target, while the Canberra force was at a point where the track to the target intersected the ten-minute circle. The strike leader contacted the Auster on R/T and called three times, 'Bombing in ten', the call being acknowledged. Now the navigator-plotter started his stop-watch and the Canberra began its bombing run. With the help of Auster 'pathfinders', the Canberras achieved a high standard of accuracy in their jungle bombing strikes. In all 101 Squadron flew ninety-eight sorties.

The squadron then had detachments at Singapore and Malta, operating from the latter in the 1956 Suez War.

After this the Canberra returned to Binbrook, where No. 101 Squadron disbanded on 1 February 1957. It re-formed in October as part of the RAF V-Force at Finningley.

Canberra B. Mk2 WK146 was released to service on 2 December 1954, and is seen here at Blackbushe in September 1956, shortly after No. 102 had been renumbered 59 Squadron. In the fin is 102 Squadron's badge, a red lion and blue bomb. There is an Atom bomb badge on the nose.

No. 102 (CEYLON) SQUADRON

English Electric Canberra B. Mk2   **October 1954 to August 1956**

No. 102 Squadron formed at Hingham, Norfolk, in August 1917, and was one of the squadrons that served on the Western Front. After the Armistice the squadron returned to England and disbanded in July 1919. It re-formed in March 1936 at Worthy Down as a heavy-bomber squadron, and at the outbreak of war was flying Whitleys. In December 1941 the squadron re-equipped with Halifaxes and continued with this type for the rest of the European war. It took part in all the major raids.

After the war the squadron was transferred to Transport Command, flying Liberators, but this was for only a short period, for in February 1946 the squadron disbanded.

It re-formed on 20 October 1954 at Gütersloh, Germany, as a Canberra jet-bomber unit in the 2nd Tactical Air Force. No. 102 Squadron remained at Gütersloh until August 1956, when it was renumbered 59 Squadron.

No. 103 SQUADRON

English Electric Canberra B. Mk2   **November 1954 to July 1956**

No. 103 Squadron formed at Beaulieu, Hampshire, on 1 September 1917, and was employed on the Western Front on day-bombing and reconnaissance duties. Disbanded in 1919, it re-formed at Andover in August 1936 as a bomber squadron with Hawker Hinds. The squadron entered the Second World War with Fairey Battles, which were traded for Wellingtons in October 1940.

No. 103 Squadron served with great distinction during World War Two, with Wellingtons, Halifaxes and Lancasters. It had the most distinguished specimen of all – Lancaster III ED 888 'M²' (Mike Squared) – which logged 140 sorties, the highest in Bomber Command. In November 1945, No. 103 Squadron was renumbered 57. After a period of nine years No. 103 re-formed on 30 November 1954, as a Canberra bomber squadron at Gütersloh, West Germany. It served throughout at Gütersloh until disbanded on 1 August 1956, bringing to an end its brief Canberra period.

No. 104 SQUADRON

English Electric Canberra B. Mk2   **March 1955 to July 1956**

No. 104 Squadron formed at Wyton, Huntingdonshire, on 4 September 1917 as a day-bomber squadron, and with its DH9 aircraft moved to France in May 1918. The squadron was soon in the thick of it, and owing to heavy losses, it had to re-form three times. After the Armistice the squadron returned to England and disbanded in June 1919.

The squadron re-formed again in January 1936, only to be absorbed into No. 13 OTU in April 1940. In April 1941 the squadron re-formed at Driffield as a medium-bomber unit of No. 4 Group, and from April 1941 to February 1945, No. 104 Squadron was armed with the twin-engined Vickers Wellington and served in the Middle East and much of North Africa. Only in March 1945 did the squadron begin to convert to four-engined bombers, these being Consolidated Liberators and Avro Lancasters. After a short period in a peacetime role, No. 104 disbanded in April 1947 at Shallufa, Egypt. It then re-formed on 15 March 1955, at Gütersloh, West Germany, as a Canberra bomber unit. It flew Canberras at Gütersloh until it disbanded there on 1 August 1956.

No. 109 SQUADRON

English Electric Canberra B. Mk2   **August 1952 to December 1954**
B. Mk6   **December 1954 to January 1957**

No. 109 Squadron formed in 1918, only to disband the following year. It re-formed from the Wireless Intelligence Development Unit in December 1940. It was a 'special duties' (wireless) squadron equipped with Anson and Wellington aircraft. In August 1942 it moved from Stradishall to RAF Wyton, and in December converted to Oboe Mosquitoes. In July 1943 it moved to RAF Marham until the end of the war, when it disbanded. At RAF Woodhall Spa on 1 October 1945, No. 627 was re-numbered 109 Squadron and equipped with Mosquito 1Xs and XV1s, but it was no longer needed and pulled out before the end of October 1945 to RAF Wickenby. In November 1946 it moved to RAF Coningsby for pathfinder duties, and in March 1950 to RAF Hemswell in Lincolnshire to prepare to receive Canberra aircraft.

No. 109 Squadron converted to Canberra jet bombers in the autumn of 1952, and flew the B. Mk2s until the latter part of 1954, when it gradually changed over to the B. Mk6 version. In January 1956 it moved to RAF Binbrook. During 1956 the squadron had detachments in Libya and Malta, from where it took part in the Suez War. The Canberras of 109 Squadron returned from Malta in January 1957, and on 1 February 1957 No. 109 Squadron disbanded.

No. 115 SQUADRON

English Electric Canberra B. Mk2   **February 1954 to May 1957**

No. 115 Squadron formed at Catterick, Yorkshire, on 1 December 1917, and moved to France with Handley Page 0/400 twin-engined bombers. The squadron was a late arrival, but managed fifteen raids and dropped twenty-six tons of bombs.

Disbanded in 1919, No. 115 re-formed in June 1937 as a bomber squadron equipped with Handley Page Harrow aircraft, which it flew until early 1939.

During the first half of the Second World War No. 115 Squadron was equipped with Wellingtons, which it traded in for Lancasters in March 1943. It flew the four-engined bombers until late 1949, and then converted to Lincolns, only to be disbanded six months later – on 1 March 1950. However, three months later it re-formed at Marham, Norfolk, with Boeing Washington aircraft. Early in 1954 the Washingtons were replaced by Canberra jet bombers. For a time the tip tanks of No. 115 Squadron Canberras were painted black. The squadron flew the Canberras until it disbanded in May 1957.

No. 139 (JAMAICA) SQUADRON

English Electric Canberra B. Mk2 and
B. Mk6   **November 1953 to December 1959**

No. 139 Squadron formed at Villaverla, Italy, on 3 July 1918, as a fighter-reconnaissance squadron equipped with Bristol Fighters. Disbanded in 1919, it re-formed at Wyton in September 1936 as a bomber squadron with Hawker Hind aircraft.

At the outbreak of the Second World War the squadron was flying Blenheims, and it won one of the first two decorations of the war. After duty in France the squadron returned to England, and on 30 April 1942 it was renumbered No. 62 (GR) Squadron in India. It re-formed in Norfolk in June 1942, and from late 1942 right up until November 1953, No. 139 Squadron flew the highly manoeuvrable Mosquito – from 1948 it had B.35s, which were traded in for Canberras in November 1953, bringing to an end eleven years with Mosquitoes.

In 1955 No. 139 Squadron strengthened its link with Jamaica when the squadron visited the island as part of the colony's tercentenary celebrations. The Jamaicans gave them a great welcome and honoured No. 139 by giving it the freedom of Kingston. Operation New World, a tour of the British West Indies which culminated in a visit to Canada, was a huge success, and it gave 139 Squadron the chance to show the Canberras to those who had subscribed to buy bombers in the early years of the war. A Jamaican newspaper, The Daily Gleaner, started a fund to buy bombers for Britain, and Jamaica herself contributed enough money to buy twelve Blenheims by 1941.

In March 1956 a detachment visited Idris for an exercise. The following month the squadron gave a display before Mr Krushchev and Marshal Bulganin of the Soviet Union, and on 23 July 1956 had the honour of flying past Her Majesty the Queen at Marham.

As a result of increasing tension in the Middle East, a detachment of the squadron, half of whose personnel were members of No. 109 Squadron, flew to Luqa, Malta, where bombing exercises took place, and the rest of the squadron left Binbrook for Nicosia, Cyprus, in October 1956. On 31 October, operations against Egypt commenced when Almaza airfield was raided, and continued until 5 November. The major role of the squadron during the Egyptian operations was target marking by night, using the techniques evolved during the detachment to Idris in March, but a number of bomber sorties were also flown. Throughout December the squadron remained in readiness for further operations in Egypt, but returned to the UK at the end of the month.

In May 1957, the squadron took part in two major NATO exercises while on detachment to Malta, and in August was visited by Sir Foot, the Governor of Jamaica, who watched aircraft returning from operational exercises. In October 1957 the squadron was based at Idris, and in April 1958 was detached to Luqa for major naval attack exercises, while in July a detachment was sent at short notice to Akrotiri, Cyprus, where it remained until November; during this period the squadron was brought to a high state of readiness in order to cover a troop movement out of Jordan. On 7 October 1958, the squadron detachment was again visited by Sir Hugh Foot, who was then the Governor of Cyprus.

In May 1959, the Canberras of No. 139 Squadron paid another visit to Malta, which was a detachment they liked; but it was to be their last visit to sunny Malta, for on 31 December 1959, No. 139 Squadron disbanded at RAF Binbrook in Lincolnshire, and by so doing brought the Canberra era to an end.

No. 149 (EAST INDIA) SQUADRON

English Electric Canberra B. Mk2   **March 1953 to August 1956**

No. 149 Squadron formed on 3 March 1918, at Yapton, Sussex, as a night-bomber unit, and three months later moved to France with its FE2bs. After the Armistice it returned to the UK and disbanded at Tallaght, Ireland, in August 1919. The squadron re-formed on 12 April 1937, at Mildenhall, Suffolk, again as a night-bomber unit. It was equipped with Heyfords, and in January 1939 it converted to Wellingtons, then Stirlings and Lancasters, the latter from 1944 to November 1949, when it re-equipped with Lincolns, but after only a few months the squadron disbanded in March 1950.

It re-formed five months later with Washingtons, and in the spring of 1953 began to re-equip with Canberras. In August 1954, No. 149 moved from Cottesmore to Ahlhorn and became the first Canberra squadron to be permanently based in Germany with the 2nd Tactical Air Force. The squadron remained in Germany until 31 August 1956, when it disbanded at Gütersloh.

No. 199 SQUADRON

English Electric Canberra B. Mk2   **March 1954 to December 1958**

During the First World War No. 199 Squadron had a brief existence from November 1917 to June 1919. The squadron re-formed at Blyton in November 1942 as a bomber squadron in No. 1 Group, and during the Second World War it flew a total of 2,940 sorties with Wellingtons, Stirlings and Halifaxes. It disbanded in July 1945, only to re-form in July 1951 at the Central Signals Establishment, RAF Warton, and was subsequently equipped with Avro Lincolns and de Havilland Mosquito N.F.36s.

After its radio countermeasures (RCM) role it moved and transferred from Warton,

Canberra WJ616, a Handley-Page built B. Mk2, which was released to service on 8 January 1954. Seen here in the markings of No. 199 Squadron at RAF Honington in September 1958

Norfolk, to Hemswell, Lincolnshire, and from No. 90 Group to Bomber Command in April 1952. Its Lincolns and Mosquitoes were supplemented and eventually replaced by Canberras and Valiants, and when the squadron disbanded in December 1959 its Valiant flight formed the basis of a re-formed No. 18 Squadron.

No. 207 SQUADRON

English Electric Canberra B. Mk2   **March 1954 to February 1956**

No. 207 Squadron dates back to 1915 and was the first British squadron used solely for long-range night bombing. When the RAF was formed on 1 April 1918, the unit became No. 207 Squadron. Disbanded at Uxbridge in January 1920, it re-formed twelve days later at Bircham Newton as a day-bomber unit equipped with DH9As. At the outbreak of the Second World War it served as a training unit and was absorbed into No. 12 OTU. It re-formed at Waddington in November 1940 for the express purpose of bringing the new Avro Manchester into operational service.

No. 207 exchanged its Manchesters for Lancasters in March 1942, and flew its four-engined mounts for the remainder of the war. It re-equipped with Lincolns in the summer of 1949, only to disband in March 1950.

It re-formed on 29 May 1951, at Marham, Norfolk, with Washingtons, and these were replaced by Canberras early in 1954. After nearly two years flying the Canberras, No. 207 disbanded on 27 March 1956. It re-formed in April 1956 as a V-Force squadron at Marham.

No. 213 (CEYLON) SQUADRON

English Electric Canberra B(I). Mk6   **March 1956 to December 1969**

No. 213 Squadron formed at Saint Pol, near Dunkirk, France, in June 1917, as a fighter unit equipped with Sopwith Camels. It remained in that role until the end of the war and it disbanded in December 1919.

In the Second World War it was again destined to be a fighter unit. The thirties were

Canberra B(I) Mk6 WT307 of No. 213 Squadron. Note the large hornet on the tail. The early tail badge was a much smaller hornet, then in the early 1960s it changed again, until the large-size hornet appeared and fitted almost half the tail. (Must have seen the film Them.*)*

Canberras at British Aerospace, Samlesbury, sitting under a light covering of snow as they await delivery to No. 213 Squadron in Germany. The giant hornets are getting impatient!

the expansion period for the RAF, and on 8 March 1937 No. 213 Squadron re-formed at Northolt, as a fighter unit, with Gloster Gauntlets, and on 1 July moved to Church Fenton. In May 1938 the squadron moved to Wittering. On the outbreak of war the squadron moved south and played a part in the Battle of Britain. Soon afterwards, the squadron was on the cards for a move to the Middle East; and it saw service in Malta, Cyprus, Egypt – where it took part in operations over the Western Desert in support of the 8th Army – and Italy, where it saw out the war. It remained overseas until it disbanded in September 1954.

In July 1955, No. 213 Squadron re-formed at Ahlhorn, Germany, as a Canberra light-bomber night-intruder squadron, but did not receive its Canberras until March 1956. It remained in this role for fourteen years, and eventually disbanded at Brüggen on 5 December 1969.

The squadron badge was a hornet, and as a fighter squadron the unit was known as 'The Hornets' at Dunkirk, during the First World War.

No. 249 (GOLD COAST) SQUADRON

English Electric Canberra B. Mk2	**September 1957 to November 1959**
B. Mk6	**November 1959 to April 1962**
B. Mk15	**November 1961 to February 1969**
B. Mk16	**November 1961 to February 1969**

No. 249 Squadron formed at Dundee on 18 August 1918, and after flying a few anti-submarine patrols off the Scottish coast, disbanded in 1919. The squadron re-formed at Church Fenton in Yorkshire on 16 May 1940 with Hurricane MkI fighters, and their fighters were soon in action. The squadron claimed its first 'kill' at 11.30 hours on 8 July 1940. After moving south, one of its pilots, Flight Lieutenant J.B. Nicolson, was awarded the Victoria Cross for heroism during the Battle of Britain. He won Fighter Command's first and only VC during the Second World War (one can read the only VC in my book, *Fighter Pilots in World War II* which is also published by Pen & Sword Books,

ISBN 1-84415-065-8). During the Second World War the squadron operated in Malta and Italy, and at the end of the war disbanded in August 1945. A few weeks later the squadron re-formed with Baltimores, and during the spring of 1946 in Kenya re-armed with Mosquitoes. The squadron received Vampires, and after a period in Egypt, moved to Jordan, where, in 1955, it re-armed with Venoms. In August 1956 the squadron moved to Akrotiri in Cyprus, but its stay was brief, for the Canberra era was blowing in the wind. In July 1957 it moved back to Kenya, where it disbanded in October 1957.

On 15 October 1957, No. 249 Squadron re-formed at Akrotiri and then detached to RAF Coningsby in Lincolnshire, where 249's crews converted to Canberras and reverted to a light-bomber role. As soon as it had re-equipped with Canberra B. Mk2 aircraft, the

Canberra B. Mk15 WH972 (ex-Short-built B. Mk6, which was released to service on 26 September 1955), seen here in Malta on 16 October 1968 with No. 249 Squadron. Squadron elephant insignia on the fin.

squadron returned to sunny Akrotiri in October 1957, as a unit of the Middle East Air Force Light Bomber Tactical Force. Routine flying training, interspersed with operational exercises, 'Ranger' flights and detachments to many parts of the Mediterranean, occupied the squadron's time until November 1959, when, on re-equipment to Canberra B. Mk6 aircraft, its role changed to providing target facilities for the Central Treaty Organization and other operational units. Between November 1961 and April 1962, re-equipment again took place with Canberra B. Mk16s and a few B. Mk15s.

Squadron markings on the Canberras varied. The early Canberras had a black serial with the RAF Station Akrotiri badge on the fin, the main feature being a pink flamingo superimposed on a white shield. The tip tanks were yellow, with a spear, the shaft black, spearhead red, with an elephant in grey on a white disc. In the early Sixties the squadron Canberras appeared with camouflage finish, yellow tip tanks, white fin marking and white serial.

The elephant, walking with right foot raised, and a bezant (a gold coin current in Europe in the ninth century) are both on 249 Squadron's badge, and imply a link with the Gold Coast, for this was one of the wartime gift squadrons.

After twelve years with the faithful Canberra, the Canberra era finally came to an end when, at Akrotiri, its sunny base for all those years, the squadron disbanded on 24 February 1969.

No. 617 SQUADRON

English Electric Canberra B. Mk2   **January 1952 to April 1955**
B. Mk6   **February 1955 to December 1955**

No. 617 Squadron has a special place in the history of the Royal Air Force. It was the only squadron formed to undertake a specific operation – the breaching of the Ruhr dams in Germany. It was formed with special Lancasters at Scampton, near Lincoln, on 21 March 1943, under the command of Wing Commander Guy Gibson. The squadron attacked three major German dams, breaching two and damaging the third. After a distinguished war record of precision attacks on vital targets, the squadron re-equipped with Lincolns in 1946, and in 1952 it was the second squadron to be equipped with Canberra jet bombers. The routine of peacetime training was broken in mid-1955 when a detachment of the squadron flew to Butterworth, Malaya, from where the Canberras took part in operations against the Communist terrorists there. They revived wartime techniques of target marking, but this time used light aircraft to mark Communist encampments hidden deep in the jungle.

After six months of this detachment, the squadron was recalled to the UK, and on 15 December 1955, No. 617 Squadron disbanded. It re-formed on 1 May 1958 as a V-Force squadron at Scampton.

CHAPTER SEVEN

Miscellaneous Canberra Units

No. 7 SQUADRON

No. 7 Squadron formed at Farnborough on 1 May 1914. It served on the Western Front and its duties were tactical reconnaissance. It disbanded on 31 December 1919.

On 1 June 1923, No. 7 re-formed as a bomber squadron, and at the outbreak of the Second World War was flying Hampdens and had a training role.

After a further disbandment No. 7 re-formed at Leeming on 1 August 1940 with Stirlings. In 1942 it was transferred to the Pathfinder Force and converted to Lancasters, which it flew for the remainder of the war. The squadron disbanded on 1 January 1956, but it was not to be out of the lists for long, and on 1 November 1956, it re-formed with Valiants, only to disband again on 1 September 1962.

On 1 May 1970, No. 7 re-formed at St Mawgan for target support duties for various marks of Canberras. It disbanded at the end of 1981 and the Canberra TT.18s were absorbed by 100 Squadron.

No. 13 SQUADRON

No. 13 Squadron formed at Gosport on 10 January 1915, and moved to France on observation and photographic reconnaissance duties. It disbanded on 31 December 1919.

It re-formed on 1 April 1924, and after the outbreak of the Second World War moved to France with its Lysander aircraft, but was back in England by May 1940. In 1941 it converted to Blenheims. The squadron moved to North Africa at the end of 1942, and then on to Egypt, where it re-equipped with Baltimore aircraft. February 1944 saw the squadron in Italy, and in October of that year Bostons replaced the Baltimores. In September 1945, No. 13 Squadron moved to Greece, where it disbanded on 19 April 1946.

On 1 September 1946, No. 680 Squadron at Ein Shemer was renumbered No. 13, and at the end of the year it moved from Palestine to Egypt. In January 1952, the photographic reconnaissance Mosquitoes were replaced by Meteor PR.10s; and these in turn were replaced by Canberra PR. Mk3s. January 1956 saw the squadron move to sunny Cyprus with its Canberra PR. Mk3s, and in May of that year it converted to Canberra PR. Mk7s.

No. 13 Squadron took part in the Suez War, and was the only squadron to lose a Canberra while on an operational mission. On 6 November 1956, Canberra WH799 took off from its base in Cyprus, and while photographing Egyptian airfields in the Nile Delta and Canal Zone, and oil pipelines, the Canberra was attacked and shot down by a Syrian MiG-15. Two of the Canberra's three-man crew survived, but the navigator was killed.

No. 13 Squadron was allocated Villafranca in Italy as a forward base, and in September 1965 it moved to Luqa, Malta, where it became the resident photo-reconnaissance unit. In 1968 the Canberras carried out an aerial survey of Muscat,

Canberra T. Mk4 WJ872 of No. 13 Squadron landing at Luqa, Malta, on 4 October 1976. The nose section of this aircraft is preserved at Hornchurch ATC.

Oman, Qatar and Bahrain. An area of more than 138,000 square miles (357,000 km²) was covered. In August 1961 the squadron converted to Canberra PR. Mk9s, and four aircraft completed a photographic survey of 90,000 square miles (233,000 km²) of the southern half of Kenya. In 1972, No. 13 Squadron was one of two squadrons of PR. aircraft – both primarily using Canberra PR. Mk9s – at Akrotiri, serving the Near East Air Force and CENTO. The squadron then reverted to mainly Canberra PR. Mk7 aircraft, and in 1979 was at RAF Wyton, flying the following PR. Mk7 aircraft: WH773, WH775, WH779, WH794, WJ815, WJ817, WJ821, WJ825, WT509, WT519, WT530, WT532, WT537 and WT538. But the end was in sight, and on 4 January 1982 the squadron disbanded, bringing to an end three glorious decades with the Canberra.

No. 17 SQUADRON

No. 17 Squadron formed at Gosport on 1 February 1915, and at the end of the year moved to Egypt. Throughout the First World War it served as a reconnaissance unit and saw service in the Western Desert and on the Bulgarian border before disbanding on 14 November 1919.

The squadron re-formed at Hawkinge on 1 April 1924 with Snipes, and the outbreak of the Second World War saw the squadron flying Hurricanes. When France was invaded the squadron gave cover for the retreating Allied troops. After the Battle of Britain the squadron moved overseas and flew defensive patrols from Burma. When the Rangoon airfields were overrun the squadron moved north, but was cut off, and the few surviving aircraft

Canberra PR. Mk7 WH803 of No. 17 Squadron.

reassembled at Calcutta. In August 1943 No. 17 Squadron moved to Ceylon and it began to take on strength Spitfires in March 1944, and with its new mounts moved back to Burma to fly escort and ground-attack missions. In April 1946 the squadron arrived in Japan to form part of the Commonwealth occupation force until disbanded on 23 February 1948.

On 11 February 1949, No. 691 Squadron was renumbered No. 17, and after a further disbandment re-formed at Wahn on 1 June 1956, with Canberra PR.7s as a photographic reconnaissance squadron in Germany, disbanding on 12 June 1969, bringing to an end the Canberra era. On 16 October 1970, the squadron re-formed at Brüggen with Phantoms.

No. 31 SQUADRON

No. 31 Squadron formed at Farnborough on 11 October 1915, and the following month left for India. It flew a variety of aircraft and saw service on the North-West Frontier of India.

At the start of the Second World War the squadron's role changed from army co-operation to bomber transport, and it flew Valentias and DC-2s, which were replaced by Dakotas. The squadron was engaged in supply-dropping missions for the 14th Army in Burma, and after the Japanese surrender it moved to Singapore, then to Java to support the Allied forces. The squadron disbanded at Kemajoran on 30 September 1946, only to reappear in the lists again on 1 November 1946, when No. 77 Squadron was renumbered 31 at Mauripur, only to disband again on 31 December 1947. The squadron then reappeared, and after a further disbandment re-formed at Laarbruch on 1 March 1955, with Canberra PR.7s for photographic reconnaissance duties in Germany. After sixteen years flying the Canberra PR.7, the squadron disbanded at Laarbruch on 31 March 1971.

Canberra PR. Mk7 WT513, the 45th built, and released to service on 28 January 1955. Seen here in the markings of No. 31 Squadron.

Canberra PR. Mk7 WH779, the seventh built from the first production batch. It was released to service on 24 March 1954. Seen here with No. 31 Squadron in Germany.

Canberra PR. Mk3 WF924 of No. 39 Squadron. This aircraft was released to service on 11 November 1953. Note the squadron number on tip tanks.

No. 39 SQUADRON

No. 39 Squadron formed at Hounslow on 15 April 1916, as a home defence unit. It moved to France in November 1918, only to disband a few days later.

The squadron re-formed on 1 July 1919, and at the outbreak of the Second World War was flying Blenheims from Tengah. No. 39 Squadron served overseas throughout the war, and in October 1945 it moved to the Sudan, where it began to re-equip with Mosquitoes, only to disband on 8 September 1946.

On 1 April 1948, No. 39 Squadron re-formed at Nairobi with Tempest F.6 aircraft, but once again it was short lived, for it disbanded on 28 February 1949. On 1 March 1949, it re-formed at Fayid with Mosquito night-fighters, and these were exchanged in March 1953 for Meteor NF.13s. In January 1955, No. 39 Squadron moved to Luqa in Malta. The following year it was on detachment to Nicosia in Cyprus, in order to throw its weight behind the Suez War, and one of its duties was defensive night patrols around Cyprus. With the Suez War over, the squadron returned to Malta; however, in 1957 it found itself back in Cyprus for another short detachment, this time on defensive patrols to prevent aircraft from dropping supplies to EOKA terrorists. Then it was back to Malta, and during 1958 yet another detachment to Cyprus, this time to provide air cover for the Air Transport Force during the Lebanon crisis.

On 30 June 1958 the squadron disbanded. The following day, No. 39 Squadron re-formed at Luqa, Malta, as a Canberra Photographic Reconnaissance Squadron, equipped with ten PR. Mk3s and one T. Mk4 from No. 58 Squadron. The PR. Mk3s were replaced in November 1962 by Canberra PR. Mk9s. The squadron Canberras had no code markings. In October 1970, No. 39 Squadron left sunny Malta, and moved to RAF Wyton, England, from

One of No. 39 Squadron's PR. Mk9 Canberras over Norway.

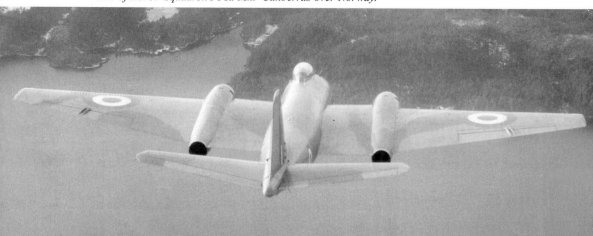

where it continued in the tactical reconnaissance role, for it was the best in the business. From October 1970 until March 1972, the squadron also had on strength a few Canberra PR. Mk7s. The squadron was on detachment, for aerial survey and night photographic duties, to many parts of the world: Africa, Fiji and Jamaica, to name but three.

On 31 May 1982, No. 39 Squadron disbanded and a few of its PR.9s, the last ones remaining in the RAF, were allocated to No. 1 Photographic Reconnaissance Unit (1 PRU) for the photo-survey role. These aircraft retained the RWR pods on the fin leading edge and in the extreme rear fuselage.

In 1992 the winds of change were again blowing through the corridors of mindless power; and No. 39 Squadron re-formed as No. 39 (1 PRU) Squadron in July 1992, its role as before and in support of NATO. During the 1990s the squadron was on detachments in Zimbabwe and Kenya for survey duties, which were fully carried out by the faithful Canberras, flying gracefully into the twenty-first century – not for reasons of sentimentality, but because in the photographic reconnaissance role it is still the best to deliver the goods.

As at December 2003, No. 39 (1 PRU) Squadron was operating from RAF Marham in Norfolk, having moved there in December 1993, with five Canberra PR. Mk9s, serial numbers XH131, XH134, XH135, XH168 and XH169; and with two Canberra T. Mk4s, serial numbers WJ866 (this was released to service on 9 September 1954) and WJ874 (this was released to service on 22 December 1954). There is another T. Mk4 – WH849 (this was released to service on 20 May 1954), but it is in storage.

Being the only Canberra squadron in RAF service, the unit does its own conversion training with two T. Mk4s.

Sadly, on 2 September 2004, Canberra WJ866 crashed on take-off, killing two pilots, Flt/Lt's Paul Morris and Lawrence Coulton. She is now in the home straight, so let us pray that there will be no more sad incidents, before the Grand Old Lady retires, and brings to an end the Canberra era in the RAF.

No. 51 SQUADRON

No. 51 Squadron formed at Thetford on 15 May 1916, as a home defence unit. It was deployed to defend the Midlands and London, disbanding at Suttons Farm on 13 June 1919.

It reformed on 5 March 1937, and was flying Whitleys at the outbreak of the Second World War. In May 1942, the squadron was transferred to Coastal Command, but returned to Bomber Command the following October and re-equipped with Halifax bombers, which it flew for the remainder of the war. In May 1945, No. 51 Squadron again transferred, this time to Transport Command, and was engaged on trooping flights to India and the Middle East. During the Berlin Airlift it flew York aircraft before being disbanded on 30 October 1950.

On 21 August 1958, No. 192 Squadron at RAF Watton was renumbered No. 51. It was

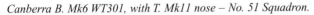

Canberra B. Mk6 WT301, with T. Mk11 nose – No. 51 Squadron.

equipped with Canberras, mostly B. Mk2s with a few B. Mk6s and Comets. These aircraft were used on long-range calibration duties. The specialist Canberras were engaged on electronic intelligence and photographic reconnaissance duties, which included monitoring Russian ships and recording their transmissions onto a tape recorder in the bomb-bay. They were attached to NATO until March 1961, when the squadron moved to RAF Wyton. In 1974, the Comets and Canberras were both replaced by the Nimrod aircraft; and thus the era of No. 51 being a Squadron with Canberra aircraft came to an end.

No. 58 SQUADRON

No. 58 Squadron – a unit with a varied history. It was formed at Cramlington in Northumberland on 10 January 1916. The squadron saw service on the Western Front flying FE.2Bs.

It entered the Second World War as a heavy-bomber unit, flying Whitleys from Driffield in Yorkshire, and first went into action on the night of 3/4 September 1939. In

Canberra PR. Mk9s in service with No. 58 Squadron.

April 1942, No. 58 Squadron was transferred to Coastal Command, and saw out the war as a general reconnaissance unit. A few weeks after VE Day the squadron was disbanded, only to reform in October 1946 as a Mosquito-equipped photographic-reconnaissance unit in Coastal Command.

In March 1950 the squadron was transferred to Bomber Command, and in 1954 traded in its Mosquito aircraft for Canberra PR.3s, which it flew until late 1955, when it traded them in for Canberra PR.7s. In January 1960 the squadron took on strength a few Canberra PR.9s and flew these alongside the PR.7s.

In 1962 the Canberras of No. 58 Squadron held the world in their hands, for they had the three Aces that president Kennedy needed in his hand. This was not a game of bluff, for the stakes were high – a nuclear war, World War Three. The Canberras had photographed the Soviet ships bound for Cuba during the Kruschev – Castro missile crisis. They had the proof that Kennedy needed.

No. 58 Squadron disbanded in September 1970. It re-formed in August 1973 at RAF Wittering, equipped with Hunters.

No. 69 SQUADRON

No. 69 Squadron formed on 28 December 1916, and in September 1917 it moved to France. In January 1918 it was redesignated No. 3 Squadron Australia Flying Corps.

It re-formed on 10 January 1941, when No. 431 Flight was redesignated No. 69 Squadron. It was based at Malta, equipped with Maryland, Beaufighter, Hurricane and Spitfire aircraft. The squadron carried out reconnaissance missions over enemy ports and airfields in Sicily, Italy and Libya.

Disbanded on 7 August 1945, it re-formed the following day at Cambrai, France, and flew Mosquito fighter-bombers until disbanded on 31 March 1946. It re-formed in April 1946, only to disband again in November 1947.

On 5 May 1954, No. 69 re-formed at Laarbruch as a Canberra reconnaissance squadron equipped with PR.3s, and it remained in Germany with Canberras until renumbered 39 Squadron on 1 July 1958.

No. 80 SQUADRON

No. 80 Squadron formed at Montrose on 1 August 1917, as a fighter squadron equipped with Camels. The squadron moved to France, where it remained for the remainder of the war. In May 1919 it moved to Egypt, where it was renumbered 56 Squadron on 1 February 1920.

With the war clouds gathering over Europe, No. 80 re-formed at Kenley on 8 March 1937, as a fighter squadron equipped with Gauntlets, which were soon replaced by Gladiators. In April 1938, the squadron moved to Egypt, then to the Libyan frontier for a period before moving to Greece in November 1940. By now the squadron had re-equipped with Hurricanes, and over the next three years saw action in Syria, Palestine, Cyprus and the Western Desert until January 1944, when it moved to Italy. The squadron was now flying Spitfires, having re-equipped with them in April 1943.

In April 1944, No. 80 Squadron returned to the UK in preparation for the invasion of Europe, and in August 1944 re-equipped with Tempest aircraft, and with these flew armed reconnaissance missions for the rest of the war. The squadron remained in Germany after the war, and in July 1949 moved to the Far East to reinforce Hong Kong, being based at Kai Tak and Sek Kong from August 1949 until it disbanded on 1 May 1955.

On 20 June 1955, No. 80 re-formed at Laarbruch with Canberra PR.7 aircraft as a photographic reconnaissance squadron in Germany, and formed part of the 2nd Tactical Air Force until disbanded on 28 September 1969.

Canberra PR. Mk7 WT530 of No. 80 Squadron about to touch down in Malta on 6 January 1969. Note the squadron bell badge on the fin – yellow bell on a white circle.

Canberra PR. Mk7 WH777, the fifth production aircraft, which was released for service on 10 February 1954. Seen here in service with No. 81 Squadron.

No. 81 SQUADRON

No. 81 Squadron formed at Scampton, Lincolnshire, on 1 August 1917, as a training unit. It disbanded in July 1918, only to re-form the following November as a fighter squadron at Wyton, but it did not become operational and was disbanded on 1 February 1920.

Between the wars it was out of the lists, and it next appeared just after the outbreak of the Second World War, when the communications squadron at Mountjoie near Amiens was redesignated No. 81 Squadron. After only a few months it returned to the UK and disbanded on 15 June 1940.

No. 81 then re-formed at Leconfield on 29 July 1941 as a fighter squadron, and in September it flew its Hurricanes off HMS *Argus* to a North Russian airfield. After only a few weeks the Hurricanes were handed over to the Russian Navy, and No. 81 returned to the UK in the cruiser *Kenya*. The squadron then became operational again with Spitfires and flew offensive sweeps from southern England. The squadron then moved overseas in October 1942, its first stop being Gibraltar, then Maison Blanche, and in June moved to Malta to help cover the landings in Sicily. After a short stay in Italy, No. 81 moved to India and then on to Ceylon (Sri Lanka), where it remained until disbanded on 20 June 1945, its Spitfires being required to re-equip Indian Air Force squadrons, which were later to be big users of the Canberra.

At the same time as No. 81 Squadron disbanded at Ratmalana, No. 123 Squadron at Bobbili was renumbered 81 Squadron, but the war ended before its Thunderbolts became operational. The squadron then moved to Java, where it disbanded on 30 June 1946.

On 1 September 1946, No. 684 Squadron at Seletar was renumbered 81 Squadron. Its equipment was Mosquito PR.34 aircraft, and Spitfires were added the following year. Meteor PR.10s gradually replaced the Mosquitoes and Spitfires, and in 1958 the squadron began to convert to Canberra PR.7 aircraft. As the rundown of the Far East Air Force took effect, No. 81 Squadron disbanded on 16 January 1970.

No. 82 SQUADRON

No. 82 Squadron formed at Doncaster on 7 February 1917, equipped with Armstrong Whitworth FK8 aircraft, and in November moved to France. In February 1919 it returned to England and disbanded at Tangmere on 30 June 1919.

On 14 June 1937, No. 82 re-formed at Andover as a day-bomber unit equipped with Hinds. The following year it re-equipped with Blenheims and with these entered the Second World War. After having a detachment in Malta in 1941, the squadron left for the Far East the following March and arrived in Karachi in May 1942. The squadron flew Vengeance dive-bombers, which were then replaced by Mosquitoes. After the Japanese surrender, No. 82 Squadron disbanded on 15 March 1946.

On 1 October 1946, No. 82 Squadron re-formed at Benson from a flight of No. 541 Squadron. The squadron flew Lancaster bombers and Spitfires, and carried out survey work in Nigeria, the Gold Coast (Ghana), Sierra Leone, the Gambia and East Africa. In 1952 the squadron began a survey of West Germany, converting to Canberra PR.3s in November 1953. In October 1954 it took on strength Canberra PR.7s, and the Canberra PR.3s were phased out in February 1955. During this period, the squadron's main role was photographic reconnaissance for Blue Steel's safe flight path to target. Blue Steel was the RAF's strategic 'Stand Off' deterrent, and its launch platform was the mighty Vulcan V-bomber.

After a detachment to the Far East with the Canberras, the squadron disbanded on 1 September 1956. On 22 July 1956, No. 82 Squadron re-formed as a Thor missile unit, disbanded on 10 July 1963.

No. 85 SQUADRON

No. 85 Squadron formed at Upavon on 1 August 1917, and after a brief period on the Western Front returned to the UK and disbanded on 3 July 1919.

It re-formed on 1 June 1938 with Gladiators, and these were replaced by Hurricanes the following September. In August 1942 the squadron re-equipped with Mosquitoes and carried out intruder missions over France. The squadron remained with Mosquitoes throughout the remainder of the war, flying all marks, Mosquito II, XII, XIII, XV, XVII, XXX and the NF.36, which it flew from January 1946 to November 1951, when it converted to Meteors, which it flew until disbanded on 31 October 1958.

Refuelling Canberra T. Mk4 WT485 of No. 85 Squadron. It was released for service on 21 June 1955.

Line-up of No. 85 Squadron Canberras at RAF Binbrook in 1969. Nearest the camera are four T. Mk19s, and the others are B. Mk2s.

On 30 November 1958, No. 89 Squadron at Stradishall was renumbered 85 Squadron and flew Javelins until disbanded on 31 March 1963. On 1 April, 1963, the Target Facilities Squadron at West Raynham was renumbered 85 Squadron and a few days later moved to Binbrook with its Canberra T.11s to provide target towing for air-to-air firing and radar interceptions. In January 1972, No. 85 Squadron moved to West Raynham, where it disbanded in December 1975, having flown during its Canberra period B.2s, T.4s, T.11s and T.19s.

Canberra B. Mk2 WE113 'Q' of No. 85 Squadron.

No. 97 SQUADRON

No. 97 Squadron formed at Waddington on 1 December 1917, as a training unit, and six weeks later moved to Stonehenge. In July 1919 it moved to India, where it disbanded on 1 April 1920.

No. 97 Squadron re-formed at Catfoss on 16 September 1935, and after a further disbandment re-formed on 25 February 1941 with Avro Manchesters. In January 1942 the Manchesters gave way to Lancasters, and the squadron flew this type for the rest of the war. In July 1946 the squadron re-equipped with Lincolns, and flew these until disbanded on 1 January 1956.

On 1 December 1959, No. 97 re-formed at Hemswell as a Thor missile unit, being disbanded on 24 May 1963. On 25 May, No. 151 Squadron was renumbered No. 97 and flew Canberra B.2s and Varsities in Signals Command until disbanded on 2 January 1967.

No. 98 SQUADRON

No. 98 Squadron formed at Harlaxton on 30 August 1917, and moved to France in April 1918 as a day-bomber unit. After the Armistice the squadron returned to the UK in March 1919 and disbanded at Shotwick on 24 July 1919.

On 17 February 1936, No. 98 re-formed at Abingdon as a training unit, and at the outbreak of the war was equipped with Battle aircraft. The squadron moved to France, but was recalled, and many of the squadron personnel were lost when the liner *Lancastria* was sunk off St Nazaire. The squadron re-assembled at Gatwick, but in July 1941 the squadron was redesignated No. 1423 Flight.

It then entered the lists on 12 September 1942, when No. 98 re-formed at West Raynham as a medium-bomber squadron equipped with Mitchells, which it flew for the remainder of the war. After the war the squadron converted to Mosquitoes and flew these

Canberra B. Mk2 WH670 'E'. Early No. 98 Squadron aircraft before fin badge applied.

until February 1951, when it converted to Vampire fighter-bombers. These gave way to Venoms in August 1953, and in March 1955 No. 98 received Hunters and changed its role to a day-fighter unit, only to disband on 15 July 1957.

On 1 August 1959, No. 98 re-formed at Driffield as a Thor missile unit, only to disband again on 18 April 1963. On the following day No. 245 Squadron at Tangmere was renumbered No. 98, and it had on strength Canberra B.2 aircraft. In October 1963 the squadron moved to Watton, which was the Signals Command main base. The squadron then took on strength Canberra E.15s before moving to Cottesmore in April 1969 with No. 90 (Signals) Group. No. 98 Squadron was tasked with flight-checking all RAF navigational, airfield and runway approach aids on a world-wide basis with its Canberras. It disbanded at RAF Cottesmore on 27 February 1976.

No. 192 SQUADRON

No. 192 Squadron formed in September 1917 as an advanced night-flying training unit to operate from Newmarket. It disbanded in December 1918.

It re-formed at Gransden Lodge on 4 January 1943, and flew Wellingtons, Mosquitoes and Halifaxes. The unit's role was radar countermeasures, and it disbanded in August 1945.

On 15 July 1951, No. 192 re-formed at Watton in a similar role, using Lincolns, Washingtons and Canberra B.2s for countermeasures training until renumbered 51 Squadron on 21 August 1958.

No. 245 SQUADRON

No. 245 Squadron formed in August 1918 at Fishguard, only to disband in May 1919. Two decades later it re-formed at Leconfield on 30 October 1939, with Blenheims. After a few months flying Battles the squadron re-equipped with Hurricanes in March 1940. In January 1943 the Hurricanes gave way to Typhoons, which the squadron flew until disbanding on 10 August 1945. That same day No. 504 Squadron at Colerne was re-numbered 245. It was equipped with Meteors, and these in turn were replaced by Hunters in March 1957, but these were flown for only a short time, for on 3 June 1957 the squadron disbanded once again.

On 21 August 1958, No. 527 Squadron, a Signals Command unit at Watton, was renumbered 245, and three days later moved to Tangmere, where it operated with Canberra B.2s until renumbered No. 98 Squadron on 18 April 1963.

No. 360 SQUADRON

Motto: Confundemus (We shall throw into confusion)

No. 360 Squadron, made up of 75 per cent Royal Air Force and 25 per cent Royal Navy personnel, formed at Watton on 23 September 1966 as a joint RAF/Royal Navy electronic warfare training squadron. Navy personnel came from No. 831 Squadron, which was also based at Watton. Canberras were to be the main equipment for the new squadron, and the first to arrive were Canberra T.4s, which the unit had held since April with the provisional number of '360'; Canberra B.2s arrived in October 1966. The following December it took on strength Canberra T.17s, which took over as the main equipment when the Canberra B.2s and B.6s were phased out in 1967.

The specialized ECM-training Canberra T.17s were well equipped for their role, and at the heart of their electronic countermeasure equipment was a 2,000 lb (907 kg) package of transmitters in the bomb-bay, these being provided with cooling air from three scoops beneath, two outlets being located behind. Small radomes on the nose and in the extreme rear of the fuselage contained 1-band transmitting aerials and electronic support measures (ESM) receivers, while the larger nose radome was for a lower-frequency aerial. Other fittings included a D-band blade aerial beneath the nose, an HF aerial from the port side of the forward fuselage to the fin tip, and a 'towel rail' aerial above the port wing, inboard of the engine.

The additional electrical power required for this formidable array was provided by two turbo-generators fed by air bled from the engines, their cooling ducts protruding from the wing undersurfaces, outboard of the engines. When carried, chaff was contained in modified tip tanks equipped with a dispenser to open and distribute pre-cut lengths, which varied with the frequency of the radar to be jammed. In contrast to the large strips of aluminium foil used in the Second World War, modern 'window' is typically a two-inch (5 cm) long needle of coated fiberglass, but is, nevertheless, equally effective.

Training required flying at any height from 500 to 40,000 ft (150 m to 12,200 m), although the usual band was somewhere between 5,000 and 15,000 ft (1,525 and 4,570 m). Despite its various protuberances, the T.17's handling and performance was similar to other Canberra marks, except the PR. Mk9, but landing required care because of the restricted view available over the nose. Without the benefit of fuel tanks in the bomb-bay, the aircraft was more 'short-legged' than its companions.

In January 1967, No. 361 Squadron was formed under the control of 360 Squadron. This unit was for deployment to the Far East, but on 14 July 1967 No. 361 Squadron disbanded and its crews joined 360 Squadron, which moved to RAF Cottesmore in April 1969, and remained there until August 1975, when it moved to RAF Wyton. This turned out to be its final home, for it disbanded there in October 1994, and its role was taken over by Flight Refuelling Ltd, a civil contractor.

No. 527 SQUADRON

No. 527 Squadron formed at Castle Camps on 15 June 1943 for radar calibration duties, and served in this role until it disbanded at Watton on 15 April 1946.

On 1 August 1952, N and R Calibration Squadrons of the Central Signal Establishment at Watton were redesignated No. 527 Squadron. The unit flew a variety of aircraft, which included a few Canberra B.2s. It was renumbered No. 245 Squadron in August 1958.

No. 540 SQUADRON

This unit formed at Leuchars from H and L Flights of the Photographic Reconnaissance Unit on 19 October 1942. It was equipped with Mosquitoes, and carried out reconnaissance sorties from Norway down to France and Italy. Many other long-range sorties were made to Germany and the Baltic ports. In preparation for the landings in North Africa, the squadron made sorties over southern France and Algeria from Gibraltar. After a move to Benson in February 1944, the squadron moved to France for the rest of the war, returning to Benson in November 1945, where it disbanded on 30 September 1946.

On 1 December 1947, No. 540 Squadron re-formed at Benson with Mosquito PR.34s, for photographic reconnaissance and survey duties. In December 1952, the squadron converted to Canberra PR.3s, and in March 1953 moved to Wyton. In September 1954, some Canberra PR.7s were taken on strength, and the squadron flew both marks up until it disbanded on 31 March 1956.

No. 542 SQUADRON

No. 542 Squadron formed at Benson on 19 October 1942, from A and E Flights of the Photographic Reconnaissance Unit. The squadron was equipped with Spitfires, which it flew for the duration of the war. It disbanded on 27 August 1945.

On 17 May 1954, No. 542 Squadron re-formed at Wyton in the photographic reconnaissance role in No. 3 Group, Bomber Command, and was equipped with Canberra PR.7s, which included WH795, WH796, WH801, WH798 and WH779. The

Tony Regan, refuelling WH702 of No. 542 Squadron at RAF Kinloss, poses nonchalantly for the camera, as if James Bond has just dropped in and said, 'Fill her up'.

Ground crew at work on a Canberra of No. 542 Squadron at RAF Wyton. Tony Regan is fitting starter cartridge in starter. Note nose-wheel doors – red stripe on white.

542 Squadron at Gibraltar in 1956, during its 'sniffing days'. Note the 'Dream Boats' on wing tip. The Canberra has a red tail and wing tips. A Shackleton of No. 224 is in the background.

unit carried out flying trials on the Avon 109 and two-speed tail planes. Two aircraft, WH795 and WH796, were to fly 600 hours in a month. The individual aircraft had to be in the air eighteen hours a day, and flew the Wyton – St Mawgan – Manston –Kinloss triangle twice. The strength of man-power was doubled and quick turnarounds were done. On 1 October 1955, No. 542 Squadron disbanded, only to re-form a month later from No. 1323 Flight at Wyton. It was equipped with Canberra B.2s (WH902, WH701, WH884 and WH573, ex-1323 Flight) and Canberra B.6s.

In December 1955, No. 542 Squadron moved to Weston Zoyland, and it was to operate world-wide – Australia, Christmas Island, Goose Bay, Gibraltar, Kinloss and Leuchars.

At the end of 1955, No. 76 Squadron joined 542 Squadron at Weston Zoyland prior to departure to carry out survey and sampling flights during the nuclear bomb tests. No. 542 was the specialist squadron in this field. 'C' Flight, 542 Squadron, was an administration exercise as far as 542 UK was concerned, for C Flight, equipped with Canberra B. Mk6s, never operated in the UK. It served only at Goose Bay in Canada and Laverton in Australia. Once again 542 UK was the expert at atomic dust gathering.

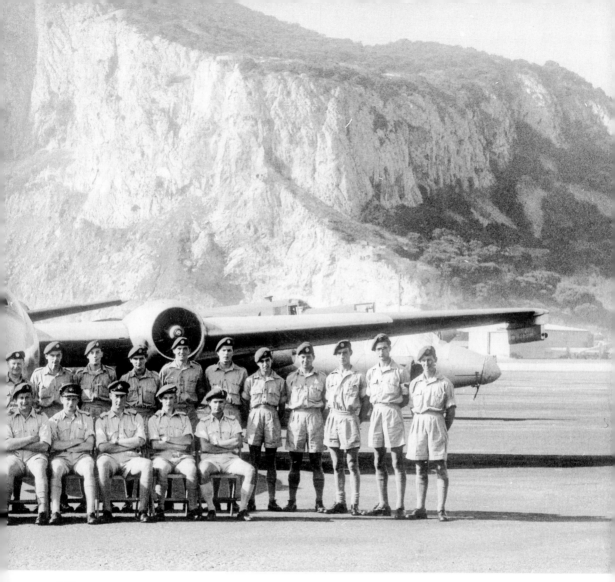

UK EXERCISE
Bagpipes – Bottling the atomic dust, Dream – Filtering the atomic dust

Bagpipes – aircraft had bottling gear in the Canberra bomb-bay. A meteor gearbox with generator, repolarized to become a motor driving the meteor accessory box and a Heywood compressor. The air to the compressor came from a tapping on the starboard engine. Two bottles were strapped in the bomb bay.

Dream – a filter box where the drop tanks fitted (see photograph). A later model, 'Cascade', was then used. The Canberras had Mk.10 filters on the bomb door at the front. The pioneer of this kind of work was 1323 Flight.

Weston Zoyland in Somerset, England, a wartime Nissen-hutted airfield, was the main base for 542 Squadron, and there was a great camaraderie spirit among the Canberra ground and air crews. No. 542 Squadron had its own rugby XV, which played in the Somerset league. Many of the squadron married local girls. The squadron was detached to Laverton in Australia until April 1957, when it then returned to England.

On 17 July 1958 it moved to Upwood, and on 1 October 1958 it was re-numbered No. 21 Squadron.

Poring over the handiwork of the Canberra PR.9 and its crew of No. 1 PRU are Lt. Doudeau, Flt/Lt Dave Ashton, Capt John Dieken, Maj Neville Youngs and Lt Donner at the Joint School of Photographic Interpretation.

No. 1 PHOTOGRAPHIC RECONNAISSANCE UNIT

Before the start of the Second World War, the German Colonel-General Baron von Fritsch commented, 'The next war will be won by the military organization with the most efficient photographic reconnaissance.' How right he was. At the outbreak of the Second World War, Sidney Cotton was put in sole charge of the very important Photographic Development Unit (PDU). It is ironic that Cotton should have had an uphill struggle to get this special unit started. At the outbreak of war Heston Aerodrome was requisitioned by the RAF, and during September 1939 the Heston Flight was formed. Within weeks the Heston Flight was designated No. 2 Camouflage Unit, but on 8 July 1940 its name was changed to No. 1 Photographic Reconnaissance Unit (No. 1 PRU). Even with a name change, Cotton still had to work hard against mountains of red tape (nothing changes). In October 1942 No. 1 PRU disbanded and a series of RAF PR squadrons were formed. On 2 June 1982 No. 1 PRU re-formed at RAF Wyton with a few Canberra PR.9s from the disbanded No. 39 Squadron. The Canberras were used on mapping and similar tasks. The PRU activities were very much reduced, being a unit from the Second World War; and the Canberra PR.9s were also relegated to less busy times because low-level tactical reconnaissance in Europe was not as easy for the large PR.9 and it no longer had the wide variety of camera options.

During its heyday in the Sixties and Seventies a full operational fit for the Canberra PR.9's fuselage comprised a forward-facing F95 low-level tactical camera in the extreme nose; two oblique F95s on either side of the nose; an F96 behind the cockpit, left side only; an F49 or a 70 mm infra-red linescan to the rear of the bomb-bay; two additional oblique ports beneath the wing trailing edge; and a vertical port further to the rear.

Sighting of the oblique camera was undertaken by the pilot with the aid of reference marks on the cockpit canopy, while the navigator had the benefit of fore and aft observation through an 'inverted periscope'.

Just a decade since it had re-formed from the disbanded No. 39 Squadron, the winds of change were again blowing, and in July 1992 it was decreed that No. 39 Squadron should re-form as No. 39 (1 Photographic Reconnaissance Unit) Squadron, equipped with the last faithful Canberras, and in 1993 it moved to RAF Marham.

As at December 2003, the Canberras are still in service, and current plans are that they will remain in service for some years to come. But they cannot remain in service for ever, can they?

The answer is 'No'. I have known for some months that No. 39 (1 PRU) Squadron will disband on 31 March 2006; and by so doing, the Canberra era in the Royal Air Force will be over and become just memories. Hence this unique book full of Canberra facts (told for the first time) and full of unique pictures, so that one can cherish those Canberra memories.

No. 231 OPERATIONAL CONVERSION UNIT

No. 231 OCU formed at RAF Coningsby in Lincolnshire in March 1947 with Mosquito T3s and B16s to train crews for Pathfinder and Photographic Reconnaissance duties. No. 231 disbanded in December 1949.

On 1 December 1951, No. 231 OCU re-formed at RAF Bassingbourn, absorbing in the process No. 237 OCU, with a variety of aircraft. Early in the new year the first Canberra B.2 aircraft arrived for the training of Canberra crews; and the unit was destined to remain in that role.

Training with the Canberras began in May 1952, and within eighteen months Canberra T.4s came on strength (the first T. Mk4 WE188 was released to service on 20 September 1953). By June 1953, the unit had twenty-six Canberras on strength. In November 1953 the unit received seven Canberra PR. Mk3s, and soon afterwards the PR Section of 231 OCU moved to Merryfield and then to RAF Wyton, where it re-formed as 237 OCU, only to return to Bassingbourn in early 1958 and be absorbed by 231 OCU.

In May 1969 the Canberras of 231 OCU moved to Cottesmore, and in February 1976 to Marham, where the unit had a six-year stay before moving to RAF Wyton at the end of July 1982. Here it absorbed the Canberra T. Mk4 trainers of the Canberra Servicing Flight. The unit's staff consisted of six pilots, three navigators and one master engineer systems instructor, plus forty-five ground crew; it continued in its role of training Canberra crews until disbanding at Wyton in December 1990, when it was renamed Canberra Standardization Training Flight (CSTF). But more changes were in the wind, and in May 1991 No. 231 OCU re-formed, absorbing in the process the CSTF. However, it was not to be, and in April 1993 No. 231 OCU disbanded at RAF Wyton.

CHAPTER EIGHT

Experimental Canberras

The Canberra's high performance, relative ease of changing engines and straightforward layout ensured that it would be used for a large number of flying test-beds, including the Bristol Siddeley Olympus and Gyron Junior turbojets, the de Havilland Spectre and Napier Double Scorpion liquid-propellant rocket motors, radar and missile trials.

All the British engine manufacturers used various Canberras for flight testing. Rolls-Royce used the following at various times: B.1 VN813, B.1 VN850, B.2 WD930, B.2 WD943, B.2 WD959, B.2 WF909, B.2 WH671 and B.2 WH854.

Canberra Mk.1 VN813, second prototype used for DH Spectre rocket motor and Nene engine development work.

Canberra B.1 VN813 was used by Rolls-Royce for a short period during November 1950 to September 1951 for development work on the Nene.

Canberra B.1 VN850 was used by Rolls-Royce for development work on the Avon R.A.2 during the period October 1950 to June 1951.

Canberra B.2 WD930 was released to service on 8 March 1951, and following service with the RRE at Defford was issued to Rolls-Royce at Hucknall for flight-testing the Avon R.A.7s for the later B.6. It later flew with Avon R.A.14s in July 1953. At a later date Avon R.A.26s were fitted, followed by R.A.29s in 1956. WD930 was finally scrapped at Hucknall in August 1960.

Canberra B.2 WD943 was delivered to Rolls-Royce in October 1951 and used in repeat trials of the R.A.7R Avon. In July 1957 WD943 left Rolls-Royce for 23 MU, where it was sold for scrap in November 1962

Canberra B.2 WD959 was released to service on 12 December 1951, and, after a period of service with English Electric was delivered to Rolls-Royce at Hucknall for reheat development work on the Avon R.A.7R and R.A.14R

Canberra B. Mk2 WJ674, the first of the last batch produced by Handley Page, and released to service on 26 October 1954. Seen here in service with No. 231 OCU at RAF Bassingbourn.

engines. It was finally fitted with Avon R.A.24s. After six years of service it was retired to Melksham as 7620M, where it stayed until at least 1962.

Canberra B.2 WF909 was released to service on 17 July 1952, and used by Rolls-Royce for general development work on the Avon for a period of about three years until 1955, when it went to de Havilland as a test-bed for the Gyron Junior, with which it first flew on 28 May 1957.

Canberra B.2 WH671 was released to service on 17 December 1952. It was delivered to Rolls-Royce from Boulton Paul in June 1954 for development flying with the R.A.24 and R.A.28 Avons. It was scrapped in November 1961.

Canberra PR. Mk3 WE139, which was the fifth off the production line and was released to service on 15 December 1952. Now preserved in the RAF Museum at Hendon – 8369M

Canberra B. Mk2 WD933.

Canberra B.2 WH854 was released to service on 20 October 1952. It was used by Rolls-Royce for relighting rests with various Avon engines.

Several aircraft were used by Armstrong Siddeley at Bitterswell for flight-testing the Sapphire: they included B.2s WD933 and WK141.

Canberra B.2 WD933 was released to service on 13 April 1951. After a short period with Vickers, WD933 was delivered to Armstrong Siddeley for installation of Sapphire AS3s. These were replaced in 1952 with the ASSA6 engines and later still with the ASS7, with which it first flew on 13 August 1954. WD933 was written off in a landing accident at Bitterswell, when it belly-landed and overturned.

Of all the test-bed Canberras probably the best remembered are the record-breaking Bristol Olympus-powered aircraft used by the Bristol Engine Co. at Filton.

Canberra B.2 WD952 was delivered to the Bristol Engine Co. for conversion to Olympus B01 engines in December 1951, flying for the first time with these on 5 August 1952. With Wing Commander W.F. Gibb at the controls, WD952 established a world aeroplane altitude record of 63,688 ft (19,412.1 m) on 4 May 1953. Subsequently re-engined with more powerful Olympus 101s, and

Canberra B. Mk2 WD952.

Canberra B. Mk2 WK141 on test.

Canberra B. Mk2 WK163 at RAE Bedford in September 1980.

later with 12,000 lb (5,443 kg) thrust Olympus 102s, it achieved a new record of 65,876 ft (20,079 m) on 29 August 1955. After a crash on 12 March 1956, it was broken up at Colerne later in the year.

Canberra B.2 WK141 was released to service on 5 October 1954, and replaced WD933 as the Sapphire test-bed. It was used by the Bristol Siddeley Engine Co. from September 1959 to March 1963 for Sapphire AS7 and Viper flight trials (Viper 8 and 11).

Several Canberras were used by the de Havilland Engine Co. and de Havilland Propellers for engine and missile test work, including B.1 VN813, B.2 WD992 and B.2 WF909.

Canberra B.1 VN813 went to de Havillands in June 1953, and was later converted by Folland to flight-test the D.H. Spectre rocket motor, which uses a propellant combination of hydrogen peroxide and kerosene. First airborne trial firing of the Spectre occurred on 18 December 1956. From these tests, Blue Steel – the air-launched nuclear missile carried by the V-Bombers, was successfully launched in 1958 powered by a DH Double Spectre rocket engine.

Canberra B.2 WD992 was released to service on 16 April 1952. This aircraft saw no RAF service, going straight to D.H. Propellers at Hatfield for missile development work. It was sold for scrap on 14 June 1965.

Canberra B.2 WF909 was released to service on 17 July 1952, and after a period of service with Rolls-Royce, this aircraft was delivered to DH Propellers for conversion to a flying test-bed for the DH Gyron Junior engine, with which it first flew in May 1957.

Canberra B.2 WK163 was released to service on 25 January 1955. It was converted by Napiers at Luton for flight-testing the Scorpion liquid rocket motor. It was first flown in this form on 20 May 1956. It was to this aircraft that the world aeroplane altitude record once again fell, when WK163 reached a height of 70,310 ft (21,430.4 m) on 28 August 1957, piloted by Michael Randrup.

The Ferranti Co. used a number of Canberras for flight tests of airborne electrical equipment; the following aircraft were used by Ferranti:

Canberra B.2 WD947, December 1966 to October 1967.
Canberra B.2 WD953, October 1961 to February 1969
Canberra B.2 WJ627, August 1959 to September 1963
Canberra B.2 WJ643, September 1954 to March 1969
Canberra B(I).8 WT327, August 1956 to April 1966
Canberra B.2(I).8 WV787, October 1959 to December 1963
Canberra B(I).8 VX185, April 1956 to October 1957
Canberra SC.9 XH132, May 1961 to September 1961

A number of these aircraft are of special note:

B.2 WJ643, for example, was fitted with B(I).8-style cockpit and nose radome to accommodate Airpass radar equipment. Later re-engined with R.A.7s in place of the earlier R.A.3s, it was also used on the laser ranger testing, for which it was equipped with laser equipment in the nose.

Canberra B.2 WV787 was delivered in August 1952 and was used by Bristol Siddeley Engines as a test aircraft in its original form. After its service with Bristol Siddeley Engines, it was modified so many times with major components from other marks that it defied designation.

Short S.C.9, XH132 was a PR. Mk9 special, converted by Short Brothers for use in conducting field trials with the de Havilland Red Top missile guidance system. It played a priceless role at a crucial time. The S.C.9 was modified to accept the Red Top homing head and various components of the missile's guidance system. It was also used to gather infra-red data on target characteristics and to evaluate target detection systems. These data turned out to be ground breaking and highly useful. This was its only role before being struck off charge.

Flight Refuelling Co Ltd used several Canberras, including B.2s WH734 and WK143, in probe and drogue refuelling trials.

The Aeroplane & Armament Experimental Establishment, as one would expect, handled many Canberras, and relatively few saw any length of service with the establishment. The following are a few of the few:

Canberra B.2 WD945 was released to service on 21 September 1951. It spent three periods at Boscombe Down, from 17 December 1951 to 30 June 1952, then departed to Defford, arriving back on 2 August 1955, departing on 15 November 1955 to Farnborough, returning for a final period with the A & AEE from 22 August 1958 to 21 April 1964, when it was scrapped.

Canberra B.2 WH638 was released to service on 27 August 1952. It spent a short period from 9 June 1953 to 24 January 1955 with the A & AEE before departing to Defford. It returned to Boscombe Down on 27 June 1962, and remained there until January 1978, when it was scrapped.

Canberra B.2 WH876 was something of a mystery. It was released to service on 29 October 1953, being the 24th B. Mk2 built by Short Bros and Harland. After RAF service it went to the Ministry of Supply for conversion to U.14, but for some reason saw out its days with the Maritime Test Flight.

Canberra B.2 WK121 was released to service on 20 April 1954, and was to be another long-serving member of the Bomber and Maritime Test Flight with the A & AEE from 16 February 1960 to February 1973, after which it was scrapped.

Canberra B.2 WK164 was released to service on 14 February 1955, and then served with the A & AEE from 9 December 1959 to 9 December 1977, when it was transferred from MoD service. After overhaul at St Athan it went to RAF service with No. 100 Squadron.

Canberra B.2 WJ638 was released to service on 30 May 1954, and after service with the RAF it went to MoS for conversion to U.10 It was later used at A & AEE for ejection seat trials, after which it was scrapped.

Canberra PR.3 VX181 was the prototype PR. Mk3. After appearing at the SBAC show at Farnborough in 1950 it was used for development at Benson. During January 1953 it flew out to Woomera in Australia, setting another Canberra record as it went. It took off from Heathrow at 08.35 hours on 27 January 1953, and arrived at Darwin at 06.44 the following day, a total time of 22 hr 9 min. Flying time was 19 hr 1 min. Refuelling stops were made at Fayid, Karachi and Singapore. On its return the aircraft served with the A & AEE for many years, finally arriving at Pershore in 1969, where unfortunately it was broken up during the period 1972–5.

Canberra PR.3 WF922 was released to service on 11 November 1953, and after RAF service was sold to the Ministry of Technology on 31 January 1969, and then joined the fleet at A & AEE where it served until 1972, after which it went to the RRE and then to Marshalls at Cambridge.

Canberra PR.7 WT503 was released to service on 20 October 1954. It was used for three short periods by the A & AEE from 20 March 1961 to 6 July 1961, and then went to Boulton Paul. It returned on 2 September 1963 until 3 October 1963, returning to Boulton Paul and then to A & AEE from 11 August to 3 November 1964. It then went to RAF Wyton for service with 58 Squadron.

Although a number of Canberra B(I).8s served at the A & AEE, special mention should be made of two that came to grief while in A & AEE service:

Canberra B(I).8 WT326 was released to service on 21 July 1955. It spun into the ground after take-off from Boscombe Down on 27 November 1955.

Canberra B(I).8 WT328 was released to service on 28 January 1956. It flew into the sea during radio altimeter trials south of Shoreham, Sussex, on 7 May 1956.

Canberra PR.9 XH133 made a number of short stops at Boscombe Down between 1960 and 1966, going to and from Short Brothers, before going to Malta in September 1966, having been exchanged with XH175, which now went to RAF Wyton in September 1966, not sunny Malta.

Canberra B.2 WV787 was the 90th off the B.2 production line, and was released to service on 11 August 1952. It was destined for a varied life, and it was the only Canberra with WV code letters. It saw service with Ferranti Limited. It had a converted B(I).8-style nose section. After Ferranti it saw service with A & AEE at Boscombe Down, and was used for airborne icing and de-icing trials before ending its days in 1988.

Canberra TT.18 WJ632, as a B.2, was released to service on 20 April 1954 and then served with the A & AEE from 22 November 1962 until 24 November 1966, when it was delivered to Tarrant Rushton. Returned to A & AEE as a TT.18 on 11 April 1968, it crashed into Lyme Bay on 1 May 1970.

Telecommunications Research Establishment (TRE) and Royal Radar Establishment (RRE)

Almost from Day One, the TRE and RRE used Canberras in the testing of various airborne radio and radar systems. Following the closure of Defford, the flying unit moved to Pershore in September 1957. With the closure of Pershore in 1978, the RRE flying unit moved to RAE Bedford. The following are some of the Canberras used by the above establishments:

Canberra B.2 WD929 was probably the first Canberra to be used by the unit. It stayed only briefly, from 15 March to 5 April 1951, before going to the RAF at Farnborough.

Canberra B.2 WD936 was allocated to the TRE in January 1952 for a few months, before going to No. 109 Squadron at RAF Hemswell. WD963 later converted to a T. Mk4.

Canberra B.2 WD953 was released to service on 11 November 1951. After serving with the RAE, the A&AEE and Ferranti, WD953 appeared with the RRE in March 1969. Later in the year it was declared non-effective and was struck off charge.

Canberra B. Mk2 WG789 served at Pershore as a trials aircraft with RAE. Has been a research aircraft all its life. Photographed for the author at RAE Bedford on 28 November 1983.

Canberra B. Mk2 WJ992, converted to T. Mk4 standard and seen here in service with the Royal Aircraft Establishment.

Canberra WT333 was released to service on 1 March 1956, and served for a period at Marshall's of Cambridge. The above photograph shows it as it started as a B(1). Mk8. Here it is seen with a very unusual nose, in service with the Royal Aircraft Establishment.

Canberra WH953, B. Mk6 modified. Released to service on 31 January 1955. Served at Pershore – seen here with the Royal Aircraft Establishment – September 1981.

Close-up of nose on Canberra WH953 at RAE Bedford.

<u>Canberra B.2 WG789</u> was released to service on 11 August 1952. It had a T.11-type nose fitted. It was transferred from Pershore in late 1976 and rebuilt at Warton in 1978–9.

<u>Canberra T.4 WJ992</u> was converted from a B. Mk2 that was released to service on 30 October 1953. It was the used for pilot continuation training. It was transferred from Farnborough.

Short S.C.9 XH132, a PR.Mk9 Special seen here in new livery at RAE Bedford for secret research. The pilot look at the camera. Note special livery, even on tip tanks. Unique photograph.

Canberra B(I).8 WT333 was based at Marshalls for a number of years and used as a trial installation aircraft for proving various modifications. It was used as the trials aircraft for the Low Approach Bombing System (LABS). These trials were carried out at A & AEE Boscombe Down, and later in Germany.

Canberra B(I).8 WT327 was modified to B.6 standard, from Pershore. It was also used by Ferranti.

Canberra B.6 XH568 had a modified nose section.

Canberra B.6 WH953 had a modified nose section.

Royal Aircraft Establishment Farnborough
The RAE Farnborough, like other establishments, used a number of Canberras for various purposes.

Canberra B.1 VN799 was the first B.1 Canberra used by the RAE for a short period in July/August 1953 for automatic approach and landing experiments.

Canberra B.2 WD931 joined the RAE on 20 February 1951 for experimental work, and was at one time fitted with wingtip cameras. It stayed with the RAE until 1958, when it went to the RRE at Pershore.

Canberra B.2 WD945 served with the RAE Met. Flight from 1955 until 1957, and was later used for target-towing developments during 1961. It later went to the A & AEE.

Canberra B.2 WD947 was delivered to the RAE on 14 November 1951, where it was fitted with wingtip cameras. It then served with the Bombing Trials Unit as (J) at Martlesham Heath and Woodbridge during 1955, and had a period with the Ferranti flying unit at Turnhouse before retiring to the RAE in 1967 and going to 15 MU in 1969.

Canberra B.2 WD953 was delivered to the RAE in December 1951, and like

Short S.C.9. XH132m in change of livery, and posing proudly like a sleek fighter aircraft, with canopy open.

WD947 also served with the Bombing Trials Unit at Martlesham Heath and Woodbridge as (K) during 1955. It then went to the Ferranti flying unit at Turnhouse in October 1961.

Canberra B.2 WD960 was released to service on 31 December 1951. It was delivered to the RAE on loan in February 1952, but suffered a Category 5 accident on 30 April 1952 and was struck off charge.

Canberra B.2 WD962 was released to service in January 1952 and loaned to the RAE for ejector seat trials. It was then transferred to the RAF, where it remained until scrapped in 1961.

Canberra PR.3 WE146 after being exhibited at the SBAC show at Farnborough in September 1953, was transferred to the MoS and joined the RAE Met. Flight, serving with that until SOC in 1976. At one period during 1967 it was converted to carry the Beech Stiletto target drone.

Canberra PR.3 WE173 was released to service on 4 November 1953, and saw service with Nos 69 and 39 Squadrons. It was then transferred to the RAE Met. Flight and was modified to carry a nose probe. It remained with that unit until SOC in the late 1970s.

Not all Canberras were as decorated as this one.

CHAPTER NINE

Camouflage and Markings

During its many years of service with the Royal Air Force the Canberra has carried a wide range of colour schemes, and squadron and station badges, markings, etc. After a number of years' service the colours were dictated by period, area of operations and whether aircraft were used operationally or for second-line work. The permutations of markings worn by long-service Canberras are virtually endless. The first prototype VN799 carried an overall blue paint scheme, with the prototype P in yellow; serials were in white.

The remaining prototypes were painted in the Bomber Command colour scheme introduced during the summer of 1947; this used a medium sea-grey upper surface with a semi-gloss black undersurface finish that extended up the fuselage sides and included the fin and rudder. Serials were in white.

This was probably the most attractive of all the Canberra colour schemes, and was used on early production B.2s up to WD986, this aircraft going to No. 617 Squadron at Binbrook on 21 March 1952.

From WD987 onwards, B.2s were delivered in a new colour scheme, being two-tone upper surfaces of medium sea-grey and light sea-grey with PR blue underside and white serials, small format on rear fuselage.

These early colour schemes remained in use for only a short period before Bomber Command introduced a natural metal overall finish with black serials for its aircraft. It was on this finish that most of the squadron and station markings appeared, making it one of the more colourful periods in the history of Bomber Command.

As the number of Canberra squadrons built up, some stations were operating four or more squadrons. It was during this period that stations introduced markings to make their own squadrons more readily identifiable.

Canberra B. Mk2 WK135 was released to service on 23 August 1954. Seen here in August 1963 at Thurleigh on runway slush trials.

Canberra WH793 began life as a standard PR. Mk7, being the twelfth aircraft off the production line, and was released to service on 20 April 1954. It was then converted by D. Napier and Son to become the aerodynamic prototype for the PR. Mk9. Retaining the PR. Mk7 fuselage, it was fitted with the PR.9's extended wing chord inboard of the engines, extended span, Avon 206 engines and powered flying controls. Seen here in service with RAE Bedford for various high-altitude test programmes. Nose and lettering in red.

Spada of the Skies.
Aero Flight WH793 - PR.Mk7, led a very interesting life. It was released to service on 21 April 1954. In early 1965 it was with RAE Bedford. Here we see it coming into land at sunny Malta in November 1971. On seeing it I nicknamed it Spada, which is Italian for Swordfish. Just right you must agree.

Binbrook, being the first operational Canberra base and also one of the largest wings, introduced a lightning flash on the nose with a different colour for each of its resident squadrons.

RAF Binbrook nose flash colours were: No. 9 Squadron – red nose flash; No. 12 Squadron – gold nose flash; No. 101 Squadron – black and white nose flash; No. 617 Squadron – dark blue nose flash.

For a time, the tip tanks of the Marham-based Canberra squadrons were each painted a different colour, as follows:

No. 35 Squadron – blue wingtip tanks; No, 90 Squadron – white wingtip tank; No. 115 Squadron – black wingtip tank; No. 207 Squadron – red wingtip tank.

The squadrons at Honington in Suffolk were only based there for a short period: No. 10 Squadron, May 1955 to December 1956; No. 15 Squadron, February 1955 to April 1957; No. 44 Squadron, February 1955 to July 1957; No. 57, February 1955 to November 1956; and No. 199 Squadron, which received Canberras while at Honington, during 1956 and 1957, and were distinguished by the white Honington pheasant on the fin.

RAF Scampton chose for its squadrons a speedbird, similar to that used by BOAC. Once again different colours were used to identify the aircraft of the different squadrons. Examples are No. 10 Squadron – a red speedbird; No. 18 Squadron – a black speedbird.

The two resident squadrons at RAF Hemswell, Nos 109 and 139, carried a triangular fin flash. This was in yellow with a black outline for No. 109 Squadron and in red with a white outline for No. 139 Squadron.

At RAF Wittering, Nos 40 and 100 Squadrons carried that station's yellow and blue chequer markings on the fin, with No. 40 Squadron having a red centre disc and No. 100 Squadron a green centre disc.

Although RAF Upwood was host to at least six Canberra squadrons at various times, most stayed for only a short while before disbanding. The only station mark carried was that of the station badge on the fin.

One event that added colour to the Canberra's markings for a short period was that event known as the Suez War in 1956. For the invasion of Egypt, invasion stripes were carried round the rear fuselage and cordwise across the wings. Unlike the D-Day markings, however, this time they were in black and yellow stripes.

Canberra B. Mk2 WD935 seen here with Suez Invasion Stripes. Speedbird badge on nose in red, and tip tank marking also red. White pheasant on fin was badge of RAF Honington squadrons.

The original 'flying tin opener' emblem of No. 6 Squadron which started out as Squadron Leader Allan Simpson's personal emblem on his Hurricane IId, and he is seen posing beside it. The photo I have (the one you see) is the only one ever taken; remember, there was a war going on, it was not Billy Butlin's Holiday Camp.

The Canberra B.2s of the Akrotiri-based strike wing were also silver overall, and as two of these squadrons were ex-fighter units it gave them a chance to reintroduce their earlier colourful markings.

No. 6 Squadron carried its red 'flying tin opener' insignia on the wingtip fuel tanks and its red and dark blue gunner's stripe across the fin – the former being a legacy of tank-busting operations with Hurricane IIds.

Long before No. 6 Squadron's Canberra days, one can read the true wartime stories of the squadron: the birth of its insignia, and unique pictures of the 'flying tin opener' insignia in war. After their first successful sortie the Hurricane IId pilots were jubilantly called the 'tin openers'; and from that came their 'flying tin opener' insignia, which was invented, designed and christened by Squadron Leader Allan Simpson, who was the first (naturally) to have the 'flying tin opener' insignia painted on his Hurricane IId. He proudly posed in front of his aircraft to show off the insignia. You can see the historic picture, published for the first time in my book, *Fighter Pilots in World War II* (ISBN 1-84415-065-8, published by Pen & Sword Books Limited) in the chapter 'Hurricane IId "Tankbuster"', and read about how No. 6 Squadron missed out on a Victoria Cross in the chapter 'Fighter Command's Only VC'.

No. 32 Squadron, an ex-fighter unit, reintroduced its blue and white stripe markings, firstly on the fin and then later on either side of the fuselage roundel, fighter style.

No. 73, another ex-fighter squadron, carried its blue/yellow/blue arrow-shaped stripe on the wing tanks; the squadron badge also appeared on the fin.

The remaining squadron, No. 249, chose to paint its wing tanks yellow with a black assegai spear painted on them. The squadron badge of a grey elephant appeared on a white disc on the fin, and for a period on the yellow tip tank; half of the spear was black, the spearhead red and the elephant in grey on a white disc. When camouflaged Canberra B.15s and B.16s replaced the earlier silver Canberra B.2s and B.6s, markings were toned down and reduced in size. With the arrival of centralized servicing in 1965, unit insignia were removed, being replaced by the Akrotiri pink flamingo outlined in black on the fin. But it was not long before the Canberras again sported the elephant. The tip tanks were black with yellow spear, starter motor yellow with black surround on engine and black section on fin with large yellow disc with black elephant.

Those Canberra B.2s that remained in service after the arrival of the V-bombers in Bomber Command, either serving with Signals Command or in the target facilities role, adopted the light aircraft-grey overall finish then in use, with some aircraft carrying large areas of orange dayglo.

The few Canberra B.2s remaining in service in the early 1980s adopted the current matt-finish dark grey and dark green upper surfaces with light aircraft-grey undersurfaces. Red/blue roundels and fin flashes replaced the earlier red/white/blue style. Markings, where carried, were toned down, with all white removed.

Canberra B(I).6 and B(I).8 Intruders
The B(I).6 and B(I).8 intruder Canberras serving with the RAF in Germany carried the usual upper-surface colour scheme of dark green and dark sea-grey. The undersurfaces however, were in semi-matt black. Initially the black was carried well up the fuselage sides, and at this time large white serials were carried on the rear fuselage and underwing.

With the lowering of the camouflage demarcation line, the serials on the rear fuselage were painted in the more usual black. One of the German squadrons, No. 16, had the most decorative Canberra B(I).8s. A black and yellow band encircled the rear fuselage, with black and yellow cross keys on a yellow outlined white disc on the nose.

Close-up that shows clearly the shark's teeth markings on a former 16 Squadron Canberra B(1). Mk8.

Squadron fin markings carried by a Canberra PR. Mk9 of No. 39 Squadron, XH174, in July 1977.

Photo-Reconnaissance Aircraft

The photo-reconnaissance Canberras have undergone as many colour scheme changes as the bomber versions. Initially Canberra PR.3s appeared in a scheme of medium sea-grey upper surfaces with the PR blue undersurfaces, but this was soon changed to dark green and dark sea-grey upper surfaces, while retaining the PR blue undersurfaces.

Before long the demarcation line between the upper and lower colours was moved lower down on the fuselage sides, with the PR blue being replaced by silver or natural metal. Those aircraft serving with the OCU and with squadrons overseas, other than in Germany, later appeared in a silver overall scheme.

The latter Canberra PR.7 generally appeared in a silver overall finish for service in the United Kingdom and with overseas units. Those serving in Germany with 17 and 31 Squadrons retained the usual dark green and dark sea-grey camouflage with silver undersurfaces.

The Canberra PR.7s that remained in service with No. 13 Squadron until it disbanded in January 1982 adopted the matt dark green and dark sea-grey finish that was in current use on the RAF's combat aircraft. The Canberra PR.9s that initially entered service with No. 39 Squadron until it disbanded in May 1982 were in the current matt finish of that period. Roundels and fin flashes were the red/blue variety. Squadron markings were toned down, with all white removed.

Trainers

The Canberra T. Mk4 trainers in service with the RAF first appeared in a silver overall scheme with yellow T bands. This later changed to gloss light aircraft-grey overall, with areas of orange dayglo on the fuselage, wings and tail unit. The final scheme for the remaining T.4s is similar to that adopted for other training aircraft, e.g. red, white and grey. The other trainer serving with the RAF, the Canberra T.11, also served initially in a silver overall scheme with yellow T bands when serving with No. 228 OCU.

When these aircraft later served with No. 85 Squadron, most were repainted in the non-combat aircraft glossy light aircraft-grey scheme, with 85 Squadron's black and red chequers on either side of the fuselage roundel and hexagon on the fin.

At least one of the T.11s appeared in a glossy dark green/dark sea-grey colour scheme with light aircraft-grey undersurfaces. It carried the usual 85 Squadron markings.

The Canberra T.22s that served with the Royal Navy retained their original light aircraft-grey scheme with dayglo orange T bands.

Other Aircraft

The Canberra B. Mk6s of No. 76 Squadron used as the Nuclear Weapons Task Force aircraft in the Pacific were in white anti-flash finish with squadron badge on the fin.

The RAF's ECM aircraft, the Canberra T.17, saw a few changes after it was introduced in 1968. Originally in a gloss dark green/dark sea-grey/light aircraft-grey scheme, it then received a matt finish in dark green/dark sea-grey/with matt light aircraft-grey undersurfaces. There was no set pattern of finish as far as the radar nose and blisters were concerned. Some aircraft had the nose and all blisters black, others had the nose grey and blisters black, while others had a combination of black and grey blisters and black or grey nose cones.

The Canberra TT.18s of No. 7 Squadron underwent great changes. Originally having gloss light aircraft-grey upper surfaces, with yellow and black target-towing stripes on the undersurfaces, they carried a dayglo 7 Squadron motif on the fin. Until No.

Close-up of fin insignia of No. 13 Squadron, carried by Canberra PR. Mk9 WJ825 in July 1977. Lynx's head is black and white on a red disc.

Canberra B. Mk2 WD944, the fifteenth produced by English Electric. It was released to service on 9 October 1951. Seen here in service with No. 90 Signals Group at RAF Cottesmore in 1970 after conversion to T. Mk4 standard. Note liberal application of dayglo patches and unit name on fuselage side.

Canberra PR. Mk3 WE139 of No. 231 OCU at Benson in September 1966. Note rescue equipment indicators below cockpit in black stencilled shapes. Aircraft's basic colour is silver (painted).

7 Squadron disbanded at the end of 1981, the Canberra TT.18s were of the current scheme of the period, matt dark green/dark sea-grey on the upper surfaces, while retaining the yellow and black target-towing stripes. The last two of the serial appeared on the fin in red, along with the squadron badge. After disbandment the Canberra TT.18s were absorbed by No. 100 Squadron, and the squadron aircraft were marked with the insignia of a triangular blue and yellow chequerboard containing a skull and crossbones, and a two-letter code marked in white, the letters appearing in large format astride the fuselage roundel and repeated, small size, on the nose. Most squadron aircraft had light grey undersides, only the TT.18s retaining the traditional black and yellow stripes to advertise their role.

It is interesting to note that the Canberra TT.18s of the FRADU retained the colour scheme as originally applied to No. 7 Squadron's aircraft, but with the addition of large black code letters on the nose and minus the fin flash. They also carried the words 'Royal Navy' above the fuselage serial. In common with training aircraft and some front-line types, the Wyton Canberras had the starboard serial removed and, as of old, no roundels carried below the wings. At RAF Wyton, to avoid confusion between aircraft during the twilight Canberra years, the station adopted double letter codes in 1981: No. 231 OCU, BA-BK; No. 100 Squadron, CA-CW and No. 360 Squadron EA-EQ. No. 1 PRU's

Close-up of 231 OCU fin badge on Canberra PR. Mk3 WE139 at Benson in September 1966. Leopard's head is yellow and black with a red tongue, eye and collar. Shield is white

Canberra B. Mk2 WH876 of A & AEE, August 1972. Very attractive trim with serials repeated on the wingtip tanks.

The fin marking on a Canberra PR. Mk7 WH774 of the Royal Aircraft Establishment in June 1979.

Fin marking carried by Canberra WK124 of No. 7 Squadron in August 1973.

The Moth badge of No. 360 Squadron.

aircraft carried no markings apart from serial and roundels. One unit, No. 360 Squadron, had a very interesting badge: the moth emblem. It is of the species *Melese Laodamia Druce*, which is a moth equipped with a receiver that picks up the high-frequency signals from the A1 radar of bats. To the moth, bats are hostile, so it transmits a signal on the same frequency used by the bat, thus effectively jamming the hostile creature's search radar and avoiding its own destruction. Thus the moth was in the electronic countermeasures business long before man thought of it, and it made an appropriate emblem for 360 Squadron, which was engaged in the same line of business.

As at December 2003, as the faithful servant, well past its retirement date, flies into the history books, we see the Canberra T.4s: one in grey/green tactical camouflage, and the other in the livery of VN799, the first prototype. The Canberra PR. Mk9s are in hemp livery.

Overseas Air Forces
In many cases aircraft delivered to overseas air forces have had a silver overall finish or have been camouflaged in a scheme similar to that in use by the RAF at the time.

In Australia the Canberra B.20s delivered to the RAAF were originally silver overall with black serials, black leading edges and black outline walkways. By the early 1960s the only change was the addition of Kangaroo roundels to the fuselage. The first Australian Canberra (A84-201) carried the Australian flag on the right-hand side of the nose, with the words 'First Australian Canberra' painted in flowing script just above the flag.

Aircraft that operated from Phan Rang in Vietnam were dark grey overall with a dark camouflage pattern on the upper surfaces, and serials were in black. No. 2 Squadron RAAF carried a red lightning flash across the fin.

The early Canberra B.57 intruders of the USAF initially appeared glossy black

Later-style fin markings of No. 7 Squadron carried on Canberra TT.18 WJ680 in July 1977.

overall, with all markings and codes in gloss red. Those aircraft destined for the Air National Guard units were stripped to bare metal, with serials and markings being in black. The ANG insignia were painted on the fin.

B.57s operating in South Vietnam were at first unpainted, but were later camouflaged in the two-tone green and tan upper surface and grey under surface colour scheme. In a few special cases black was used as an undersurface colour on some B.57s.

Target-towing B.57s were in natural metal with large areas of red or orange dayglo on nose, fin and wing tanks.

The Canberras supplied to Argentina had grey and green topsides with light grey undersurfaces. During the Falklands War the FAA Canberras retained the camouflage and markings with which they were painted in Britain, and no special markings were used during the fighting.

CHAPTER TEN

Armament

Marshall of Cambridge (Engineering) Ltd was primarily responsible for all developments and modifications of Canberra aircraft from 1953 to the cancellation of TSR-2 in 1964. In association with the RAE Weapons Department, Marshalls designed and trial-installed the first LABS weapon delivery systems for the Canberra. These initial installations catered for the E role (American 1,650 lb (748 kg) store). Subsequently the firm designed and trial-installed the integrated wiring system, again in association with the RAE. These systems catered for the E and B roles (B role – British 2,000 lb (907 kg) store).

Following these installations, Marshalls was involved in the development programmes, culminating in the introduction of the 2,100 lb (952 kg) system and the WE.177 system to full AMAC (Armament Monitoring and Control) requirements. All check-out requirements for the AMAC specification were carried out by Marshalls. The senior designer in charge of this project visited Germany during the period that the profile missions were carried out.

Rear view of Canberra B-109 (ex-RAF WH875/G-27-163, delivered on 9 September 1971) clearly shows the upper surface camouflage and the Argentine roundel on the left wing only, with the serial on the right wing. This pattern was reversed under the wing.

Armament of a Canberra. The aircraft in the photograph is a B(I). Mk6. At the front, laid out, are SNEB rockets. Behind them are four (white) 8½ lb practice bombs. Under the nose of the aircraft is Hispano 20 mm gun ammunition. Looking to the left, the large equipment is bomb-bay gun pack (see fitted to flying shot of WT307 in this chapter). To left of bomb-bay gun pack the two bombs are 540 lb bombs.

At the front left the two small bombs are 4 lb practice retard bombs. Behind them on the left four (black) 20 lb fragmentation bombs. On their left four (white) 25 lb practice bombs. Behind them on the left two larger (black) cylinders, which are Lepus flares. To their left the large white object is a CBLS 100 Carrier. Behind that on the extreme left under the wing are three free-fall 1,000 lb bombs. Next to them are two Matra launchers for the SNEB rockets. The equipment is the same on the right side.

Close-up of missile, rockets and bomb on Canberra wing. Nearest wing fitment is launcher for Nord AS30 missile. The other fitment (BAC) is Matra 155 launcher for SNEB rockets. On the trolley is a 1,000 lb (454 kg) free-fall bomb.

Closely associated with the weapons delivery systems, Marshalls designed and trial-installed a series of practice bomb facility installations that catered for the changing service requirements in this field, including the LABS instrument system to Canberra T. Mk4 aircraft for the training of pilots in the LABS delivery-flight profiles.

A comprehensive design study was carried out to investigate the fitment of the Bullpup weapon to wing pylons. This design study covered all the implications of structural design, including wing loading, aerodynamic performance, pylon design and all associated circuitry.

The above weapons system work was supplemented with modification programmes to improve the conventional weapon role, including the introduction of 2 in. (5 cm) air-to-air rockets in both the selective firing and single-shot configurations, this coupled with the design and manufacture of a series of modifications to introduce a universal sole plate for wing pylons together with the relevant airframe modifications to cater for a range of wing stores to include the ML Twin Carrier, various 1,000 lb (454 kg) conventional stores, practice bomb carriers, Rocket Launcher No. 1 Mk2 Lepus Flares and Napalm.

The introduction of the F.49 Mk4 camera to Canberras PR.7 and PR.9 involved Marshalls in a major design exercise, which included the design of a complex sealed camera pack. During the eleven year period in which Marshalls was primarily responsible for the development of Canberra aircraft, the company introduced and trial-installed some 400 modifications, of which not fewer than 140 were directly related to the weapon delivery systems and the practice bomb facility.

Armament Monitoring and Control (AMAC)
This was the system developed by the Americans for control and monitoring of the fusing system, etc. of each of their nuclear store, once fitted in the aircraft. Obviously it was a classified system, so one didn't actually get to know very much as to how the system operated. All Marshalls of Cambridge did was to install the 'black boxes' to USA drawings. A similar system was later developed for the UK nuclear store, and this fusing and release system was fitted on the B.15/B.16 aircraft.

Underneath shot of Canberra WT307, the first Interim Interdictor aircraft, showing the gun pack fitment in the fuselage and on each wing a 1,000 lb (454 kg) free-fall bomb.

Canberra B(I). Mk56 '244' of the Peruvian Air Force, which clearly shows the wing fitments. On the wing tip the wingtip fuel tank. Next to it at Rib 5 the launcher for Nord AS30 missile, with Nord AS30 missile fitted. Inboard of it at Rib 3 Matra launcher 155 with SNEB rockets. On the ground 1,000 lb free-fall bomb.

Low Approach Bombing System (LABS)

This was an American system used for releasing bombs (both conventional and nuclear) at either low or high altitude. At low altitude there were two alternative manoeuvres, either 'forward toss' or 'over the shoulder'. The release point was automatically programmed once the pilot had pressed his 'pickle button' (which in fact was the gun trigger) at a predetermined point. The system consisted of vertical and horizontal gyros, a calibrator, timer, accelerometer and dive/roll indicator. Bomb doors operation and bomb release were automatic. The system was first fitted to the Canberra B(I).8 squadrons in Germany, and later to the B.15 and B.16 Canberras based in Cyprus. The release sequence was timed from a predetermined landmark known as the IP, 'Initial Point'.

CHAPTER ELEVEN

Bombing-up
of Canberra Aircraft

'Day One' Problems

T he main person to work on the Canberra armament and ejection seat after it came into squadron service at RAF Binbrook in Lincolnshire was Squadron Leader Ken Wallis, a wartime bomber pilot who was the senior armament officer. Wallis was posted from RAF Scampton to RAF Binbrook in December 1951. After three or four months his views on armament aspects were starting to be heard. By this time he had made a long list of all the problems, from serious to minor, totalling more than 100. Wallis was very, very experienced in this field, and his views were very much respected, so much so that an Air Ministry and English Electric delegation eventually arrived at RAF Binbrook. The mountain had come to Muhammad. It was a great pity that the top brass, more or less, regarded Wallis as a trouble-maker rather than as one trying to help, and so their visit to RAF Binbrook was to find the truth, and this it seemed to do. The Air Ministry and English Electric delegation arrived with the obviously clear intention of sorting out this armament officer who was spreading such alarm and despondency. But as soon as they were shown the facts they changed their minds, and Wallis was invited, with his second-in-command, Flying Officer MacTaggart (who subsequently rose to considerable rank), to discussions at Warton.

Wallis System – The ex-wartime Type-F bomb trolley, but fitted with rails on which the bomb cradles can run, to transfer to the bombing-up trolley.

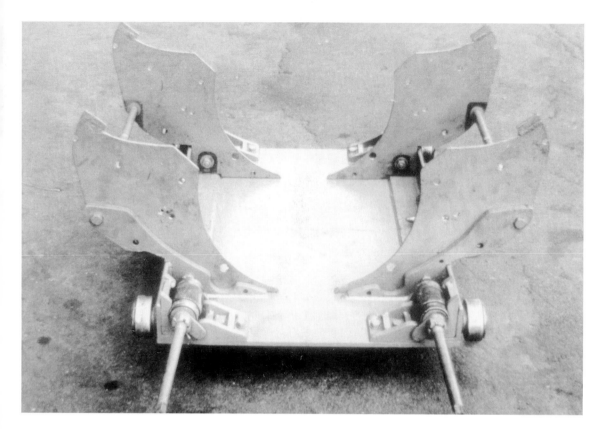

Wallis System – Bomb cradle, mounted on four rollers, which run in the channel-shaped rails on the bomb trolleys. The cradle will accept a clutch of three 1,000 lb bombs or one 5,000 lb bomb. In this case it is set for three 1,000 lb bombs.

Wallis System – Modified Type-F bomb trolley, with two cradles set up for three 1,000 lb bombs each.

Wallis System – Ex-wartime Type-F bomb trolley, modified to Wallis design, with Canberra bomb load of two clutches of three 1,000 lb bombs. Bombs are transported from the bomb dump to dispersal pan on this trolley.

Wallis System – Transporter and bombing-up trolley rail ends engaged, prior to bomb cradle transfer.

Wallis System – A clutch of three 1,000 lb bombs being transferred from the transporting trolley to the Canberra bombing-up trolley. Note that bombing-up trolley is lifting the transporter's wheels clear of the ground – RAF Binbrook, May 1952.

Wallis System – Transfer of 5,000 lb bomb from bomb transporting trolley to Alvis bombing-up trolley – RAF Binbrook, May 1952.

Wallis System – Bombing-up trolley after transfer of three 1,000 lb bombs, being moved away.

Wallis System – The modified Alvis bombing-up trolley with platform partly raised. Note hydraulic controls and lifting hand wheels, etc.

Wallis System – 5,000 lb bomb on cradle, locked on transporter (ex-Type-F) bomb trolley.

Wallis and MacTaggart arrived at Warton with the list of more than 100 points to discuss, and on their arrival, the first question asked of Wallis was whether he could resign his commission and become their armament designer! He didn't think that was likely!

The points raised by Ken Wallis varied from quite serious shortcomings to little more than 'cosmetic', and some of the suggestions they had made had also been foreseen by English Electric, who showed them drawings similar to their ideas. They also showed Wallis and MacTaggart a letter stating that the proposals had been turned down by either the Airframe or the Armament Modification Committee at MOSAP.

Months later a new Canberra arrived incorporating the ideas in the airframe, that modification committee having approved it. Unfortunately, none of the armament electrics could be plugged into this improved airframe. It appeared that it was a case of the right hand not knowing what the left hand was doing, for while one modification committee had approved the modifications, the other had turned it down. One would have thought that they would consult each other. It was many months before the modified bomb beams, etc. came through that would marry up with the airframe. This was not the fault of English Electric.

The major armament changes were done independently of English Electric. Firstly, the Canberra was so low (a jet can be lower than a propeller-driven aircraft, of course) that the nose-wheel hydraulic retraction had to have special controls to allow it to be retracted independently of the main wheels. This was to allow for access of the bomb lifting and transporting trolley under the rear fuselage to the bomb-bay, lowering the nose naturally lifting the rear.

This put the aircraft in a considerable nose-down position. The raising of the nose-wheel had obvious possibilities of error. The operation required aircraft fitters to be involved in armament work. Wallis's solution was ridiculously simple. He made adaptors for the tops of standard hydraulic jacks, to fit under the main-wheel legs. By jacking up the main wheels a small amount, a greater movement upwards occurred to the rear of the

Wallis System – Pulling away the Alvis Canberra bombing-up trolley, after transfer of 5,000 lb bomb from the transporting trolley.

Sitting on the sideline at RAE Bedford in November 1983 are WH952, which saw service at Farnborough, and WG789, which saw service at Pershore.

bomb-bay, allowing access to the bomb trolley. The Canberra's hydraulics were simplified, and even dim-witted armourers could be allowed to jack the main wheels.

A bigger problem was that of the bomb transporter/lifting trolley, an expensive and complicated beast (necessarily so, because of all the movements required) made by Alvis. This trolley carried a clutch of three 1,000 lb (454 kg) bombs, half the load of the 'Canberra'. One trolley was provisioned between three aircraft, as was the arming-up crew. However, since the trolley would have to return to the bomb dump many times (generally quite a considerable distance), the delay in turning round the aircraft would be considerable and the armourers would be wasting much of their time. Further, the very special trolley was vulnerable to mud and dirt, and could easily be damaged during the many miles of transportation.

At the time there were still hundreds of the old wartime bomb trolleys around; many of these had been sold to farmers for £5 each! Wallis's idea was to use these wartime trolleys to transport six 1,000 lb (454 kg) bombs in two 'clutches', or one 5,000 lb (2,268 kg) bomb. Thus, three such laden trolleys could be waiting on the dispersal pan for the three returning aircraft, ready for rearming. If a system could be devised for carriage of the bombs in a clutch on the transporter, together with a simple transfer to the lifting trolley at the dispersal, the armourers could do a quick reloading operation.

Squadron Leader Wallis devised the 'Wallis Canberra Bombing-up System', and he described it to his chief at Group HQ at RAF Bawtry. It was received enthusiastically, but his chief said, 'Ken, they'll not agree to this at Bomber Command, just from drawings and words. Make it up in model form, then it will mean more.'

This was no problem, for Wallis was an expert modelmaker, and following submission of the detailed working models, with solid steel miniature bombs, to Bomber Command in early February 1952, Wallis was given the 'go ahead' in early March 1952 to modify their then only Alvis bomb-lifting trolley and, of course, the old standard Second World War Type-F bomb trolleys.

The models, solid steel bombs and bomb trolleys, made by Wallis to show the 'Wallis System' for bombing up the new Canberra aircraft, are shown in the two pictures

(A)

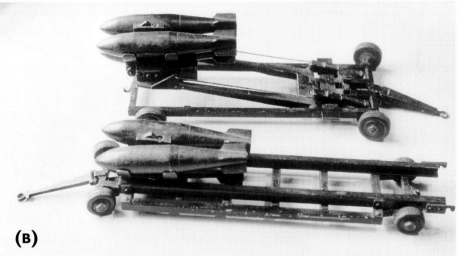

(B)

(A) and (B), which were photographed on 15 January 2004 at the home of Wing Commander K.H. Wallis. Here is his description of them.

'In the two pictures you see Wallis-made models of wartime Type-F bomb trolleys to transport bombs, then connecting up with Alvis bomb-lifting and transporting trolleys, specially made for bombing-up the new Canberra. The Alvis trolleys were provided one to three Canberras, and they carried only half the load of six one-thousand-pound bombs for the Canberra. Hence, dreadful delays if three Canberras returned from a bombing raid before they could be bombed-up again. By using the Second World War Type-F trolleys, the bombs could be available on site, there to be transferred to the Alvis, the latter to be used only for bombing-up.

The two model bomb trolleys in picture (A) are 'mated up' so that bombs can be moved from transporting to lifting trolley, on site, by the use of roller bearings in channel steel. The Alvis lifting trolley engages, then lifts the transporter until its rear wheels are just clear of the ground. A pin can then be removed and the three one-thousand-pound bombs, or one five-thousand-

This photograph is referred to in the text. Bombs were stored well past the bomb dump huts, thus almost a mile for each round trip made by the transporter bomb trolleys.

pound bomb, can be rolled across to the Alvis lifting trolley.

Picture (B) shows the models after the first three one-thousand-pound bombs have been transferred to the Alvis bomb-lifting trolley and it has disengaged with the modified Type-F transporting trolley. It is now ready to put the first three bombs on the Canberra, before again 'connecting up' with the Type-F transporting trolley for transfer of the remaining three one-thousand-pound bombs.

The equipment was sent to No. 4 MU at Ruislip, and Squadron Leader Wallis went on temporary duty (he was given ten days' leave which he never got back) to Ruislip, to superintend the major modification of the Alvis bomb-lifting trolley and the construction of the cradles and modification of the old standard Second World War Type-F transporter trolleys. The work was done very quickly and, in the words of Wallis, on a 'saw it here, weld it there, drill it here' basis. After about ten days the work was completed, and the modified trolleys to the 'Wallis System' were delivered to RAF Binbrook, where they were tried out and worked exactly as planned. Squadron Leader Wallis did receive a letter from Sir Pugh Lloyd, Headquarters Bomber Command, dated 27 August 1952, and one from the Air Ministry concerning the modification. He also received a small award (£400) for his idea, and because of the modification, it was possible to cancel a number of very expensive trolleys, and something like £180,000 was saved by the 'Wallis System', apart from the quicker turnround time achieved and increased operational efficiency.

The 'Wallis System' was adopted on all subsequent Canberra units. With regard to Wallis's idea of jacking the main wheels to allow the bomb trolley access to the bomb bay, he received a letter from P.R. Inventions, dated 24 October 1956, with a heading: 'Bombing-up of Canberra Aircraft'. It states: 'Action has been taken under normal procedure to amend the existing scale, to include the 15-ton Hydraulic Pillar Jack 4Q/2657, together with Jack Adaptor Head Mark 27.' Thus, the 'Wallis System' was used, as was the 'Wallis Canberra Bomb Trolley System'.

While at RAF Binbrook, Squadron Leader Wallis also continued his investigation

into the failures and accidents with the 25 lb (11 kg) Smoke/Flash Practice Bomb. Wallis's first letter, warning of the hang-up danger, was dated 23 June 1952. This problem affected not only Canberra aircraft, but any bomber operating at the operational heights then usual.

Wallis submitted a written detailed description, and full detailed drawings of his idea for a cure, to the Ministry of Supply and Air Publication. Their reply to No. 1 Group was that 'the idea is fundamentally unsound and cannot possibly work'. Luckily, the group armament officer knew Wallis fairly well, and asked 'off the record' whether he was sure the idea for the practice bomb firing mechanism would work. Wallis confidently said it would work, and he knew why.

The idea was again submitted. Eventually Wallis received a telephone call from an old friend at the Ordnance Board. He knew of his idea and was very surprised to see that he had not been invited to a meeting to be held at Hobbies Limited, at East Dereham, to see the first experimental bombs. Wallis telephoned Hobbies and attended at the firm's invitation. It was as well he did, for a vital feature of the idea had been changed by some desk-bound idiot, and the bomb would not have worked. Many letters were exchanged, and eventually the bomb was introduced; but those long years of needless delay cost many lives. On 31 October 1958, the Air Ministry wrote to Wallis thanking him for his good services etc. and awarded him £150. However, this was only after Wallis had seen an Air Publication while serving at Strategic Air Command Headquarters in the United States, describing the No. 2 Mark 1, 25 lb (11 kg) Practice Bomb, which employed the 'Wallis System', Wing Commander Wallis said, 'Truly, it can be an uphill struggle to try and help.'

As senior armament officer, Squadron Leader Wallis had many ideas and modifications for the Canberra. Another was for the ejector seat. The ejector seat was newly introduced, and accidents were happening from ignorance and lack of appreciation of the hazards. Wallis recalls one being fired accidentally in the hangar, when the upper cartridge was being removed. To remove the upper cartridge, a box spanner had to be employed over the cartridge breech. To get the box spanner in position, the normal safety pin, fitted whenever the aircraft was on the ground, had to be removed. Then one false move would fire the seat up through the unblown canopy. This did happen, and after this serious accident, Wallis devised a very simple modification to the box spanner (more

correctly a 'tube spanner'). By suitably cutting it away, it was possible to fit it in place with the safety pin still in place.

Things were certainly a mess for the poor old Canberra, and this was from Day One, for it had been sent out 'half-baked'. RAF Binbrook had not got a Canberra that could drop a bomb for months. It is a fact that without the expert help of Wallis it would have been downhill for the Canberra. The expensive Alvis lifting trolley was never thought out for the job; and it only carried half the bomb load, so it was used only for bombing-up, not transporting. The very design of the Alvis trolley shows it to be usable only on a surface such as concrete or tarmac – not grass or in mud, which is often the case on airfields. The design team obviously never thought about how the bombs were going to be brought from the bomb dump, which, for obvious reasons, was some distance from the hangars and dispersal areas for the bombers. In the photograph of RAF Binbrook, which was up in No. 5 Squadron crew room, and taken down by the author when the station closed, the bomb dump can be seen marked out. No. 5 Squadron hangar is just in the picture on the right. You are looking towards Grimsby.

That is how it was done, thanks only to the senior armament officer, Squadron Leader (later Wing Commander) Kenneth Wallis, whose fertile, inventive brain saved the taxpayer a lot of money; and saved the Canberra, by solving the bombing-up of the Canberra with the 'Wallis Jacking System' and 'Wallis 'Canberra' Bomb Trolley System'; and, by solving the serious 'Day One' problems. When interviewed on 1 November 2004, over lunch at his club (first proof stage for the Canberra book), Wing Commander Wallis said,

> 'I certainly have strong memories of those times, including the dreadful task of searching through every bit and piece of the wreckage at Canberra crash sites searching for the detonator ring that was to be used to cut the elevator controls, when the canopy was blown prior to use of the ejector seats, so that the control wheel would go forward and the pilots would not get their knees damaged by the control wheels, as they went up on the ejector seat.

There were three crashes in mysterious circumstances, at night or in bad weather. The suspicion was that they resulted from inadvertent firing of the explosive detonator ring, which was in my department, as the station armament officer.

I was pleased to find, on each occasion, that it had not detonated, and the mystery accidents were eventually found to be due to a runaway of the electrical trim system for the stabiliser.'

What a man, and he added,

'It certainly sounds as if the history of the Canberra is being well recorded. It's a bit of the recent history of Lincolnshire.'

Sadly, Wallis never got the rightful credit or recognition for his work... But, he has now.

Today – 2005, that special breed of men like Wing Commander Wallis are as rare as rocking horse manure. No wonder James Bond 007, had to enlist his help, for it was Wallis who invented, built and flew 'Little Nellie' in the 007 film 'You Only Live Twice'.

If Wallis had not been on hand, the Canberra would have been like the wartime Manchester bomber. There was always tight security around the very troublesome Manchester, and there were many crashes. The Canberra also started off in the same vein, with many fatal crashes. The Manchester very easily caught fire. Only half of the Manchester bombers were operational at any given time. However, good came out of bad, for from the ill-designed Manchester came the mighty Lancaster bomber.

The Canberra, like the Manchester, was fine on the drawing board but was not so in reality. Thankfully, as you are now well aware, that in the Canberra's case, Wing Commander Kenneth Horatio Wallis... a man born into a Family of 'those magnificent men in their flying machines'...was on hand. It was Wing Commander Wallis's father, H.S. Wallis, and his uncle, P.V. Wallis, who built the Wallbro (Wallis Brothers) Monoplane, the world's first successful aeroplane of all steel tube construction for all its primary structure which, flew during the summer of 1910.

In August 1978, at Royal Air Force Swanton Morley, the replica of the world's first successful aeroplane with all-steel tube for its primary structure, the 'Wallbro', takes to the sky (see photograph opposite). The pilot is Wing Commander K.H. Wallis RAF, Rtd, the son of H.S. Wallis, who, with his brother P.V. Wallis, completed the original 'Wallbro' (Wallis Brothers) monoplane in May 1910. It was ahead of its time, but the original was destroyed in its shed during a freak wind storm in October 1910.

So, the Canberra, Britain's first jet bomber, was in very good safe hands; and it repaid Wing Commander Wallis by being one of the best.

Index

CANBERRA

COLOUR PROFILES

created by Dave Windle

English Electric Canberra B.Mk2

No. 100 Squadron

Bomber Command Development Unit
April 1954 to August 1959
RAF Wittering and RAF Wyton

Target Facilities
February 1972 to September 1991
RAF West Raynham, Marham and Wyton

English Electric Canberra PR.Mk3

No. 231 Operational Conversion Unit

Photographic Reconnaissance

RAF Wyton

Operated by a special flight of No. 540 Squadron, the fifth production PR.Mk3, WE139 won the London to New Zealand Air Race on 8 October 1953 in a time of 23 hours and 51 minutes. The aircraft later served with No. 69 Squadron and No. 231 OCU. WE139 is now an exhibit at the RAF Museum, Hendon.

English Electric Canberra T.Mk4

No. 231 Operational Conversion Unit

Training

1 December 1951 to 15 December 1990, RAF Bassingbourne. Disbanded 15 December 1990 and reformed 13 May 1991 at RAF Wyton. Disbanded 23 April 1993.

D I WINDLE 2004

English Electric Canberra B.MK6 (B.MK2)
Jet Warbird G-BVWC

As a test bed for the Napier Double Scorpion rocket motor, WK163 set a height record of 70,310 feet on the 28 August 1957.
Delivered to the RAF in 1955 as a B.Mk2, WK163 was refitted with B.Mk6 wings and engine in 1968, and a new nose from Canberra B.Mk6 XH568 in 1969.

English Electric Canberra B(I).Mk6
No. 213 Squadron

Interdiction

March 1956 to December 1969
Ahlhorn & RAF Bruggen

English Electric Canberra B.Mk6 (Mod)
No. 51 Squadron

Electronic Intelligence

August 1958 to February 1963, RAF Watton
February 1963 to October 1976, RAF Wyton

D I WINDLE 2004

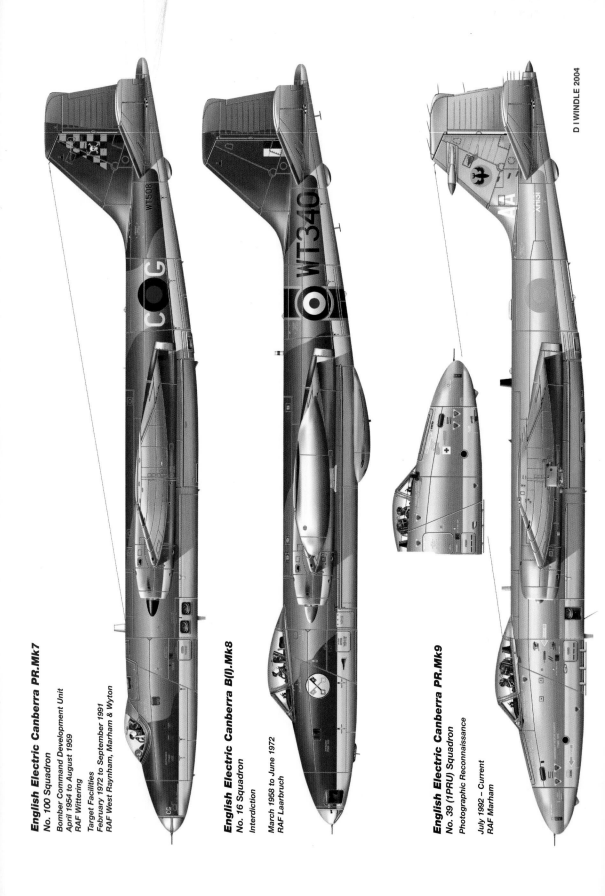

English Electric Canberra PR.Mk7

No. 100 Squadron

Bomber Command Development Unit
April 1954 to August 1959
RAF Wittering

Target Facilities
February 1972 to September 1991
RAF West Raynham, Marham & Wyton

English Electric Canberra B(I).Mk8

No. 16 Squadron

Interdiction

March 1958 to June 1972
RAF Laarbruch

English Electric Canberra PR.Mk9

No. 39 (1PRU) Squadron

Photographic Reconnaissance

July 1992 – Current
RAF Marham

D I WINDLE 2004

English Electric / Shorts Canberra SC.Mk9

Royal Signals & Radar Establishment and Ferranti

Pershore 1972

English Electric Canberra T.Mk11

No. 85 (Target Facilities) Squadron

Air Interception Training
April 1963 to December 1975
RAF Binbrook

English Electric Canberra T.Mk17

No. 360 Squadron

Electronic Warfare Training
December 1966 to October 1994
RAF Watton, Cottesmore & Wyton

D I WINDLE 2004

English Electric Canberra TT.Mk18

No. 7 Squadron

Target Tug

1 May 1970 to 5 January 1982
RAF St Mawgan

English Electric Canberra B.Mk20

(A84-205)
No. 6 Squadron
Royal Australian Air Force

English Electric Canberra T.Mk22

Fleet Requirements and Air Direction Unit (FRADU)

Fleet Air Arm Air Direction Training & Target Facilities

1973-1986

D I WINDLE 2004

English Electric Canberra TP.Mk52
Kunliga Svea Flygflottilj 8 (Royal Svea Air Force Wing 8)
FRA – Foersvarets Radioanstalt (Defence Radio Establishment)

Electronic Intelligence
Barkaby, Stockholm
1960-1974

Martin RB-57A Canberra
(Glen L. Martin Company)
Kansas Air National Guard
Photographic Reconnaissance

D I WINDLE 2004

Martin EB-57B-MA Canberra
(Glen L. Martin Company)
Vermont Air National Guard
Electronic Counter Measures Training

Martin B-57G Canberra
(Glen L. Martin Company)
Tropic Moon III
13th Tactical Bombing Squadron
8th Tactical Fighter Wing
United States Air Force

Night Attack
Thailand 1970-1972

General Dynamics / Martin WB-57F Canberra
NASA 926 (63-13503)
High Altitude Research Program
NASA Johnson Space Center
Ellington Field, Houston